Also by Sean Moncrieff

PUBLISHED BY POOLBEG

Stark Raving Rulers

PUBLISHED BY BLACK SWAN

Dublin

GOD
A USER'S
GUIDE

SEAN MONCRIEFF

POOLBEG

Published 2006
by Poolbeg Press Ltd
123 Grange Hill, Baldoyle
Dublin 13, Ireland
E-mail: poolbeg@poolbeg.com
www.poolbeg.com

1 3 5 7 9 10 8 6 4 2

A catalogue record for this book is available from the British Library.

ISBN 1 84223-283-5 559338
ISBN 978-1-84223-283-5 (From Jan 2007)

Typeset in Sabon 11.5/15

Printed by Creative Print & Design, Wales

About the Author

Sean Moncrieff began his media career in print journalism, working in Ireland and the UK. Later he joined RTÉ where he wrote and presented a number of television and radio shows. On radio, he has worked on *It Says In The Papers* and *The Right Side* and as a contributor to *The Arts Show*, *The Marian Finucane Show* and *A living Word*. On television, his credits include *The End, Good Grief Moncrieff, Black Box, Don't Feed The Gondolas, Ireland Undercover, The Restaurant* and most recently *HQ – The Holiday Quiz*.

Sean hosts a daily radio show on Newstalk 106FM, Ireland's newest national radio station. As well as writing a weekly column for *The Irish Examiner*, he also happily rents himself out as a voice-over artiste to promote a number of high-quality goods and services, all of which he thoroughly believes in. He is the author of a novel, *Dublin*, and *Stark Raving Rulers*, also published by Poolbeg.

Sean Moncrieff lives in Dublin. He is married and apparently has four children.

For my parents

Preface

FIRSTLY, A word on the order of the chapters. They appear to be going backwards not because the typesetter has a drink problem but because this is a chart: the number twenty spot going to Rastifari, right through to Christianity, currently the world's most popular religion. Chart positions were awarded on the basis of the number of adherents. Those of you with a beef about the figures quoted can take it up with the website that I (and pretty much everyone else who writes about religion) stole them from: www.adherents.com

Secondly, I might as well say it, though it probably won't make any difference: by writing this book, I am not setting out to offend anyone; but almost certainly, offence will be taken.

As I think this book demonstrates in abundance, there's nothing quite like religion to get some people riled up; and usually because someone had the temerity to have a different point of view.

So let me try to explain what I'm at. If I have a hidden agenda, then it's hidden even from me. I'm not setting out here to rubbish religious belief or to recommend it; I'm not trying to prove that one belief system is better than any of the others: I was simply interested in finding out about the vast range of religions in the world, how they came about and what they believe. Whether you are religious or not, the fact that so many billions of others do feel there is something greater than themselves must say something significant about the human condition. You can figure out yourself what that might be.

However, writing this book did present me with one problem; particularly the 'How they came about' explanation for each belief. All religions, by definition, claim to have been divinely revealed by God; otherwise they wouldn't be much of a religion. Depending on the religion in question, adherents can be horrified, and, yes, even *offended* by the suggestion that their belief was influenced by a pre-existing one.

Yet if you view religion from a solely *historical* point of view, this does seem to be the case. And not just for one or two.

Thus for the purposes of this book I am, for the record, dealing with Religion, not Faith. Faith is belief in God and an after-life; religion is the all-too-human business of figuring out what God wants us to do, and organising that worship.

Not everyone will agree with this division, and it is far from perfect. But humans, unlike deities, are imperfect creatures.

Of course, you could argue that the evolution of religion in various societies – with one influencing the other – was divinely inspired; and there's no evidence to disprove this.

I'm not putting it forward as a theory, but just pointing out a pattern which, as you read this book, you'll probably notice yourself: historians theorise – *theorise* – that there may have once been an Indo-European belief system, which in various forms covered the area from western Europe to northern India; perhaps even further. The common element was its pantheon of gods: for war, for various elements of the weather, for fertility. There is a striking similarity, for example, between some old Celtic gods and those of Vedic Hinduism of 5000 years ago. The theory is that those gods remained, perhaps with name changes, in some later Greek, Roman and central European beliefs, while also in Hinduism. In India, Buddhism, Sikhism and Jainism were offshoots of Hinduism; in China, Buddhism and Hinduism mingled with traditional Chinese belief systems. In Japan, Buddhism influenced Shinto, which in turn gave us Tenrikyo. In Vietnam, Cao Dai absorbed bits of all of the above and Christianity.

West of India, Vedic Hinduism definitely influenced Zoroastrianism in Persia, which influenced Judaism, which begat Christianity. Christianity and Judaism gave us Islam and Rastafari. Islam also gave us the Baha'i faith. Christianity mixed with a range of indigenous beliefs to produce hybrid religions practised by millions. In Europe, Christianity was gently grafted over the old Pagan beliefs – many of which were resurrected two thousand years later.

Perhaps this is Intelligent Design. Perhaps it is a series of accidents, similar to evolution. You can make up your own mind about such things. As Dave Allen used to say: may your God go with you.

20

Rastafari

AS WE work our way through the various religions, you may begin to notice something: many of them are not as dissimilar as you might have thought beforehand. Many of them have been influenced by (or have pilfered ideas from) other belief systems. We'll see evidence of this, to varying degrees, in pretty much every chapter of this book. But as an example of this phenomenon, Rastafari is a humdinger. A mixture of Christianity, Judaism and some African beliefs, Rastafari began with a magazine article written by a man who never became a Rasta. The religion originally contained some distinctly racist ideas and although mainly based in Jamaica worships a God from Ethiopia. Or, depending on your point of view, a man from Ethiopia who denied he was a God and never became a Rasta either.

And before you say it: the religion is called Rastafari – not Rastafarianism. Rastas disapprove of 'isms' of any kind and so find the term offensive. There is also some debate, both within Rastafari and without, as to whether it is a proper religion at all: it could be viewed as a Christian or even a Judaic sect, or simply as a religious movement. Certainly, there are Rastas who are members of other churches, but as we'll see in other parts of this book (see **Shinto**), this is not so unusual. There are many Rastas who reject the 'religion' term as being a western concept; they prefer to describe it as a way of life.

It may have borrowed a bit here and there, but Rastafari has its own unique concepts of God and creation, of what happens when we die, methods of worship and a moral code: enough to qualify it as a religion in its own right. However, because many adherents have a semi-detached relationship with Rastafari, the exact number of people who count it *solely* as their religion is difficult to pin down: probably more than a million have some connection, though it's more likely that the number of church going (or more correctly, dope-smoking) Rasta is more like 600,000.

Not a bad figure for such a young belief, because it only began as recently as the 1930s – or if you prefer the Rasta version of events, it began 4000 years ago when Abraham started his search for the Promised Land. Pay attention now, because this takes some explaining: Rastas believe that they are the true Israelites. And this is how it happened: in about the tenth century BC, the queen of Sheba went to visit King Solomon of Israel, armed with a raft of difficult questions to test his legendary wisdom. Now many (though not all) academics believe that Sheba was a part of modern-day Ethiopia.

The Queen's visit is recorded in the Bible with the following quotation: "And King Solomon gave unto the

Queen of Sheba all her desire, whatsoever she asked, beside that which Solomon gave her of his royal bounty. So she turned and went to her own country, she and her servants."

Now 'royal bounty' is a phrase which could be open to interpretation, but according to Ethiopian tradition, the Queen returned to Ethiopia carrying Solomon's child. This story is contained in an Ethiopian book called the *Kebra Nagast* (Book of the Glory of Kings), which purports to tell the story of the Royal Family of Ethiopia. The book is at least seven hundred years old, though as to its veracity in describing a royal line which goes back 3000 years; well, that's anyone's guess.

Anyway, the Queen heads back to Ethiopia and has a son, Menelik the First. A few years later Menelik goes to visit Dad to absorb some wisdom, and while there steals the Ark of the Covenant: the container which houses the stone tablets on which the Ten Commandments are carved. (See **Judaism.**) According to The Ethiopian Orthodox Church, the Ark is still located at the Church of Our Lady Mary of Zion in the city of Axum in northern Ethiopia, where Menelik brought it. It is guarded day and night and never shown to anyone.

Now you might think this was a pretty sneaky thing to do. But remember; Menelik was a son of King Solomon, and therefore a direct descendant of the House of David. Therefore Menelik was an Israelite: one of the chosen people. The story also claims that Menelik brought with him one of the twelve tribes of Israel: who would have intermarried with the native Ethiopians, making them Israelite too.

Menelik established a dynasty which ruled Ethiopia in a pretty much unbroken line until the mid-1970s.

The Israelite connection is impossible to prove one way or another, though in Ethiopia there *are* Jews: they are known as Beta Israel (House of Israel) and have existed there for centuries, though with little contact with other Ethiopians, who have traditionally regarded them as outsiders. Some have theorised that they are a tribe who fled ancient Israel to escape civil war or that they are one of the Lost Ten Tribes. However, DNA tests have indicated that they are probably native Ethiopians who converted. How this happened though, remains a subject of conjecture.

Unusually for an African country, given the western penchant for colonialism, the Ethiopian dynasty survived into modern times. The most recent hereditary Ethiopian ruler was Haile Selassie I, who came to power on November 2nd, 1930. Now Rastas regard Haile Selassie as a living God, despite the fact that he died in 1975.

To explain how this happened, we need to zip over the Caribbean to Jamaica.

A little bit of history: the first people to arrive in Jamaica probably came from South America sometime between 500-1000BC. The next people to arrive were the Spanish in 1494. And, as was the fashion at the time, the Spanish killed them all. The British took over the island in the following century and basically turned it into one huge sugar plantation – but to do that they needed cheap labour. And in them days, there was nothing cheaper than slaves from Africa. Indeed, so many slaves were brought in that by the 19th century, blacks outnumbered whites by 20 to 1. Now as you might expect, this led to a certain amount of bad feeling: the threat of revolt was constant, and eventually black slaves achieved full emancipation in 1838.

Then again 'freedom' is a relative term. About the only thing the black residents of Jamaica were free to do was what they did before: work on the sugar plantations. A proto-independence movement sprang up, and with that, a growing sense that black Jamaicans should reject the Christian/Western culture which the white world had foisted upon them: that they should embrace their African roots.

And one person at the forefront of this drive was a chap called Marcus Garvey. Born in 1887, Garvey was a truly remarkable individual, being a publisher, journalist, entrepreneur and political agitator. In 1914 he established the Universal Negro Improvement Association and African Communities League, which had the modest aim of uniting all Africans to establish their own government and country. Thanks mostly to Garvey's own lecture tours, the League established 1,100 branches in 40 countries.

However, while some in the League fancied upping sticks and bringing all black Jamaicans back to Africa, Garvey was more interested in self-improvement, encouraging education and setting up a series of industries including several corporations and even a shipping line.

Unlike many other activists at the time, Garvey wasn't into Black Supremacy – the idea that black people are superior to whites – but did approve of the idea that the races should be separate: so much so that he once had a meeting with Edward Young Clarke, then Imperial Giant of the Ku Klux Klan. That must have been fun.

In many respects, Garvey was a one-man movement for

social change in Jamaica. Hugely charismatic and intelligent, he was regarded by many poor uneducated Jamaicans with awe; some with almost religious devotion. Which is where we have a little difficulty: although Garvey is credited as being one of the founders of Rastafari and one of its prophets (some regard him as a reborn John the Baptist), there is little evidence that he wanted anything to do with the religion. Garvey was raised Methodist and later became a Roman Catholic.

The Back-To-Africa movement in Jamaica was far more than just political: it was an attempt to re-create an *entire culture* which was Afro-centric, including its own religion. Many had already taken a particular interest in Ethiopia: the only independent African state with an unbroken line of rulers – who claimed to be descendants of Abraham. When Selassie became Emperor, his other titles were *King of Kings, Lord of Lords* and *Conquering Lion of Judah*: titles which match those of the Messiah in Revelations. The Lion of Judah is an Israelite symbol, and also appeared on the Ethiopian Imperial flag.

Thus a central part of the movement was to re-create God in their 'black' image. As early as the 1920s, an associate of Garvey's from the US, the Reverend James Morris Webb, published a series of monographs employing Biblical evidence to prove that a black messiah would return to rule the world, and that Jesus was in fact black. And he wasn't the only one proposing this idea. A preacher named Fitz Balintine Pettersburg (everyone in Jamaica seems to have a cool name) penned the self-explanatory Royal Parchment Scroll of Black Supremacy, while Robert Athlyi Rogers, who was born in the West Indies, compiled a book called the Holy Piby – later called the Black Man's Bible. He also established the Afro 'Athlican' Constructive Church, with branches around the Caribbean and the US. Once again, Piby's basic thesis was that Ethiopians were the chosen people ('Ethiopian' was quickly becoming a synonym for 'African') and that the early Popes had deliberately distorted the Bible (hostility to Catholicism is a distinguishing feature of Rastafari) to make it seem as if Jesus and the Israelites were white. The Piby was an attempt to re-create the 'real' bible. The book also named Marcus Garvey as a prophet.

Predictably, this message didn't go down too well with the Church or political authorities at the time, so the Piby became an 'underground' book. It was, however, widely distributed in east Jamaica – fast becoming a hotbed for the new counter-culture.

It's not known how Garvey felt about being named a prophet, though he did deliver some speeches along religious lines, at least one of which seemed to posit the idea that after death humans go through a form of melding into nature rather than ascension into heaven. He also said this: "If the white man has the idea of a white God, let him worship his God as he desires. If the yellow man's God is of his race let him worship his God as he sees fit. We, as Negroes, have found a new ideal. Whilst our God has no colour, yet it is human to see everything through one's own spectacles, and since the white people have seen their God through white spectacles, we only now started out (late though it be) to see our God through our own spectacles. The God of Isaac and the God of Jacob. We Negroes believe in the God of Ethiopia, the everlasting God – God

7

the Father, God the Son and God the Holy Ghost, the One God of all ages. That is the God in whom we believe, but we shall worship Him through the spectacles of Ethiopia."

Now this could be interpreted as meaning that God is in Ethiopia, but more likely Garvey's intent was that black people should worship God *the way they do in Ethiopia* – and in Ethiopia, they didn't regard their emperor as a God.

For Garvey, Ethiopia was a source of political and cultural inspiration for Jamaicans and all Africans, particularly the forthcoming coronation of Haile Selassie I, who had offered to give up land to Jamaicans seeking to come 'home' to Africa. Now there is some dispute over certain things Garvey said. Some claim that in a Kingston Church in 1927, he stated, "Look to Africa for the crowning of a Black King; He shall be the redeemer." (But this could have been Webb.) However, what is indisputable is that in 1930, Garvey wrote in his own publication, *The Blackman*, a glowing review of the coronation which included some Biblical-sounding language about prophecies of 'princes emerging from the east'; and while Garvey was probably writing metaphorically, some took these words, combined with previous speeches, at face value: God had arrived on earth.

For an influential figure like Garvey to apparently endorse an idea which had already been touted by many street preachers in Jamaica suddenly gave it huge credibility. Garvey's Universal Negro Improvement Association and African Communities League subsequently went to some lengths to distance itself from the deification of the Emperor, and seven years later, Garvey himself penned a vicious attack on Selassie, accusing him of being an idiotic coward who had sold out his own people. But by then it was far too late: as far as the fledling Rastafari religion was concerned, God had arrived and Marcus Garvey had prophesied it.

Oh, and by the way: the pre-coronation name of Selassie was *Ras (Duke) Tafari Makonnen*: hence Ras Tafari.

But while Garvey may have made the 'prophecy' another man was largely responsible for transforming this into a religious belief. His name was Leonard P. Howell. Howell was born in 1898, and at the extremely tender age of 16 headed for the United States where, among other things, he served in the US Army. The other things included meeting a lot of militant black leaders, including Garvey, and doing two years in prison for larceny – after which he was deported back to Jamaica in 1932.

He was probably coming back anyway, because Howell had also come to the conclusion that Ras Tafari was God returned to earth: he quickly became a familiar figure in Kingston where he preached and sold pictures of Selassie. He also visited east Jamaica, where it's believed he spent some time at one of the many communes which had sprung in that part of the island (where they were relatively safe from the authorities) and almost certainly read the Holy Piby.

At the time, the set of beliefs around Ethiopia and the black version of religious history had grown organically, and as a result varied from preacher to preacher. Howell is significant in the development of Rastafari in that for the first time he gave the belief system six fundamental principles:

9

1) Hatred for the white race
2) The superiority of the black race.
3) Revenge on the white race
4) The destruction of all legal and political bodies in Jamaica.
5) Preparation for the 'return' to Africa.
6) Recognition of Haile Selassie as God and ruler of all black people.

Yes, it was scary stuff, and even though Rastafari largely rejected Black Supremacy not much later (after Selassie made a speech to the UN condemning racism), it was enough to seriously put the wind up the British authorities (Jamaica was still a colony).

Howell was a marked man – especially so when he published *The Promise Key*, an account of his alleged attendance at the coronation. All the usual claims about Selassie's Godly nature were made, but what did for Howell was the accusation that the then King of England was an impostor: along with the idea that Africans were the chosen people came increasingly fantastical theories as to how the 'white' race managed to keep it quiet.

Fantastic or not, the British authorities jailed Robert on charges of sedition in 1934. But within two years he was out again, and, no doubt inspired by what he had seen in east Jamaica, established the Pinnacle commune.

Set on a 200-hectare stretch of land bought with money contributed by followers, Pinnacle quickly became Rasta heaven. At its height the commune was home to 1000 people, and survived until 1954, despite constant attempts by the authorities to close it down. Pinnacle became famous throughout Jamaica and a major symbol of the Rastafari way of life.

The people in Pinnacle made their living from selling baskets and various farm products: oh, yeah, and truckloads of cannabis which Howell apparently exported to the UK. When the place was finally closed down, the police claimed they found evidence of staggering wealth. Howell escaped the raid and after that somewhat faded out of Rastafari life: the revelation that Pinnacle was a money-making concern as well as a religious retreat probably damaged his reputation, as did the fact that he never grew dreadlocks or a beard – both expressions of religious belief in Rastafari.

Rastafari had spread rapidly as a religion in Jamaica at this time and was also in the process of developing a unique theology. However, it was still regarded by most as a belief system for outsiders; the stoned ramblings of a bunch of weirdos.

Two factors changed that perception: one, as you might imagine, was music and the other was a visit from God.

Most of the time, Rasta Fari himself regarded the Rastas with polite puzzlement. Then again, it was probably better than the reaction he got from Ethiopians, many of whom regarded him as a despot. Selassie had met with Rasta elders and had come good on his earlier promise to donate land for any Jamaicans who wanted to 'return' to Ethiopia. (There is now a large community of Rastas in the town of Shasamane, about 150 kilometres north of Addis Abbaba. The Ethiopian government, however, has refused them citizenship.) But at no stage did he ever claim to be a God. Indeed, he once asked the leadership of the

Ethiopian Orthodox church to convert the Rastas to Christianity.

Nonetheless, he did visit Jamaica on April 21, 1966 and received an ecstatic welcome. Up to two hundred thousand Rastas gathered at the airport to meet him and at first were so unruly that Selassie refused to get off the plane. But the sheer size of the crowd announced to the world that Rastafari was a proper religion and not just a weird cult. Conveniently, a long drought ended with rain soon after he arrived.

His visit attracted even more Jamaicans to the religion, including the wife of Bob Marley, Rita, who claimed she saw the stigmata on the Emperor. Rasta Fari also brought with him a major theological change: he encouraged the Rastas not to move to Africa, but to improve conditions in Jamaica.

The visit brought Rastafari a degree of respectability in Jamaican society, which in turn enabled reggae musicians like Bob Marley and Peter Tosh to be open about their religious beliefs. While some Rastas regard it as selling out to 'Babylon', the worldwide fame of Marley has probably been the most significant factor in the mainstream acceptance of Rastafari in Jamaica.

So let's back-up just a little bit and examine exactly what Rastas believe. The personal nature of Rastafari is all important: adherents are encouraged to take their own spiritual path and so can come to their own (and often contradictory) conclusions. However, pretty much all of them believe that they and all black Africans are descended from the ancient Israelites. Because of the slave trade and an attempt by Christianity to 'whiten' religion, this has been kept secret. However, there will be a day of judgement, when Haile Selassie will lead all Africans back to their homeland and establish heaven on earth.

Selassie is, inconveniently, quite dead now, so his availability for judgement day might be a problem. However, many Rastas believe that he didn't die at all and is in hiding. Haile Selassie means 'power of the trinity', so Rastas think he is God the Father and the Son (Jesus was simply a previous incarnation) and that humankind embodies the Holy Spirit

The Rastafari attitude towards the soul is a little vague. Because it remains a religion without any hierarchy or central authority, beliefs do vary. But generally speaking, Rastas don't believe in heaven or hell. They reckon the body simply re-combines with the universe to come back in different forms, while the soul attains a oneness with God. However they do believe an elite in Rastafari will retain their physical body and live for ever.

Put another way, Rastas *don't believe in death at all*: when Bob Marley was diagnosed with terminal cancer he refused to make a will, reasoning that this would somehow be giving in to death. Because of this, there is no funeral rite in Rastafari.

Seeing that Marley did die, this would seem to have been a pointless gesture: but that's typical of Rastafari, which to an extent deliberately flies in the face of western 'logic'.

In fact all things western, corporate and authoritarian are regarded as enemies of Rastafari and are referred to under the catch-all phrase, Babylon: it being where the Israelites were brought to in chains, and so for Rastafari a symbol of oppression. Thus many things can be referred to as 'Babylon': an idea, a country or an individual. What it doesn't mean is white: Rastafari has mostly dumped its black supremacist philosophy and now largely takes an anti-racist line. In many western countries there are white Rastas.

The opposite of Babylon is Zion: literally the name of a hill near Jerusalem. Over time it has come to mean Jerusalem, the Promised Land and Ethiopia as well as the way of life which rejects Babylon and is loyal to Jah – the Rastafari term for God. (A shortened form of the Biblical Yahweh).

Language is extremely important in Rastafari. It's unlikely the original slaves from Africa were fluent English speakers, but rather had their native tongue 'stolen' and replaced with English: so Rastafari has adapted English to reflect Rasta ideas. 'Overstanding' (understanding), 'Livication' (dedication), 'Downpression' (oppression). As we've already said, Rastas avoid using any 'ism' terms. Also extremely important is the use of the letter 'I': for instance, Rastas will refer to God as Rasta Fari-*I* to reflect the concept of 'I and I': that God is within each of us and we are all linked to each other. Thus Rastas will tag the letter I on the end of a range of phrases.

Rastafari also has a number of dietary laws, mostly taken from the Old Testament, which allow consumption of a limited range of meats (though many Rastas are vegetarian) and ban alcohol. This is an integral part of what they see as living a more 'natural' (and African) lifestyle. Over time Rastafari has developed its own healthy cuisine which is widely popular throughout the Caribbean islands.

No drink, healthy food, but loads of ganja. In Rastafari, it's not mandatory to smoke, but most do, regarding the drug as an aid to increasing perception and bringing smokers closer to Jah. The fact that it is illegal in most countries is of no surprise to the average Rasta: this is a typical reaction of Babylon, which wants to keep the truth from people. Dope-smoking, according to the Rasta interpretation, is also heavily encouraged in the Bible, which does make repeated references to 'Herb'.

So while all the other religions go to boring old church or temple at the weekend, Rastas have a weekly event called a Reasoning. This can take place anywhere: Rastafari doesn't have churches, believing that one's own body is the temple of God. The Rastas will sit in a circle. One says a short prayer, then lights up a spliff which is passed clockwise around the group as they discuss religious, ethical and social issues. Apart from the weekly reasoning, there are other annual holidays, including Ethiopian Christmas (January 7) Bob Marley's birthday, the anniversary of Haile Selassie's visit to Jamaica, (also known as Grounation Day), the birthday of Emperor Haile Selassie, the birthday of Marcus Garvey and the coronation of Haile Selassie. There's usually feasting, dancing, music and perhaps the odd bit of cannabis.

"They shall not make baldness upon their head, neither shall they shave off the corner of their beard, nor make any cuttings in the flesh" is the quotation from the Bible which Rastas believe encourages them to wear their hair in dreadlocks. Originally inspired by pictures of the Mau Mau fighters in Kenya in the 1940s, the wearing of dreadlocks is seen as yet another statement of the Rasta opposition to Babylon: razor, scissors and comb being regarded as Babylonian instruments. The growing of the dreads (which, obviously takes some time) is also intended to remind Rastas of the patience required for their own spiritual journey through life. Us non-rastas, by the way, are known by the flattering term, baldheads.

Like all religions, Rastafari has developed and changed over the years. The status of women has improved, though it's hardly at the cutting edge of feminism. Generally speaking, Rastafari women – known as 'queens' – are regarded as inferior to men, their main job being to cook and clean for the 'kings'. Women cannot be leaders and cannot even join the religion unless introduced by a man. They are not allowed to wear make-up or revealing clothes and are forbidden birth control: contraception being a western tactic to suppress the African population. Abortion is also not allowed.

Rastafari does not have any marriage rite. All the couple have to do is live together to be regarded as hitched.

The religion has also morphed into three main variations or Mansions of Rastafari:

Bobo Ashanti, also known as the Priestical House of Rastafari, the Ethiopian Africa Black International Congress or Church of Salvation for Bobo Dreads. It was founded in the 1950s by Charles Edwards, who later rewarded himself with the title Prince Edward Emmanuel Charles VII. The vast majority of the Bobos live in their own community in Bull Bay, Jamaica. Bobos wear turbans and robes and carry brooms to signify cleanliness.

In Bobo, the holy trinity consists of Prince Emmanuel (as high priest) Marcus Garvey (as prophet) and Haile Selassie (as God, or Jah).

Like other Rastas, they believe the Israelites were black

– but here Black supremacist ideas have survived: black people are not only chosen, they are better. And black men are the best: women and children are also regarded as inferior and must adhere to a dress code. Nearly all the men in the community are regarded as priests or prophets. Naturally. The Bobos also observe the Jewish Sabbath and fast twice a month

Nyabinghi otherwise known as the Nyabinghi Theocracy Government. It's named after a legendary Amazon queen of the same name. This version of Rastafari is probably best known for its music, as it employs a wide range of chants and drums, (including one called a 'Vatican Basher'), developed from a combination of traditional Jamaican and African musical styles. Nyabinghi has been hugely influential on a host of reggae musicians.

Yet despite the music, Nyabinghi is considered the strictest mansion. Committed pacifists, their idea of heaven is a global theocracy headed up by Haile Selassie: a situation which they believe is inevitable.

The Twelve Tribes of Israel is the largest of the mansions. It was founded by Vernon Carrington, also known as the Prophet Gad.

The main theological difference of the Twelve Tribes of Israel is their acceptance of Jesus as God (though they call him Jah). Haile Selassie is regarded as a divinely appointed king and as a living symbol of the covenant with God – but not as a God himself. The Twelve Tribes is anti-racist and accepts members from all ethnic backgrounds. Bob Marley was a member of this sect.

The different sects enjoy fairly convivial relationships, and given the *laissez-faire* nature of the religion, most Rastas aren't too pushed about the theological differences. What's important for them is living the Rasta lifestyle which, given the amount of cannabis most of them smoke, is no doubt a constantly happy experience.

19

Unitarians

HERE'S the tricky bit: technically, the Unitarians shouldn't be in this top twenty. By their own count, they have only about 350,000 adherents around the world – less than Rastafari, (600,000), or even the believers in the science-fiction-tinged theology of the Scientologists, (500,000).

So why include them? Well, because for the Unis, all those official, soul-destroying statistics don't really matter, man: in a survey conducted in the US in 1990, a whopping 500,000 Americans claimed to be Unitarian, despite the fact that only about a third of that number are enrolled members. Add that figure to the number of congregations in Canada and around the planet and you get, (very) roughly, a figure of 700,000.

But we're not manipulating the figures here just because the Unitarians may be nice people. That two-thirds of its

American following have never darkened the door of a Unitarian Church sits quite comfortably with the Uni philosophy; it's such an all-embracing, liberal religion that there are virtually no rules: to be a Unitarian, (or at least some versions of the religion) you don't have to turn up to any services or join a congregation. To be a Unitarian, you don't even have to believe in God.

The Unitarians are the right-on hippies of the religious world, (they prefer the term 'Association of Congregations'). In 2004, the Red River Unitarian Universalist Church in Denison, Texas was denied the tax-exempt status usually given to religions because the State Comptroller felt it didn't have 'one system of belief'. The status was later restored, but Ms Comptroller's confusion was understandable. Modern Unitarianism contains a dizzying and apparently contradictory range of beliefs: there are humanists (a moralistic philosophy centred on the needs of humans rather than those of any God), agnostics, atheists, Buddhists, Christians, neopagans and people who describe their belief as 'earth-centred'. Something to do with gardening, presumably.

Critics of Unitarianism, (usually conservative Christians of various hues), agree with the comptroller: that it's not a religion at all but a yuppie, self-development fad which offers salvation without any pain; that all it promotes is a cult of the Self.

But let's not be sneery: as we'll see elsewhere, many of the denominations in the Unitarian mix have traditionally preferred to slaughter each other rather than come together, so for it to work at all is something of an achievement: especially for a group of people who, on principle, make no attempt to convert anyone to their religion. Or Association.

It's a modern, new-agey belief system born partially from the idea that dogmatic belief in religion has been the source of far too much conflict in the world – while also accepting that all religions have something to offer. Yet its history is also one steeped in controversy and blood, way back in the 1500s.

Unitarian ideas (we'll explain shortly what they are) are almost as old as Christianity itself: the first Council of Nicaea discussed and rejected them in 325 – thus establishing the dogma of the Trinity. Prior to that, there had been many theories circulating as to what the Trinity was. However, the man credited with founding Unitarianism – though somewhat by accident – is one Michael Servetus. Born some time around 1510 sixty miles north of Zaragossa, Spain, Michael began studying under a Franciscan monk, Juan Quintana. And the study of religion was, in those days, rife with controversy. The great split of the Reformation had already taken place and both the Catholic and fledgling Protestant churches were somewhat touchy: even a hint of heresy and you could find yourself at the top of large bonfire. The invention of the printing press had added – pardon the pun – fuel to the flames. Prior to that, only clerics had access to the Bible and so could spin their own interpretation of what it meant to the great unwashed congregations. But now anyone could get their hands on a copy of the Good Book and, dangerously, make up their own minds.

This willingness to incinerate anyone with heretical ideas, however, was not simply due to religious zealotry.

As we'll see in subsequent chapters, many 'religious' disputes were really more about political power, and in some cases, simple cash. Young Michael Servetus had been born into a Europe where the Catholic Church was the local superpower – where national governments would kow-tow to its wishes. The emergence of Protestantism, however, had created a sort of religious Cold War, with both brands of Christianity determined to hang onto the territory they had, perhaps even gain some more – though not at the cost of a full-scale conflict though an actual war did eventually break out. The constant threat of heresy was a handy way for both sides to keep dissension at bay. These were paranoid times.

Young Michael, however, seemed cheerily heedless of this. Even as a teenager he began asking questions about the Catholic doctrine of the Trinity and later, while at University in Toulouse, was shocked to discover that there is no explicit mention of the Trinity in the Bible. After two years in University, Servetus returned to the service of Quintana, but became even more disillusioned: a trip to Italy left him disgusted at the vulgar opulence of the Church and the almost pagan adoration of the Pope. So he switched sides. He travelled to Basle in Switzerland and joined the Protestants.

For the some months he stayed in the home of a local pastor by the name of Oecolampadius. No doubt, pronouncing his host's name created some difficulties, but altogether more tricky was Servetus' insistence on banging on about the Trinity. So Michael moved again, this time to Protestant Strasbourg, which had a reputation for being more tolerant. There, he published two books: *De Trinitatis*

Erroribus (On The Errors of the Trinity) and *Dialogorum de Trinitate* (Dialogues on the Trinity), both of which expounded his re-definition of the Trinity, while also introducing some new crowd-pleasers: like the suggestion that there was no such thing as original sin.

So, Michael's basic thesis: after centuries of debate, the Council of Nicaea in 325 defined the Trinity as being Father, Son (Jesus) and Holy Spirit; three aspects of the one being – but each of these aspects was eternal. In other words, Jesus was in heaven *before* he came to earth. From 325 on, anyone who disagreed with this was a heretic. Michael agreed that Jesus had God within him, but crucially, argued that he was also a man who *hadn't* existed before Christmas Day on the year zero. Jesus continued to exist after his death and is a sort of mediator between us and God, being part man. Effectively, Jesus was demoted to the number two spot, thus implying that there is no such thing as the Trinity, and only one God.

Ergo, Unitarianism.

Michael didn't go all the way in saying this, (though others did later): he proposed a kind of alternative Trinity. But it was more than enough to get him in trouble.

He further rejected the idea that through crucifixion, Jesus had atoned for humanity's sins: this concept, he argued, was invented by humanity to make mankind seem more important to God, whereas the Big Man was really more concerned with his great cosmic battle with the Devil. (The battle, he predicted, wouldn't last that long: the Archangel Michael would bring deliverance and the end of the world around 1585. Hey, you can't get everything right.)

The papacy, he contended, was actually part of the Devil's organisation, with child baptism mirroring child sacrifice rites of pagan times. Michael also had a somewhat sunnier view of humanity than both the Catholics and Protestants, believing that all humans – rather than the Christian elect – were capable of receiving God's grace. He even believed that – gasp – non-Christians could be saved.

Strasbourg was tolerant, but not that tolerant. Michael's ideas were about as popular as a dose of plague, not just because many disagreed with them, but also because even the suggestion that they were indulging such heresies might prompt the Catholic armies to return and start building some more bonfires. His books were confiscated and he was invited to leave town: several of them. For a while, poor Michael couldn't find any Protestant area willing to accommodate him, and going home to Spain was now out of the question: the Spanish Inquisition had also heard about his wacky ideas and wanted a chat. Given that many of their chats took place in torture chambers, Michael was, understandably, not that keen. Instead he fled to Catholic Paris, changed his name to Michael de Villeneuve, got a job as a book editor and enrolled at university to study medicine and mathematics. He kept the head down, but even here couldn't resist the odd bit of quiet religious debate: it was during this period that he first met one of the poster-boys of Reform Protestantism, John Calvin. But the debate didn't last too long: Calvin had to leave town in a hurry for being too flagrantly Protestant – an episode which reminded Michael that, for the time being at least, it was best to keep quiet. Yet the two men had begun a conversation, one that was to end tragically some years later.

The studies went well: during his time at the University of Paris, Michael published a pioneering description of the blood's circulation through the lungs. But it seems as if the young fella couldn't resist a bit of drama: following allegations that he was mixing medicine with astrology, (of which he was cleared), 'Michael de Villeneuve' decided it was best to leave town. This was becoming a bit of a pattern.

Obviously, this all happened a long time ago, so some of the details are fuzzy. But it seems as if Michael had to leave before completing his degree; but sure, that's only a piece of paper anyway. How difficult could being a doctor in 16th century France be?

Not that hard at all, it seems: Michael moved to Vienne, near Lyons and became personal physician to the local Archbishop there – a job he held for twelve years without having to leave town once.

But while he was mild-mannered Doctor Michael de Villeneuve by day, he was still Michael Servetus at night – and in the process of preparing his major theological work *Christianismi Restitutio,* (The Restoration of Christianity). A secret postal dialogue with John Calvin had now also re-started.

By this time Calvin was a big noise in Geneva and the most prestigious figure in Reform Protestantism. But this had been hard won: when in college in Paris with Servetus, Calvin had been a bit woolly on certain theological matters – including the existence of the Trinity. Servetus smelled a possible convert to his point of view. However, what he didn't realise was that, while in Switzerland, Calvin had been accused of heresy on this very issue. He'd been cleared, but since then had been somewhat over-zealous in maintaining his pro-Trinitarian credentials.

So when Michael dispatched a copy of his yet-unpublished *Restitutio* to Calvin, the leader of Reform Protestantism was underwhelmed, to put it mildly. "If my authority is of any avail," Calvin wrote to a colleague, "I will not suffer him to get out alive." Oh-oh.

After a brief exchange of abusive letters and the publication of the *Restitutio*, Calvin took the rather unsporting decision to grass up Servetus' real identity to the Catholic Church in France: effectively selling him out to the enemy. Michael was arrested and the bonfire builders got busy.

But here's the thing about the penal system in the 16th century – and it's a theme we will revisit throughout this book – the quality of the prisons was scandalously poor. In jig time, Servetus had managed to escape, (he convinced a guard to let him out of his cell to urinate), and started to make his way to Northern Italy where he fancied there were people more receptive to his ideas. But while Michael was a dab hand at radical theology and prison breaks, he was less gifted at keeping a low profile: the route he took was – rather stupidly – via Protestant Geneva where he was spotted, arrested and put on trial for heresy.

The verdict was, of course, a foregone conclusion. Michael was found guilty of antitrinitarianism and opposition to child baptism. In a sudden rush of compassion (or possibly guilt), Calvin asked that Servetus be put to death through the slightly-more-merciful method of beheading. The Council of Geneva, however, insisted on the bonfire.

Witnesses report that Michael Servetus went bravely to his death. He did call out to Jesus for help, but still refused to recant his heretical beliefs. Some months later, Servetus was also executed by the Catholic Inquisition in France, this time in effigy.

To have been executed by both the major Christian religions in Europe was some achievement, and got some Protestants wondering if perhaps the sentence was not a wee bit harsh. Calvin continued to defend his action, saying that putting Servetus to death protected the souls of the faithful. But another leading Protestant, Sebastian Castillio, wrote, "When the Genevans killed Servetus, they did not defend a doctrine; they but killed a man . . . when Servetus fought with reason and writings, he should have been repulsed with reason and writings."

The irony about Servetus' death was that, in life, he posed virtually no threat to Trinitarian Protestants or Catholics: he had no followers at the time and even the groups in Northern Italy – later known as the Socinians – agreed with only a part of his theology. Being burnt at the stake, however, gave Michael something of the rock-star mythology of the Martyr – which the newly-formed Unitarians were later happy to adopt while quietly ignoring wackier parts of his writings.

At the time, however, the term 'Unitarian' had yet to be coined. Various small groups had come to similar conclusions to Servetus, at least in relation to the Trinity and Original Sin, but didn't see themselves as one movement – and certainly not as a religion. Some might have labelled them as anti-Trinitarians, yet still they preferred the label 'Christian'. At the time, the Reformation was an ongoing process, so it at least seemed as if the issue of what a Christian should believe was up for debate.

Then again, you don't want to be stupid about it: Servetus' double-bonfire appearances were a warning to anyone with similar views so, understandably, the first proto-Unitarian churches appeared as far away as possible from the Catholic and Protestant zealots: in Poland and Transylvania, with at least some of the congregations made up of the Socinians from Northern Italy. Not that it was all hugs and everyone getting along famously: the occasional bonfire was built and in the mid-1600s, most of them were banished from Poland. Yet they had been left alone long enough to develop their own ideas. They still regarded themselves as Christians, (in Poland they were known as the Minor Church), but it is believed to be around 1570 – seven years after Servetus went up in flames – that the term 'Unitarianism' (or *unitarius*) was first used.

The ideas also began to travel: partly due to books and partly due to anti-Trinitarians being exiled. It arrived in Holland and parts of Germany and poked its head up in England, though initially without much success: the English authorities of the sixteenth century were enthusiastic heresy-roasters, so it wasn't until the middle of the next century that anti-Trinitarian views were allowed any sort of free expression. The groups went through various name-changes until the late 1700s when a distinct Unitarian Church emerged in the British Isles: first when William Robertson left the Anglican church in Ireland, followed swiftly by Theophilus Lindsey doing the same in England. Whiz forward to 1825 and we see the formation of the British and Foreign Unitarian Association, which amalgamated various Unitarian groups and set about forming links with Unitarians in Europe and the US. At this stage, of course, building bonfires had gone out of fashion, though there was still the occasional bit of stone-throwing at Unitarian chapels.

However, it was in the United States that the next set of interesting changes were to take place. As with Europe, anti-Trinitarian ideas grew in the US via a hodgepodge of groups and individuals, all operating within the established Protestant churches and in some of the centres of learning: Harvard College most notably becoming a hub of Unitarian thought. Based mainly around Boston and New England – and initially influenced by English Unitarianism, congregations began springing up, (or more typically, voting to switch over), in the late 1700s. By 1825 the American Unitarian Association was formed. But even at this early stage, there was a marked tendency towards anti-sectarianism. Over the rest of the century, the idea developed that Unitarians don't know it all; that you can still be Unitarian (or 'pure Christian') without agreeing all the fine print; that what sums up Unitarianism is 'love to God and love to man'. Simple as that. A national Unitarian conference in 1885 declared that "...nothing in this constitution is to be construed as an authoritative test; and we cordially invite to our working fellowship any who, while differing from us in belief, are in general sympathy with our spirit and practical aims." Even at this stage, Unitarians were scandalously encouraged to study texts from other, non-Christian religions – not just the Bible.

Of course, not everyone was in sympathy with these aims. In an America still largely composed of immigrants, many of whom had fled religious persecution, hanging onto their cultural and religious identity was seen as hugely important; indeed, the notion of throwing in one's lot with a bunch of foreign proto-hippies was regarded by many as obscene.

Yet some were attracted: especially the Universalists. We'll come back to them.

In the meantime, the less-than-graceful-sounding International Council of Unitarian and other Liberal Religious Thinkers and Workers was founded, which helped spread the American, more liberal, ideas back to Europe. At this stage, the Unitarians were at some remove from most Christian thought – and many Christian denominations felt that by rejecting the Trinity and Original Sin, Unitarians weren't Christians at all. Some of the smaller Protestant denominations, however, did maintain friendly links with the Unitarians, partially out of a genuine sense of ecumenism and partially because the Unitarians seemed to provide a version of Christian history not dictated by the Catholic Church. It was links such as these which provided the Unitarians with a small but steady stream of new members and probably ensured its survival. Because of their belief that faith is a personal matter and that the details of theology are not that important, Unitarians, as we've said, have never actively tried to seek converts, and still don't.

Chief among those to establish links were the Universalists. Universalism was a strictly American invention in the late 1700s in some of the eastern and southern states. As with Unitarianism, the Universalists evolved out of a rejection of the drab Calvinist idea that humans were essentially damned creatures and that only an elect would eventually get to see the pearly gates. They believed everyone would be redeemed, and because of this opened their doors to the marginalised sections of American Society: all colours were welcomed and the Universalists were the first denomination in America to ordain women.

Such crazy ideas weren't wildly popular at the time, so there was the inevitable bit of rock-throwing and pressure from the mainstream Protestant political establishment, leading to another central plank of Universalist belief: that Church and State should be separate. The inclusion of minorities in Universalist congregations also led to a greater awareness of social justice issues; as a result, many prominent Universalists fought for the abolition of slavery, for reform in the penal system and mental hospitals.

Parallel to this, the Unitarians were developing along pretty much the same lines. And apart from the fact that Universalism was more evangelic, it was hard to find any major point of difference between the two beliefs. As one Universalist preacher put it: "Universalists believe that God is too good to damn people, and the Unitarians believe that people are too good to be damned by God." You say tomato . . .

Nonetheless it was some decades before the two Unis got together. In the meantime both of them progressed on an increasing liberal path, becoming involved in various social issues and steadily developing the notion of inclusivity: pretty much anyone was welcome to join and bring whatever beliefs they had with them. Gradually, whatever remaining links there were with Christianity fell away. Not that there weren't Unitarians and Universalists who still regarded themselves as followers of Jesus; there were. But these people were now part of a movement which paid equal respect to people who followed Buddha or wood nymphs. By effectively accepting that there isn't One True Religion, they ceased to be 'Christians' in the formal sense.

In 1961, what everyone expected finally happened: the Unitarians and Universalists got together to form the Unitarian Universalist Association. They followed this up in 1995 by forming the International Council of Unitarians and Universalists.

But being UU's, not all congregations – or fellowships – are the same. Each is independent and can vote on how they want to run things. A typical – in as far as the word can be used – Sunday service resembles something in a Protestant church, with hymns and a sermon. What you tend not to get is baptism, communion or confirmation. Some have replaced these with coming-of-age ceremonies, 'water communion' and 'flower communion'. However, some churches within the wider Unitarian movement still maintain the Christian rites: these would mostly be in Europe and would consider themselves Unitarians rather than UUs – but would still belong to the International Council.

So in broad terms, you have four schools of modern Unitarianism:

1. Biblical

They believe in the Christian God, and believe Jesus is the son of God, but not God himself. This form of anti-trinitarianism is practised in Transylvania, France, Hungary, the UK and parts of Africa and India. The Khasi people of India also practise a form of Unitarianism which has evolved from a mixture of Christianity and their traditional beliefs.

2. Rational
Again, anti-Trinitarian, but rejecting all of the miraculous events in the Bible. They believe interaction with God is mostly a personal matter and so discuss scientific and humanist issues when they meet. The rationalist Unitarians have no ministers.

3. Unitarian-Universalist
The most liberal of the bunch, most UUs don't consider themselves Christians, containing, as we've already said, refugees from all the major religions as well as New Age and Pagan beliefs and people who don't believe in God at all. Only a minority of their members would have had a Christian background. UUs are often engaged in political activism, particularly in civil rights, gun control, gay rights and various feminist causes: they are extremely right-on. The first gay marriage in America happened in a UU church – despite the fact that they were illegal and the ministers involved risked prosecution.

4. Evangelical Unitarians
These are a mostly American phenomenon, created out of evangelical groups which in the nineteenth century adopted an anti-Trinitarian theology. However, in a most un-Unitarian fashion, they believe scripture is divinely inspired and inerrant – a dogmatic idea which puts them at a remove from other Unitarians. Evangelicals are not members of the International Council and include various groups, such as the Jehovah's Witnesses.

Versions 1 and 2 are mostly European, while versions 3 and 4 are most common in the US and Canada.

So: you have this worldwide community of people, some of whom believe in God and Jesus, some of whom don't. Most of them would differ about what's 'true' in the Bible; some wouldn't believe a word of it and prefer other sacred texts. Some don't believe in sacred texts at all. What could such a disparate group of people have in common? How could they be regarded as a religion (or association) at all?

Not surprisingly, the Unitarians often wonder this themselves.

The answer is a fundamental belief that diversity is a good thing – that despite containing members whose beliefs might even contradict each other, the Unitarians feel a common bond *because* they are different to each other: what unites them is the idea of basic goodness in people, despite the differences. It's kind of like the United Nations. Except it actually seems to work.

Unitarianism will never take over the world. Indeed, its insistence on not seeking converts might one day bring about its demise. And if Michael Servetus came back to earth for a visit, he might be horrified by what he had helped bring into being. When he was on the bonfire, he is said to have cried out: "O Jesus, Son of the Eternal God, have pity on me!" People attending the execution observed that if he had said: 'Jesus, the Eternal Son of God', this would have been taken as a recantation and he would have been saved. As the Unitarians might say, the Devil is in the detail.

18

Neopagans

AND if you are a Neopagan, you've probably started complaining already. Firstly, not all people in this religious category call themselves Neopagan; some prefer Heathen or just plain Pagan. But because 'Pagan' and 'Heathen' are used by some as pejorative terms – and understood by others to be synonyms for Satanism, (which they are not), most adherents prefer the term Neopagan. And technically, Neopagan is the most correct term: these are people who have revived/reinvented some ancient religions; there is virtually no evidence that these are religions which have been *continuously* practised since pre-history. Some Neopagans, or Pagans, dispute this however. Oh yes, there's a lot of disputing in Neopaganism.

There's even disputes over whether Neopaganism is a religion at all.

Admittedly, Neopaganism is more of an umbrella term for a clutch of beliefs which, in any formal sense, have only the loosest of ties to each other. The Unitarians have a strict and dogmatic set-up by comparison. (Indeed, you can be a Neopagan *and* a Unitarian.) However, even a cursory examination of what the Neopagans are about does reveal distinct points of similarity between them – and difference to everyone else.

Firstly, Neopaganism draws its inspiration from pre-Abrahamic societies – Celtic, Norse, Greek, Roman, Sumerian, Egyptian – and as such Neopagans can claim that they are practising a (reinvented) form of a religion which pre-dates Islam, Christianity or Judaism. But because Neopaganism is a product of the modern age it is (with a few exceptions), extremely PC, particularly in relation to respect for the environment.

Neopagans rarely worship in temples or any formal gathering place. Weather permitting, they do it outside. (And, disappointingly, with their clothes on in the vast majority of cases.) Many Neopagans practise their religion by themselves. Neopagans can believe in one God, in a range of different gods, in a female God, in a God that co-exists in the earth or one that lives very far away, yet most Neopagans hold to the principle of respect for other beliefs – which is probably why there is such a dazzling variety of Neopagan groups. Indeed, some Neopagan beliefs, such as Wicca, actually encourage this variety: once a coven (yes, that's what they call them) has reached more than thirteen members, it is encouraged to split into two – and each coven is allowed to develop its own culture and practices.

Because of this loose organisation, solid figures on the number of Neopagans worldwide are hard to come by. A study by the City University of New York found 307,000 in the US who would identify themselves as Neopagan, while a poll conducted by a group called the Covenant of the Goddess in 1999 claimed that there are 768,400 adherents in the US and Canada. However, the most widely accepted Best Guess is that there are at least one million Neopagans around the world.

So how did it all start? Obviously, Pagan beliefs have been around for thousands of years, and in many western countries the old rituals and holy days were simply supplanted by Christian ones. Christmas, for instance, replaced the traditional winter solstice celebrations common in many pre-Christian religions: and some argue that the practice of decorating Christmas trees actually dates from the pagan era. Many Pagan gods (such as Bridget in Ireland) were transformed into Christian saints.

However, this is not to say that the old beliefs survived intact. Most of these religions date from an era where little was written down, so contemporary knowledge of what, say, the Celts believed is patchy. And when Christianity took hold of Europe, non-believers were generally given the tough choice of converting or being burned at the stake. Thus it is highly unlikely – despite the claims of some Neopagan scholars – that Druidism or witchcraft was practised for two thousand years without anyone noticing.

The Pagan religions effectively died off, but every now and again did prompt the interest of various academics: after all, dyed-in-the-wool heathens like Plato and Aristotle had made huge contributions to philosophy, cosmology and various other sciences. Some, like the philosopher Thomas Aquinas, fused parts of Greco-Roman thought with Christianity, while during the Renaissance, artists borrowed at will from Greco-Roman mythology.

But borrowing and believing are two different things: the tinkering with pagan mythology still took place through the filter of Christianity. It wasn't until the eighteenth century and the birth of Romanticism that Neopaganism became a serious religious contender.

Romanticism was a cultural and artistic movement which was essentially a reaction against The Enlightenment: the age when science and rationalism were prized most of all. The Romantics wanted to re-establish the importance of emotion, even the bad ones like horror which they regarded as somehow more 'genuine'. Subjective experience was, for the Romantics, a means of experiencing Truth.

And along with the stress on the subjective came a new belief in individualism: characters in novels were now portrayed as sensitive, passionate and usually a bit tragic; the likes of William Blake took this idea even further by employing it as his life philosophy. "I must create a system," he wrote, "or be enslaved by another man's."

A lot of this being sensitive and tragic found its inspiration in Nature, the idea being that while society, with its strict codes and repressive class system, might crush the individual, in Nature one could find awe and the mystical connections between man and God. Long-ignored writings from the Middle Ages suddenly became trendy again, with their stress on nobility and a sense of magic: the ancient myths, it seemed, told the stories of people more tuned in to a sort of natural spirituality. In the United States especially, the idea of the 'Noble Savage' was born.

Yes, you guessed it: the Romantics took a lot of drugs.

But while the Romantics passed around the opium pipes and stared at trees, there were a number of parallel political developments: the idea of individualism in art had spread into civil society and with that a growing rejection of the old social orders. Nationalism and Republicanism were all the rage, especially after the French revolution, and the Romantic ideas of the 'purity' of ancient languages and folklore were employed in many European countries to re-build a sense of nationalism. It led to the *Völkisch* movement in Germany (*Völkstum* means Nationality) and the Celtic Revival in Ireland, where the likes of WB Yeats and others produced re-worked versions of ancient Irish myth for the stage. In fact it is as a result of this work that the term Neopagan was first coined. Writing about Yeats' and Maud Gonne's stage productions, the Irish MP F. Hugh O'Donnell branded it as "Neopagan . . . An attempt to marry Madame Blavatsky with Cuchulainn."

(The aforementioned Madame Helen Petrovna Blavatsky was one of the inventors of Theosophy in the 1870s. (Theology + Philosophy, geddit?). Theosophy was (and still is) a fairly spacey belief system which borrows heavily from esoteric Buddhism and claims a lineage back to Plato. Yeats and many other writers and artists have been fans. It has little to do with Neopaganism. But we thought you might like to know.)

The dawn of Theosophy, however, came towards the end of the Romantic era: much of the 1800s had been taken up with hugging trees and discovering our Inner Elves, so it was inevitable that someone would start exploring the pre-Christian religions. Who that person is, naturally, is hotly disputed, though a lot of smart money is one Iolo Morganwg.

Cool name. And much better than Edward Williams, which was what Iolo was originally given by his parents. Iolo Morganwg the person and the name itself are both Welsh, the latter translating as 'Ned of Glamorgan'.

Ned was originally a stonemason, but got caught up with the whole mystical thing and in 1792 founded the first *Gorsedd,* or Druidic Coven, in Primrose Hill in London.

Ned also produced a number of works, some of which claimed that the Druidic tradition has survived intact in Wales, despite the Roman conquest and two thousand years of Christianity, among other difficulties. Alas, it is widely considered that the 'evidence' produced by Iolo was forged.

Yet despite the odd bit of forgery, Iolo did leave a lasting legacy for Neopaganism in the form of the Gorsedd prayer or Druid's Prayer, which is still a staple of Neodruidism.

Oh: and he was addicted to laudanum for most of his life. But that's probably not relevant.

There's not enough room here to go into all the detail, but people similar to Iolo were popping up all over Europe at this time – all claiming to have revived (or simply continued on) the practice of the local ancient religion; many using the reborn native religion as a method of encouraging greater nationalism. This was particularly the case in Germany and Iceland. We'll get to them to shortly, but in the meantime we'll stick with Britain.

While interest in neo-Druidism grew, the occult became hugely popular among the Victorian middle classes. Various societies were established including the Hermetic Order of the Golden Dawn and the Ordo Templi Orientis, both of which could fix it for you to chat to your dead relatives via a medium. Once again, the ever-credulous W.B. Yeats was at the top of the queue. The net result of all this was a huge degree of interest in the supernatural and magic: never before, and possibly not even since have such ideas received such a degree of acceptance from mainstream society. Neopagan ideas began to mingle with some from the regular scientific world. *The Golden Bough*, published in 1890 by the anthropologist Sir James George Frazer, scandalised public opinion at the time by suggesting that primitive religions in Africa basically deal with the same archetypes as Christianity.

At this stage though, Neopaganism was still pretty much a minority interest, and it wasn't until the twentieth century that it really began to kick off. In the 1920s, the British Egyptologist Margaret Murray published *The Witch Cult in Western Europe*, which claimed that underground covens of witches had existed from pre-Christian time to the Middle Ages, when witch-burning became popular. Many academics then and since have refuted her claims, pointing out that her evidence was misinterpreted, exaggerated and in some cases simply falsified. (One denounced Murray's work as 'vapid balderdash'.) Yet Murray stoutly defended her thesis, and went on to claim that historical figures such as Thomas à Becket, Henry I and Joan of Arc were actually pagan martyrs. And despite the criticism, there were many who listened to what she had to say: covens began to be formed in Britain using Murray's description as their template.

It was probably one of these covens which initiated a former civil servant named Gerald Gardner in the late

1930s or early 1940s. Gardner had travelled extensively around the world and had previously written about Malay Native Customs, but he kept quiet about what was going on in England until 1954, when he published *Witchcraft Today*. It was here that he first coined (or revived) the term 'Wicca' – the name used for much of the Neopagan religions today, especially in the US.

Curiously, some Neopagans still criticise Gardner for publishing his book, arguing that he was giving away the secrets of what is supposed to be a secret religion. Gardner, however, said that by publishing *Witchcraft Today* he was simply trying to save Wicca from extinction. True or not, what is beyond dispute is that it was Gardner's work which brought Wicca to a worldwide audience. Before not too long it had spread to the US and Canada, and not too long after that began the inevitable process of splitting up. Today there is a dizzying range of different sorts of Wicca, ranging from 'Gardnerian' to the women-only 'Dianic'.

We'll come back to this – and also attempt to explain what it is devotees of Wicca believe and what they do. But first let's see what was happening elsewhere.

The Germans were also mad keen into the Neopaganism. As with the rest of Europe, a mixture of nationalism and Romanticism generated an interest in the old religions in the 19th century and into the 20th, with the establishment of the Gemeinschaft Glaubens-Germeinschaft (Germanic Faith Community). There is an impression that the Nazis flirted with Paganism, but this isn't strictly true: some, like Rudolf Hess, tinkered with mysticism via an outfit called the Thule Society. Influenced by the aforementioned Madame Blavatsky, the Thules believed that the earth was hollow and that Germans were descended from Aryan Supermen. The Thule Society was actually merged into what eventually became the Nazi party, but this connection was played down subsequently; the Führer, apparently, didn't want anyone thinking they were a bunch of nutters. As for the genuine Neopagans, some of them were sent to the gas chambers.

Understandably, growth of the religion stalled somewhat after that until a second revival in the 1950s – though this time with some aspects of Neopaganism taking on a distinctly neo-Nazi hue – specifically the Artgemeinschaft founded in 1951. Happily, however, they remain a tiny minority within German Neopaganism. Since then a number of non-political and expressly anti-racist groups have sprung up, including a re-launched Gemeinschaft Glaubens-Germeinschaft, (which nowadays takes an aggressive anti-Christian line). The Germans, however, seem particularly keen on having splits and feuds. German Neopaganism is often less than harmonious.

It's not even specifically German, because what we are talking about here is *Germanic* Paganism: a collection of ancient religious practices which at one stage covered much of northern Europe and has roots in Germanic, Anglo-Saxon and Nordic cultures. As with Neopaganism elsewhere, it comes in all shapes and sizes and adherents routinely squabble over whose is the 'truest' interpretation. Most notable of these is Ásatrú, which means, via Danish and Icelandic, belief in the Asir – the gods. It is widespread across the Nordic countries (though it has a variety of names) and in Iceland was officially recognised as a religion in 1972 following a prolonged campaign by the Icelandic poet Gothi Sveinbjorn Beinteinsson. In Norway, followers of

Ásatrú are even allowed to perform marriage ceremonies.

They are, however, a little touchy about who uses the name, not seeing themselves as part of the neo-pagan tree but as a completely different tree altogether. There is some legitimacy in this, in that much of the original Ásatrú practices and beliefs were recorded – whereas with most of the other Neopagan beliefs, a degree of re-invention was required. The Ásatrú have also suffered because other Germanic Neopagan groups (most notably in the US) have hijacked the religion to promote neo-Nazi ideas. As a result, the Ásatrú go to some lengths to promote their PC credentials and are very choosy about who they are seen out in public with.

So this is the story with Neopaganism so far: romanticism and nationalism gives birth to an interest in the occult and ancient cultures, opening the door for people around Europe, and then the US to practise long-dead religions. Of course what this doesn't tell you is *what* these people believe and how they do their worshipping. We could make some generalisations here, but to avoid being cursed by outraged witches and Druids, it would probably be more useful to make a whistle-stop tour of the major Neopagan beliefs and what they do. So here we go: hang on to your broom.

Neo-Druidism: This is an attempt to re-create the old druidic religion as practised by the Celts of the British Isles. Druids, however, will stress that Celtic Druidic culture was at one time spread all across Europe. Some attempt to create a new form of Druidism for the modern age; others concentrate on the old practices – or at least as much as is known. As Celtic culture was mostly oral, not much information survives, except for what was written down by Greek and Roman historians.

The Druids aren't too pushed about what god you worship: you can be, for instance, a Christian and a Druid. What they do believe is that the energy of a creative force is in Nature. They also believe in the spirits of place and of ancestors.

But there are some Celtic gods to worship if you fancy it; about three dozen in all, including Arawn, Brigid, Cernunnos, Cerridwen, Danu, Herne, Lugh, Morgan, Rhiannon and Taranis, though some Neo-druidic groups simply prefer terms like 'earth-mother' and 'Lord of the Groves' meaning the sun.

Traditional Druidism believes in an after-life and a moral code that stresses honour, loyalty, hospitality, honesty, justice and courage.

Much modern druidic practice divides adherents into three 'grades':

Bards – in charge of poetry and lore

Ovates – in charge of herb-lore and the 'deeper secrets'

Druids – the top of the Druidic tree. Once they have passed through the other two grades they are deemed wise enough to offer counsel.

One of the more interesting practices the Druids go in for is divination: they predict the future through a variety of methods: meditation, the study of the flight of birds, dream interpretation, and the interpretation of patterns of sticks thrown to the ground.

Regularity of worship varies with each group. Some meet weekly or at significant astrological times. Invariably they take place outside and can consist of the ritual consumption of *uisce beatha* (Scotch or Irish whiskey; they're not fussy), the singing of religious songs, (understandable, after a few drinks), ceremonial chanting, the occasional sermon, the occasional ordination and a Life Sacrifice: plant, not animal.

However, all Druids celebrate a number of festivals throughout the year. Each starts at sunrise and lasts for three days. Bonfires are built on hilltops and couples who take part can assure their fertility by jumping over them. Some of their main feast days include:

Samhain: The 'end of warm season'. November 1

Imbolc: February 1, marking the Return of Light.

Beltaine: (or *Bealteinne*). May 1 is the celebration of The Fires of Bel, the peak of blossom season.

Neodruidic groups are spread all across Britain, Ireland, mainland Europe and the United States. They vary in practice and belief and splinter groups are regularly formed.

Wicca: we've already learned a lot about how this came about. The word Wicca in Old English means a 'wizard' or 'magician' – or simply 'witch', depending on which etymologist you speak to. Naturally, it's disputed, as to what actually defines a Wiccan. Not all devotees of Wicca are witches, and not all witches are Wiccans.

Again, Wiccans don't insist that you believe in any particular God and allow followers to subscribe to other religions also. However, most of them worship a Goddess and a God – the names of which vary from coven to coven. Others worship a range of gods, some of which have been borrowed from the Celtic and Germanic religions. However, in Wicca there is a decided stress on the female nature of God (or gods). Many Wiccans adhere to the (unproven) theory that pre-Christian, pre-literate societies worshipped female gods and so tended to use the visual part of their brains. The Abrahamic religions came with a male God and writing – switching to the other part of the brain. Having male and female gods, goes the logic, balances this up.

Wicca is also regarded as a learned skill as much as a religion as it requires the study of spells and herb lore. However, Wicca does *not* involve black magic. If you insult a Wiccan, they won't make your ears fall off. They'll swear at you like any regular person.

Generally speaking, Wiccans celebrate eight feast-days a year, all of which are borrowed from the Celts and the Germanics, as well as Esbats – full moons. A typical rite would involve congregating inside a Magic Circle, blessing the area, saying prayers, casting spells (this usually means directing 'positive energies' towards groups or individuals who may need them – though in Wicca you cannot make someone the recipient of a spell without their permission), a cleansing ceremony followed by a meal.

Other Wiccan ceremonies include marriage (or 'hand-fastings'), while some covens observe the very sensible idea of trial marriages for a year and a day.

And yep: some Wiccans do attend religious ceremonies naked (or skyclad as they call it), though many others opt for robes or Harry Potter-type outfits. The ceremonies also involve a number of tools – including chalices, wands, magic books, candles and yes, even brooms; the non-flying kind.

Some practise alone, some are members of covens and quite a few like to give themselves cool names like Starhawk or Eldri Littlewolf. Many Wiccans believe that the ideal number for a coven is 13 – and that if the coven exceeds this number it should be split into two.

In terms of morality, their philosophy can be boiled down to the precept: 'If it doesn't harm anyone, it's OK', though Wiccans tend to phrase such ideas in olde-worldy language.

Most Wiccans believe in reincarnation – meaning that people return in human form time and again. A sort of Karma operates here. If you've lived a bad life, you tend to pay for it in the next. However, they don't believe that as soon as you die you immediately pop into another body. In between, souls reside in the very pleasant-sounding Summerlands where they get a chance to reflect on the life just lived.

Admittedly, these are generalised features of Wicca. There are many variants, and variants on the variants:

Gardnerian Wicca: the original form of Wicca as described by Gerald Gardner in his book.

Alexandrian Wicca. formed in the 1960s and named after the great library of Alexandria, which brought together all the knowledge of the world. Apparently. They focus on training and have a hierarchical structure.

Blue Star Wicca. Established in the 1970s, it has borrowed from several other Wiccan traditions but is unique in its focus on music and tattooing. Blue Star covens employ the septegram (or heptagram; a seven pointed star), as a symbol, instead of a pentagram.

Celtic Wicca: Wicca borrows heavily from Celtic religions anyway; Celtic Wicca just borrows a bit more. Celtic Wiccans stress being in tune with nature and generally worship the Celtic Pantheon of gods. Some of them, however, dispute the 'borrowing' claim and maintain they are practising a thoroughbred ancient religion. Nothing new there.

Correllian Nativist Church: Based in Illinois, this is a sort of family business which melds Wicca with Cherokee spiritual customs. It's run by the High Correll family via a website which offers witchcraft lessons.

Dianic Wicca: pretty much the same as traditional Gardnerian Wicca except with a bit more of a political edge. Dianics are big on protecting the environment and in promoting diversity: for everyone, that is, except men. Dianic covens are for the most part female only. As you might expect, they worship only the Goddess and are really keen on the theory that society was matriarchal before recorded history. But seeing as that history was never recorded, we'll never know.

Eclectic Wicca: this is the branch of Wicca to join if you've a low boredom threshold. All or any of the elements from the other traditions are included, as well as any bit adherents might fancy in other religions. Buddhism features largely here.

Feri Tradition: Wiccans have the somewhat annoying habit of never spelling words correctly. By *Feri* they mean fairy; but the weird spelling gives it a more *Lord of the Rings* feel. The Feris are the most Out There of the Wiccans. They harness 'fairy power' in order to further their mystical journey – a journey which includes sensual experience. In other words, the Feris don't object to the odd bisexual orgy.

Kemetic Wicca: otherwise known as Egyptian Wicca.

They worship old Egyptian gods and ape some of their religious rituals.

Odyssean tradition: inspired by Homer's Odyssey, this form of Wicca stresses that life is a spiritual journey. It is regarded as a 'sister tradition' to Blue Star Wicca

Seax-Wica: a form of Wicca which draws its inspiration from ancient Saxon practices.

Stregheria: as we've said, not all Wiccans are witches and not all witches are Wiccans, and Stregheria is a prime example of this. Stregheria is Italian witchcraft (the word actually means 'witchcraft' in old Italian) and thus qualifies as a distinct branch of Neopaganism. Revived in the early '80s, it is a mixture of old Tuscan beliefs and Medieval Christian heresies, though it claims an unbroken history from pagan times: because the Italians didn't burn as many witches during the Renaissance, or so goes the theory, a few slipped through undetected.

In many respects it is similar to Wicca, though there are some differences in the feast-days celebrated. However the stregheria practise 'ancestor reverence' by communicating through spirits known as Lare, and have a more avid belief that their spells can affect the real world; especially in relation to battling negative energies from the astral plain. We've all done it.

The stregheria go to pains to point out their difference to Wicca and aren't even keen on the Neopagan tag, because, (you guessed it), stregheria is a genuine religion which has been practised in secret for centuries.

Church of All Worlds. The CAW claim to have first coined the phrase 'Neopaganism' in its modern context. It came from Tim Zell, who also founded the religion after reading a book. The book was *Stranger in a strange land* by the science-fiction writer Robert Heinlein. (No, me neither.) In the book, a human born on Mars comes to earth and sets up his own religion called the Church of All Worlds. It is organised into 'nests' and emphasises non-possessive love and 'joyous expression of sexuality as divine union'. Adherents would refer to each other as 'God' and 'Goddess' – referring to their inner divinity rather than any exterior God in heaven.

So Tim and a few others set up a religion exactly like the book. It was the '60s, they were in college and no doubt keen on the joyous expression of sexuality as divine union within a non-possessive framework.

But Tim liked his Church and he stuck with it – finally (after some legal battles) achieving the tax-exempt status enjoyed by religions. In the 1970s the religion took a greener turn when Zell developed his Gaia Thesis: that being that the earth is a living organism, which of course has its own spirit. CAW adherents actually believe in a pantheon of differing spirits, most of which are aspects of nature.

Not that they get hung up on what gods people believe in. The CAW's only creed states:

"The Church of All Worlds is dedicated to the celebration of life, the maximal actualization of human potential and the realization of ultimate individual freedom and personal responsibility in harmonious eco-psychic relationship with the total Biosphere of Holy Mother Earth."

So that clears that up then. The CAW has had mixed

fortunes over the years but claims now to have a healthy membership spread across the US. However, the largest concentration, unsurprisingly, is in California. Nests tend to meet weekly and hold a form of liturgical service where they sit in a circle and pass around a chalice of water.

Zell is still involved in the CAW, though he has since passed on the leadership. He now calls himself Otter.

Dievturiba. Founded in 1925 by artist and folklorist Ernest Bratins, it is a religion based on ancient Latvian folklore and mythology.

Whether Dievturiba bears any resemblance to the religion actually practised by the ancient Latvians is disputed; as usual, there's not much evidence.

Unusually for a Neopagan belief, Dievturiba is a monotheistic religion, but with God having three aspects, rather like the Christian Trinity. There is also a host of lesser spirits, many of whom also possess three natures.

Even people have something of dual nature. Dievturiba believes that at death, the dvesele (soul) returns to heaven, but the velis – a sort of astral body – hangs around the physical body, gradually melting away over time.

Romuva. A Lithuanian pagan religion that's big on fire. It's a polytheistic faith which regards Nature as sacred. However, adherents also believe that their dead ancestors live in the hearth of any fire they light. Small offerings of food and various plants are thrown into the fire in an attempt to connect with the gods and dead ancestors. Hey: we've all tried it.

Germanic Paganism. Some call themselves Heathens, based on an old Norse word; others call it Asatru or Odinism or Forn Sed, meaning Old Custom or Theodism, the Anglo-Saxon variant. Some of the belief systems are similar; others are wildly different. Some are extremely Right On; others have Nazi sympathies. Most of them look down on the other variants of Germanic Paganism and regard only their own as genuine.

The religion is practised in Germany and Scandinavia, but also in Britain, the US, Australia and New Zealand.

In terms of organisation, some groups elect Kings or forms of government based on the old Viking parliamentary *Things*. (A hierarchical structure is relatively unusual for Neopaganism.) Most stress the importance of positive personal attributes, such as honour and self-reliance, though there aren't many rules forbidding bad behaviour; in Germanic Heathenry, pretty much everyone gets to the after-life; either Valhalla (if you died in battle), or Hel, which despite the name is a place of calm.

As you'd expect, they worship the ancient Norse gods, such as Thor and Odin, with regional variations. Their rites usually take place outdoors, and have a macho tinge, (celebrating war dead is a favourite theme). Invariably, they involve eating and drinking home-brewed mead, every Viking's favourite tipple. Apparently.

Hellenismos. Otherwise known as Hellenism or Hellenion, it is basically the worship of the old Greek gods. Adherents are encouraged to do as much research as possible into the old rites and put them into practice: lighting flames, offering libations and the like.

Hellenism comes with a moral code which stresses hospitality, self-control and moderation. Surprisingly, most of these Greekophiles live in California.

There are also Neopagans who worship the ancient Roman Gods or combinations of Greek and Roman.

Judeo-Paganism. This is a new one, which seems to have its main presence on the internet. Since the late 1990s, a number of websites have sprung up which explore the roots of Judaism and its pre-monotheistic links with the religions of the Canaanites, Phoenicians and Assyrians, among others. Another term which has appeared on these websites is Jewitchery; describing Jews who also practise Wicca.

Natib Qadish. This is a polytheistic religion based upon the religious practices of ancient Canaan. As we shall see later on, the Hebrews, along with some other Middle-Eastern peoples, are probably descended from the Canaanites. (Early Judaism was polytheistic.) However, Natib Qadish appears to have little in common with Judeo-Paganism.

Adherents make offerings to a huge range of different gods and study mythic tales which genuinely date from three thousand years ago when the religion was practised. They also have a number of feast-days and lunar observances. And once again, they all live in California.

Summum. Not an old religion re-born so much as one made up from bits of other belief systems. Founded in the

US, Summums don't believe in a God *per se* but a kind of 'universal mind' of which we are all part.

Central to their belief is the practice of meditation to establish 'spiritual psychokinesis' – a way of tapping into the big universal brain.

Summom claims that Moses was given 'Higher' and 'Lower' levels of wisdom. The 'Lower' is what we know as the Ten Commandments, but the 'Higher' are Summom's 'Seven Aphorisms'. In Utah, followers of Summum have asked that the Seven Aphorisms be publicly displayed alongside the Ten Commandments. So far, the local authorities there haven't been keen to take up this suggestion.

One Summum practice which displays a reverence for the dead combined with a keen business sense is that followers of the religion practise mummification, both for dead humans and pets. They do it so well, apparently, that Egyptologists have studied their methods. A mummification, however, can reportedly cost $67,000.

Maausk/Taarausk: these are two religions which actually have no connection to each other, apart from the fact that both come from Estonia. The Estonians have the curious distinction of being one of the most un-religious people in the world. Thanks to decades of communism and hundreds of years of invasion from larger powers, only around 25 per cent of Estonians have any religious belief: many still regard Christianity as a belief which was brutally enforced upon them.

In 1928, a decade after Estonia gained independence, a group of Estonian intellectuals attempted to do something about this by re-establishing the ancient Estonian religion:

part of a wider movement to re-establish an Estonian cultural identity.

But as with many other Neopagan beliefs, not much documentary evidence remained of what the old Estonians believed, so it turned into a mixture of what was known about the old religion and bits taken from Christian traditions. It became known as Taarausk: a monotheistic religion which worshipped the God Taara.

But when the Germans and the Russians invaded, the religion was suppressed. The belief still survives, but now in a more new-agey form. Modern adherents worship a pantheon of gods. They believe time began in 1918 – when Estonia became independent.

Maausk is more difficult belief to define, as it incorporates not just Estonian spiritual beliefs but culture, nature and old customs. Adherents have revived a number of old folk-practices, such as bonfires at midsummer, the tying of ribbons to trees by newly-weds and the lighting of candles in graveyards on Christmas Eve – which they regard as the end of the year.

Yet Maausk doesn't have priests, a God or gods or even a specific set of rules. It does believe in an otherworld, but also that the souls of the dead regularly come back to earth for a visit: an old Estonian custom, (even for non-believers), is that candles should be lit at certain times of the year to guide these spirits. Maausk is predicated on the idea that there is no divide between the spiritual and the real. A form of nature-worship is central to the religion: *Maa* in Estonian means land, earth, or Estonia itself. Adherents believe that time began about ten thousand years ago when the Baltic finally broke through to the Atlantic. As a result, the sea level dropped and most of modern Estonia emerged.

OK, OK, that's enough Neopagan religions; you get the idea. Obviously, this is not an exhaustive list, but a selection of some of the larger and more interesting Neopagan beliefs. New ones are being founded every day by people who no longer feel that they have to adhere to mainstream religion to find God. And while this usually involves the resurrection of an old religion, there's something about Neopaganism that's very modern indeed.

17

Tenrikyo

SEARCH the *New York Times* website for Tenrikyo and you'll find four passing references; search *The Guardian* and you'll find none. Yes, you've never heard of it. That's probably because Tenrikyo was founded in Japan and enjoys its largest following there. Will you hear of it again after reading this chapter? Quite possibly. With at least two million adherents around the world and a distinct evangelical streak, Tenrikyo, or Tenriism, is almost certain to keep growing.

And you can relax: compared to the religions we've looked at already, Tenriism is a more straightforward, easy-to-understand belief. Apart from their creation story. That comes later.

Tenrikyo has the distinction of being the only major world religion to be founded by a woman, but before we tell you about her, it might be useful to learn a little of the religious and political history of Japan. We will return to this later in the book, but for the moment a quickie will suffice.

Shintoism is the official religion of Japan and has been around as long as Japan itself. It's big on nature and animals and has a range of gods. Over time, other religions have been introduced, but the really big competition came in the form of Buddhism from China in the 6th century.

As we'll see later in this book, by nature, the Japanese aren't too hung up about religious distinctions and so happily practised both. Buddhist temples were built beside Shinto shrines, and sometimes it became difficult to see where one faith ended and the other began. This air of liberalism was such that in the 18th and 19th centuries, several breakaway Shinto sects were formed, some of which were quite radical.

But this *laissez-faire* attitude to spirituality came to a crashing halt in 1868 when Emperor Meiji came to power – thanks to a revolution.

Technically, Japan had been ruled by emperors for the previous 1500 years, but in reality the real power lay with various oligarchies. Prior to Meiji, Japan was run by the Shogun, who had managed to keep Japan economically and culturally isolated from the outside world for the best part of two and half centuries: two Dutch ships a year were allowed to dock at Nagasaki, along with the occasional craft from China.

And this was the way large swathes of Japan wanted it, regarding foreigners as little more than long-nosed savages. Everyone was happy to keep the foreigners out, except for anyone trying to make a few bob from the import-export business.

Fed up with the Japanese lack of entrepreneurial spirit, the Americans decided to instil it into them – at the point of a gun. Over two centuries of isolation had done little to improve Japanese military technology, so the Shogunate relented, agreeing to strict trade terms with the Americans, British, French, Dutch and Russians.

Domestically, not a good move. The Japanese warrior class, the Samurai, were outraged at the arrival of these white-skinned devils and immediately began plotting to depose the Shogun, the plan being to re-instate Emperor Meiji as head of state.

But they soon learned that they might need more than a few swords and some cool judo moves to grab power, and so, in a blaze of breathtaking inconsistency, turned to the foreigners for help: the British provided guns with which to arm a peasant army and soon afterwards the Shogun were out-gunned. Sorry.

Meiji was installed as emperor, but of course wasn't really in charge of anything – by all accounts he was a bit of a poetry-writing fop anyway. Power remained with the leaders of revolution, who by now had performed a gymnastic *volte face* in their attitude to the long-nosed devils. Not only did they realise that Japan needed to trade with the outside world; they decided Japan needed to *be* more like it. Thus the so-called 'Meiji Revolution' is actually what happened after he had been installed: a complete modernisation of industry, the military and politics.

And they weren't slow about learning: number one on the agenda was a bit of spin to keep the peasants happy, specifically with the aim of building a sense of nationalism around loyalty to Meiji.

To do that, they re-branded and re-marketed the old notion that the Emperor had divine lineage: by tradition, Meiji's ancestor Jimmu was the first Emperor, enthroned around 660BC: and he was a descendant of the Shinto sun goddess, Amaterasu. Thus loyalty to the Emperor was also loyalty to the Gods.

And you couldn't have an Emperor related to a Shinto god if the people weren't too pushed about what religion they followed. Thus Shinto suddenly became the only belief in town. Christianity was banned outright, Shinto and Buddhism were separated, often by force, the Shinto breakaways were suppressed and the three mainstream branches of Shinto were merged into one: State Shinto. From then until the end of World War Two, religious belief and loyalty to the State became meshed into the same thing.

In the process of modernising Japan, the leaders of the Meiji Revolution established an old-fashioned theocracy.

Not the best time to start up a new religion, but if God tells you, what ya gonna do?

So: this is how it all started. Miki Maegawa Nakayama was born on April 18, 1798 in what is now Nara prefecture – about halfway along the string of islands which make up Japan. Her family were well-off farmers while Miki was a devout, dreamy girl whose main ambition seemed to be to become a Buddhist nun.

But her parents had other ideas. They forced her into marriage – at the age of thirteen – which, according to the official version, Miki endured with patience and virtue. Quite a lot of patience, it seems, because things remained that way until October 26, 1838, when Miki was forty years old. Miki, her husband and son Shuji developed sudden severe pains, but rather than call for a doctor, a Buddhist priest was dispatched to perform an exorcism. It's not recorded if the father and son were afflicted by evil spirits; Miki, however was suddenly able to self-diagnose: she was 'infected' with God.

According to Tenri belief, Miki became more than just a medium for God; God was actually inside her, finally returned to earth. According to Tenri scripture, God said: "I am the General of Heaven. I am the true and original God. I have descended from Heaven to save all human beings, and I want Miki to be the shrine of God".

Notice the wording here: *I am the true and original God.* Although it happened before the Meiji revolution, this was still controversial stuff: both Shinto and Buddhism are polytheistic religions – yet this was distinctly monotheistic – even a little bit Christian; and at the time, Japan was no place for them weird foreign beliefs. Yet for more than a century afterwards, Tenrikyo managed to be perceived as a Shinto Sect: a perception they didn't publicly reject until it was safe to do so.

It may be a little unfair to suggest this, but in the meantime, the issue was helpfully confused by having one God with many names: *Tenri-O-no-Mikoto,* – Divine King of Heavenly Reason; *Tsuki-Hi* – Moon-Sun; *Oya* – God the Parent. Miki also got an extra name: from this point on she is referred to by adherents as *Oyasama* – Honoured Mother.

Now you know what it's like: the normal family stuff is going on and then suddenly Mammy announces she is the emissary of God. It was bound to cause some domestic friction. There are a number of ways of looking at what happened to Oyasama. One is that what she claimed is literally true, another is that after grinning and bearing a miserable marriage, she finally snapped and began 'acting out' her original ambition, to become a Buddhist nun. Or perhaps it was a combination of the two.

Whatever the truth, what is a fact is that Oyasama's family were less than thrilled with this development, especially when she began giving stuff away, her stated aim being to plunge herself into poverty. Despite becoming isolated from her family and the community around her, she continued this process for the next twenty years. In 1853, her husband Zenbei – the only breadwinner – dropped dead, further impoverishing the family. Oyasama responded to this by having her house dismantled and giving it to the poor.

The death of Zenbai probably also enabled Oyasama to start taking a more evangelical approach to her beliefs. To put it cruelly – and despite all the people she had helped by giving away her possessions – she was regarded locally as little more than the village nutcase. Her youngest daughter, Kokan, was dispatched to Osaka to start preaching, while Oyasama also began engaging more with the outside world: this time relieving not just poverty, but pain. Oyasama started practising as a faith healer, and seemed particularly gifted in helping women give birth without pain. (In Tenrikyo, this is known as the 'Grant of Safe Childbirth'; a 'Grant' being similar to a blessing.) By all accounts, the results she achieved were spectacular. Before long, Oyasama had a following: she was healing, preaching, and even aiming the odd bit of criticism at some Buddhist teachings. Her followers began to call her a living goddess.

Understandably, this didn't go down too well with the local Shinto and Buddhist priests, who denounced her from the pulpit; or whatever you get denounced from in Japan.

And they had reason to worry: the number of Oyasama's followers swelled dramatically, to the extent that by 1864, work began on a building in her home village, Shoyashiki – later to become the World Headquarters of Tenrikyo. Called the Place for the Service, it was, well, a place to conduct religious services. In parallel to this, Oyasama was composing the service itself and the songs and dances to go with it, known as the *Mikagura-uta*.

In 1869, she began work on her first scripture, the *Ofudesaki*, (The Tip Of The Writing Brush – it was literally written with a writing brush), while in 1875 she revealed where humankind had been first conceived. Luckily, it happened in Shoyashiki.

By now, of course, the quasi-divine Emperor Meiji had been installed and Shinto was the state religion. Opposition from the religious authorities was joined by the State. Tenrikyo services were regularly broken up and Oyasama taken into custody on a number of occasions. According to the official accounts, she bore all this with good grace, politeness, and perhaps even a little humour: whenever the cops arrived, Oyasama would thank the policemen for coming, and then tell her followers that she was going out to work.

And for a while at least the suppression had the desired effect: Oyasama's followers did suspend holding services, fearful of what effect regular spells in prison might have on the now quite elderly leader. Not that Oyasama regarded herself as old: according to her writings, the average lifespan for a human should be around 115; at ninety, she was almost a young wan.

So it's interesting the way the official Tenrikyo accounts phrase it: on January 26, 1887, then in her 90th year, Oyasama fell asleep and 'withdrew from physical life', deliberately cutting short her normal lifespan. Tenri believe in reincarnation, but this will not happen to Oyasama because officially, she's not dead. She remains at the Kyosoden, or the 'Sanctuary of the Foundress,' in what was her home village of Shoyashiki. She is served three meals a day, is run baths, while priests, who perform 'Perpetual adoration' rituals, stand guard constantly at the doors to her 'residence'. It is believed Miki will emerge when Tenrikyo becomes the religion for all mankind.

Again, this part of the story has distinct Christian overtones: the clear implication is that Oyasama deliberately 'withdrew from life' so as to inspire her followers; she sacrificed herself to help them. Leadership (or *Shin-Bashira* – 'True Pillar') of the religion was then taken over by Iburo Izo, a long-time supporter whose previous job was a carpenter: indeed, Tenri scripture is filled with carpentry allusions.

And most important for the carpenter was to negotiate a way for the religion to survive. The authorities were less than pleased that Tenriism seemed to be flourishing, despite the death of Oyasama. However, what bugged them was not the fact that, theologically, Tenrikyo was evolving into a completely different religion – this little development seemed to pass them by. Their beef was that, as a Shinto sect, Tenrikyo was too obsessed with Oyasama and not enough with Emperor Meiji: who, after all, was kin to a god. So in typically pragmatic Japanese style, Izo made some minor adjustments to Tenri theology, accommodating the State view of who was Top God.

Some believe that before she withdrew from life, Oyasama opposed such an accommodation, though there's little evidence either way. What's indisputable is that Tenrikyo came under far less pressure after that, being officially recognised as a Shinto sect in 1908.

During this period Master Iburi also went on to write the third Tenri holy book, The *Oshashizu*, which outlines the religions doctrine and philosophies in more literal terms. After Iburo's death, the leadership was passed on to one of Oyasama's descendants and has remained within the Nakayami family ever since, each one building on the missionary zeal of their predecessor. The faith spread both within Japan and overseas, especially among emigrant Japanese. Shoyashiki has over the years been extensively developed into a complex of buildings around the 'Jiba' – the spot where, Tenrikyo teaches, the world began and will end. It now has fifty thousand residents and contains a complete education system – from kindergarten right up to university, a museum and one of the largest libraries in the eastern world. But the complex is a work in progress, especially the Oyasatoyakata which has been under construction since 1954. When completed, this will be a structure of sixty-eight interconnected wings with the Jiba in its centre. The idea behind it is to build a physical model of the 'Joyous Life': the spiritual state all Tenri aspire to.

So far twenty-four wings have been built. And by the way, Shoyashiki is now called Tenri City.

The system of State Shinto was dismantled after World War Two, yet it wasn't until 1970 that Tenrikyo declared itself as a separate religion: cautiously waiting for the hangover of religious nationalism from the war to melt away.

Today there are around 37,000 Tenrikyo centres of worship in Japan, and at least 1000 overseas, mainly in the United States, South Korea, Thailand, Brazil, Taiwan, Mexico, Canada, Argentina, Australia and France. But these are conservative estimates: at least two million people have taken the Besseki Pledge which signifies official conversion to Tenrikyo, but the figure could be higher than three million. In certain territories where Tenri evangelists operate – such as China – the religion understandably keeps quiet about how many new converts there are.

So what exactly do all these people believe? For the Faithful, Tenri philosophy extends to all areas of life, not just worship. It stresses the importance of group effort, but also – unusually for a Japanese belief system – values the importance of the individual and their particular skills: so you have Tenri teachers who operate in *Daikyokai* (Great Teaching Groups), disaster relief corps, medical professionals, musicians, dancers, artists and even athletes: there is a form of Tenri Judo which has produced many champions within Japan. This is all central to the Tenri idea that through hard work and collaboration, the world can be made a better place. These forms of Tenri 'evangelism', however, are not heavy-handed: they seek to convert through example rather than brow-beating – though all

Tenri followers are taught to consider themselves as missionaries and to live by the maxim: 'You are saved by saving others'.

Central to Tenri belief are the aforementioned three scriptures. The twelve-part *Mikagura-uta* (Songs for the Service) consists of lyrics, gestures and melodies which are performed at various times of the year, usually the 26th of each month. The *Mikagura-uta* is the first text taught to new members, and as such forms the foundation of Tenri belief. The second text, the *Ofudesaki*, (The Tip of the Writing Brush) also written by Oyasama, clocks up 11,711 verses and is basically an expanded version of the *Mikagura-uta* dealing with sin and salvation, how the world was created and disease healing. The final text was written by Master Iburi, Miki's successor. The *Oshashizu* (Divine Directions) is the longest of the three scriptures, running to a whopping thirty-three books and 7,790 pages. As we've said, it gives a more prosaic account of what Tenrikyo is all about.

Tenrikyo literally means 'Teaching of Divine Reason': a teaching which describes how adherents can achieve *yoki gurashi*, (joyous life) through charity and by the eradication of greed, selfishness, hatred, anger and arrogance.

The religion describes itself and the world through a series of Japanese characters, many of which bear more than a passing resemblance to ideas in contemporary Buddhism. There is *Yo* (positive), the same character as *Yang* in the Chinese Yin and Yang; *Ki* (spirit), the same character as *Chi* in Chinese. *Yusan* (excursion), which promotes the idea of working to make the world better and *Gurashi* (livelihood), which describes ordinary, day-to-day existence.

God is described as *Tenri-O-no-Mikoto,* (Divine King of Heavenly Reason), who, as in Christianity, is regularly referred to as the creator and caring parent of all mankind. Also similar to Christianity is a slightly Trinitarian view of God: that there are three 'levels of understanding'. As a Tenri develops in spiritual maturity, (which involves wading through the massive scriptures), they will move from *Kami* which is God as understood in everyday terms, then *Tsukihi* (Moon Sun), God as the creator of nature, and finally *Oya* (Parent), which is God as the parent of human beings. To help that understanding, most Tenri at some stage go to *Shuyoka* – a three-month study retreat.

The Christian influence is probably something to do with the fact that it was Christian missionaries who first translated the *Ofudesaki* scripture from Japanese. To this day, Tenrikyo and Christianity enjoy good relations. Indeed, in the *á la carte* manner we've mentioned before, many Japanese Christians subscribe to Tenrikyo philosophies and attend their services. However, there is a certain amount of bad blood between Tenrikyo and some Buddhist sects, probably dating back to the oppressive times of the 1800s.

So: Tenrikyo teaches that we should rid ourselves of greed, arrogance and all the usual bad stuff, and work to make the world a better, or more spiritual place – a process which will be aided with a degree of stoicism. The principle of *Tanno* encourages a more constructive attitude towards illness and difficulties in life: it's all sent by God.

There is, they believe, a sort of reciprocity here: the increase in spirituality will touch God, who will in turn inject more 'spirit' into the world. The more you give, the more you get. (And note how God is carefully genderless in Tenrikyo; Oyasama was quite big on female equality.)

Good works will also improve the world through the process of reincarnation, which is described as a 'taking off of old clothes and putting on of bright new ones'. (Tenri believe that we 'own' only our minds; our bodies are on loan.) By living a good life, you increase your karmic bank balance and carry this through to the next – though in Tenrikyo they don't use the word Karma. The closest English translation is 'causality'.

In terms of what constitutes 'good' and 'bad', Tenrikyo is deliberately vague, leaving it up to the individual to make their own mind. Indeed, various Tenrikyo websites are much taken up with debate as to what attitude adherents should take towards various issues, such as same-sex unions; as a religion, the stress is far more on what you should do, rather than what's not allowed.

Only eight things are explicitly *verboten* – miserliness, covetousness, hatred, self-love, grudge-bearing, anger, greed and arrogance – and even if you indulge in one or all of these things, the worst that can happen is a crappy deal for your next life. With no belief in any sort of Devil or Hell, Tenri don't think there's any such thing as evil people, only 'those whose minds are stained with specks of dust'.

Nokori or 'Dust' is the Tenri approximation of sin, the idea being that sin-dust falls on our souls on a daily basis; the devout Tenri must be consistent in brushing it away. Tenri prayers actually include a hand-motion to symbolise this brushing.

It's a sort of spiritual dentistry: if you brush every day,

your spirit will be pearly-white and in prime condition to accept the occasional *Sazuke* or 'divine grant'. As practised originally by Oyasama herself, a well-aimed *Sazuke* can relieve physical and mental suffering – but only works on those who have sincerity in their heart.

A more low-level version of this is the *Setsubun*, a folk ritual that pre-dates Tenrikyo, which has been incorporated into Tenri practices. Originally designed to drive out demons, it's the Tenri equivalent of soul-dusting the family home. Beans, usually Soya beans, are scattered inside and outside the house. Family members are then required to eat one bean for each year of their life. Their current life, that is; not all of them put together.

It's not mandatory, but adherents of Tenrikyo can attend morning and evening services, which take place every day at sunrise and sunset to give thanks for the blessings received as well as to pray for God's unlimited blessings. However, the most important observance among Tenri is the Service or *Kagura*, which is staged on the 26th of each month. Involving ten performers – five men, five women, all wearing masks – it tells the story of how humans were first created by God. The performers chant and sing and dance and also outline ten aspects of God's providence. Blessings are also dispensed upon individuals and all of humanity.

The creation story is central to Tenrikyo because, as we've said, the *Jiba*, or place where creation took place, is in Tenri City. And it also, according to Tenrikyo belief, will be the location for The End.

Happily, it won't be a fire-and-brimstone-type conclusion. Perhaps optimistically, Tenri believe that the entire world will eventually convert to Tenrikyo. The details of exactly how this will happen are sketchy, but the plan is that six billion people – or whatever the population of the planet is at that time – will gather at the Jiba to welcome the return of God and a re-awoken Oyasama; after which we'll all enjoy heaven on Earth. So book your flight early.

With God descending to earth and people coming back from the dead (or a long nap), the Tenrikyo version of the End of Days has a distinctly Christian ring. The story of how we came about in the first place, however, sounds positively Darwinian. Whether Oyasama had thumbed through a copy of the *Origin of The Species* isn't known, but the tale of creation as penned by her does seem to contain elements of what could be considered evolution. Concentrate now; this is how it all began:

In the beginning, the world was covered by a muddy ocean. God didn't really like the look of it, so hit upon the idea of creating humans so they could appreciate the joyous life and share the joy.

After some negotiations, God took a fish, a serpent, a killer whale and a turtle and ate the lot of them. Now God wasn't just after a good fish dinner: he was 'testing their natures' so he could decide which bits to use in the creation of people. But people are complicated, so the fish-eating continued: God gobbled back an eel, a flatfish, a black snake and a globe fish, and then all the loaches (a loach is a small fish related to the carp) in the ocean. No doubt feeling a bit stuffed, God now had the raw materials to make people.

First he made a kind of prototype man and woman. In the woman God placed some seeds: nine hundred million, ninety-nine thousand, nine hundred and ninety-nine of them. This early-version woman carried the seeds for three years and three months and then began giving birth to children; a process which took seventy-five days. Ouch.

But these kids were only half an inch high, eventually growing to three inches. After ninety-nine years they died. The prototype woman then began this process all over again, conceiving nine hundred million, ninety-nine thousand, nine hundred and ninety-nine babies which were born after ten months. This time they grew to three and a half inches.

The process was repeated once more, with the mini-people now reaching four inches. After that, human beings were reborn eight thousand and eight times, but as various creatures: worms, birds etc. Eventually a female monkey gave birth to ten humans, five male, five female. These kids grew up and reached a towering one foot eight inches.

Now all of this was happening under the sea, so God reckoned it was time to start re-organising the earth. With human development well under way, God moved some terrain about so that the land and the water were separate from each other. Meanwhile, a new generation of humans reached three foot and began to speak. When they reached five feet, they left the sea and began living on the land.

January 26 2006 was the 120th anniversary of when Oyasama withdrew from physical life. It was marked by record numbers of Tenrikyo visiting the *Jiba* in Tenri City. For Tenri, a visit to the *Jiba* is a bit like a pilgrimage to Mecca – it should be undertaken at least once in a lifetime. Which is understandable, given that this is the spot where the world began and will end. And which is also why the authorities in Tenri City always have someone on hand to greet visitors with the words: 'Welcome home'.

16

Zoroastrianism

ALL the big religions use age as a selling point; to say a religion is ancient implies that it embodies a certain road-tested wisdom. On a merely practical level, any belief system which has survived for one or two thousand years must have something going for it.

So forget all the others: Zoroastrianism is the Mother of all Religions – possibly the first in the world to embrace monotheism; at one time one of the biggest faiths on the planet. From a strictly historical perspective, without Zoroastrianism, Judaism, Christianity and Islam wouldn't be what they are, and Jews, Christians and Muslims wouldn't believe many of the things they do. It's an historical irony that, for many years, Zoroastrianism was viewed as a religion on the edge of extinction: estimates ranged from 100,000-150,000 adherents across the world. However, those estimates have more recently been revised upwards; especially since the US military interventions in Afghanistan and Iraq. Because of the whole despotic-regime-thing going on in those two countries, Zoroastrians – or Parsees – have only recently become more open about identifying themselves as such, which in turn has led to a general re-assessment of Zoroastrianism numbers within the Middle East. Many world almanacs now estimate the planetary Zoroastrian total to be between two and 3.5 million: a far more healthy figure. And why wouldn't it be? After all, this is a celebratory, ritual-rich belief that stresses equality, care for the environment and tolerance: it was a Zoroastrian leader who allowed the Jews to return to the Promised Land. In India, Zoroastrians are widely respected and regarded as honest – by people from other religions. And best of all: Freddie Mercury was a Zoroastrian. It's a kind of magic.

Sorry.

It all started over three thousand years ago. At least. Estimates vary wildly on when exactly the religion's founder, Zoroaster, was born. (Which means it can never be definitely proven who was the first monotheist: Abraham or Zoroaster.) We're not even entirely sure what his name was. Zoroaster is a Greek version of Zarathustra, while he is also known as Zarathusti in Persian and Zaratosht in Gujarati. Estimates as to when he was doing his religious thing vary from 3,500 BC to 600 BC, though most of the smart money is on around 1200 BC.

So: Zoroaster was born in either northeast Persia (Iran) or southwest Afghanistan. Obviously, neither of these countries existed at the time. Young Zoroaster was brought up in what was basically a Bronze Age culture. Not that much is known about the religion of the time, though it's thought that it bore some similarities to early forms of

Hinduism. It was polytheistic, and involved animal sacrifice and the use of various narcotics. Unsurprisingly, chunks of this belief-system ended up in Zoroaster's teachings – another reason why Zoroastrianism is so unique: not only did it hugely influence the beliefs that came afterwards; it also provides clues about the Indo-Iranian culture which eventually produced Vedic Hinduism, and before that, even older Indo-European beliefs which morphed over the centuries into the ancient Greek and Roman religions. In many ways, the history of Zoroastrianism is the history of religion itself.

According to tradition, Zoroaster was marked out as special from birth. He was born smiling: a sign, apparently, of future wisdom, and nothing to do with Mammy's narcotic intake. His family seem to have been pretty well-to-do, and appointed young Zoro a tutor before he was six years old.

But even back then, there were some who didn't like the look of him: when he was just eleven, so the story goes, unknown assailants tried to poison him with black magic. Why they didn't use ordinary poison remains a mystery.

Anyway, by fifteen, Zoroaster had opted to become a priest and by twenty had moved out of the parents' gaff and into a place of his own: a cave in the mountains, where he remained for the next seven years. There, Zoroaster pondered life, the universe and everything – and came to the conclusion that there was only one God: Ahura Mazda. The other 'gods' worshipped at the time were in fact more like angels, or in same cases, evil spirits.

Interesting stuff. As long as you kept such crazy notions to yourself. Which he didn't.

The society Zoroaster grew up in was ruled by princes

and priests, so they certainly didn't want to hear that all those drugs and dead animals were a bad idea; or that commoners were as good as the ruling classes. And such nonsense should definitely not come from one of their own. Don't forget: Zoroaster was a priest.

So as soon as Zoroaster started spouting this sedition, he almost immediately became a social outcast. Not that the status quo was under any particular threat. Zoroaster's early attempts at winning converts were, to put it kindly, less than impressive: exactly one person became a follower. And as that person was Zoroaster's nephew, (or cousin, according to some versions), it almost doesn't count.

Nonetheless, the oppression continued. The local despot, King Vishtaspa, eventually threw the young prophet in prison. But we've told you before about the penal system in the olden days. In jig time, Zoroaster had escaped. And it was then that he had his first lucky break. The details are sketchy, but it seems that Zoroaster somehow happened upon King Vishtaspa's horse – which was ill. It may be that Zoroaster had secretly trained as a vet, or it could have been Divine intervention; whatever the truth, the young prophet did manage to cure the King's sick horse – prompting the King to re-evaluate the man he had previously thrown in prison.

Before long, Zoroaster was preaching again, but this time to more sympathetic ears. And chief among them were the regal lugs of King Vishtaspa. Vishtaspa and his wife converted, quickly followed by the royal court and most of the Kingdom. Vishtaspa's 'kingdom', however, was no more than a small town, and it took a little bit longer for Zoroastrian ideas to spread further: some of the neighbouring despots were less than keen on this new religious development, and for a while Vishtaspa had to physically defend his people. Yet this defence didn't have to be maintained for too long: Zoroastrianism spread so quickly that Zoroaster himself was transformed from outcast to something of a celebrity. Not that much is known about Zoroaster's life from this point on, though it is believed that he took two wives: the Vizier (a sort of government minister) of King Vishtaspa kindly donated a daughter, while Jamaspa, brother of another King, Frashaoshtra, made a similar donation. It's believed Zoroaster composed a section of the Zoroastrian holy book, the *Avesta*, (though this was done orally; Zoroastrian scripture was not written down for some centuries afterwards), and that he died in his seventies. The afore-mentioned Jamaspa took over after his death. Well worth the price of a daughter, no doubt.

After that, we have a bit of a gap in the story: little is known about the development of Zoroastrianism during the next six hundred years, other than it *did* develop, spreading to western Iran and becoming a widely established religion. But as is often the case, it was politics which gave the religion its next great boost. Spin forward to the 6th century BC and Persia is a changed place: no longer a patchwork of small fiefdoms, but a dynastic kingdom with serious imperial ambitions. It was a contender.

This period of Persian history largely falls into two distinct phases; with a bit in between when the Greeks invaded. Phase One was influenced by Zoroastrianism; Phase Two used the religion for its own ends.

The Archaemenian period of Persian history began

around 549 BC when Cyrus the Great of the Archaemenian family seized power and went on to build the first Persian empire: an area stretching almost as far east as India and which, were it not for the resilience of the Greek armies, would have spread into Europe.

Yet despite all the conquering, Cyrus was a devout Zoroastrian and attempted to rule in accordance with the Zoroastrian law of *Asha* – truth and righteousness. He wasn't exactly a big softy, but his religious faith did make him relatively liberal: as we've mentioned, it was Cyrus who allowed the Jews to leave Babylon and return home – a gesture which had a huge impact at the time, and still does: Judaism retains many influences from Zoroastrian philosophy. (According to some, ideas such the immortality of the soul and Last Judgements are direct imports from Zoroastrianism to Judaism.) And despite the fact that Zoroastrianism was effectively the state religion, other beliefs were tolerated: by Cyrus and all the Archaemenian kings (or Shahs), who followed him.

Like all religions, Zoroastrianism changed and developed over time. We'll talk in more detail about Zoroastrian beliefs later on, but it is worth noting that it was during this period that Zoroastrianism developed a distinctive 12-month 360 day calendar – with a thirteenth month added every six years to keep in line with the seasons: a deeply unfortunate move for anyone born in the thirteenth month who liked birthday parties.

They also came up with the idea of the *Saoshyant*.

The *Saoshyant* would be the saviour of the world, and would be born from the long-dead prophet's seed to a virgin mother.

79

Sound familiar?

Hundreds of years before the birth of Christ, the Zoroastrians were already pioneering immaculate conceptions.

But the caring-sharing period of Archaemenian rule finally came to an end. In 331BC. Alexander of Macedonia – or Alexander the Great to his friends – steamed over the borders and within five years he had conquered most of the Persian territories.

As the state religion of the defeated empire, Zoroastrianism also received a severe kicking. Priests were killed and many of the holy texts destroyed. Luckily though, this repression lasted only twenty years or so: when Alexander died another Greek mob, the Seleucids took over. They adopted a more benign approach to Zoroastrianism, allowing it a good deal of regional autonomy. In 141 BC, a third Greek outfit, the Parthian Arcasids, overthrew the Seleucids. The generous attitude towards Zoroastrianism not only continued, it expanded, with many of the Parthian leaders converting to the Persian belief and ruling according to the laws of *Asha*. After the destruction meted out by Alexander, a campaign was begun to gather up any surviving Zoroastrian texts.

The religion also began to extend its influence abroad: many Biblical scholars believe that the Three Wise Men who brought gifts to Jesus were Zoroastrians from the Parthian Empire, while Mithraism, a spin-off faith from Zoroastrianism, became hugely popular within the Roman Empire.

So now we move to Phase Two. Although the Greeks had ruled Persia for a few hundred years, it was along

Banana Republic lines: a Persian King who would do what he was told was kept in place. But when Ardashir, a relative unknown, succeeded to the throne, he rebelled and managed to kick the Greeks out of Persia. The Persians, however, weren't universally thrilled about this: the Greeks may have been an occupying power, but they made the camel trains run on time.

So Ardashir employed one of the oldest tricks in the political book – back then, a relatively new trick – he used religion to assert his authority. He claimed that them smelly, foreign Greeks and their Persian proxies weren't real Zoroastrians, and set about establishing a centralised Zoroastrian religion under the control of the State. Zoroastrianism was aggressively marketed both at home and abroad: meaning that if you didn't convert, you got killed. As a result, the religion spread through the now growing Persian Empire: as far afield as Armenia and even down the Silk Road into China where it became officially recognised in a number of Chinese states. The religion survived there in substantial numbers until the eleventh century, and the influence of Zoroastrianism on the development of Buddhism is acknowledged by many scholars.

Meanwhile, back in Persia, non-Zoroastrian beliefs, especially the new-fangled Christianity, were being repressed. A single canon of Zoroastrian texts was compiled and some new ones composed – and were now being written down.

They also made a stab at reforming the eccentric 360-day-12 month/13 month-every-sixth-year Zoroastrian Calendar, but in a rather half-hearted way. Rather than change the lengths of some of the months, they simply slapped on another five days at the end of the year – a change which still causes problems with the timing of some Zoroastrian festivals.

For Zoroastrianism, all these changes were something of a triumph, but also a tragedy. With the backing of the state, the religion became immensely wealthy and powerful and free of 'contamination' from some of the newer, competing religions. But in doing so, it had become oppressive and rather corrupt: losing something of the tolerant spirit which had informed it from the start.

Not that it lasted. Next in the now-lengthening queue of invaders were the Arabs, who arrived with their shiny new religion, Islam. Like Alexander, the Arabs slit a few throats and burned a few libraries, but didn't altogether suppress Zoroastrianism. The Muslim invaders came to the view that Zoroastrians were, like Jews and Christians, *dhimmis*: People of the Book.

In practice, this meant while the Arabs wouldn't actively suppress the practice of these religions, they didn't entirely approve of them either. *Dhimmis* were required to pay additional taxes in the hope that they would eventually get some sense and convert. (Confusingly, Islamic law bans mass conversions to Islam.)

And see sense they did: gradually, first the towns and then the country areas became followers of the new prophet. Zoroastrianism became a minority belief. Further invasions by the Turks and Mongols, (both of whom quickly converted to Islam), didn't help matters either.

Indeed, the situation became so dire that a large group of Zoroastrians fled Persia in the tenth century and headed for India. Once there, they were given refuge in Sanjan, (now Gujarat), on condition that they refrained from missionary work and married only within their own community – a practice the Indian Zoroastrians still largely observe today. The Indian branch of the religion became known as Parsi – because they came from Persia.

The Parsis are still there today, and despite one thousand years apart, the Zoroastrians of India and Iran have only a few relatively minor cultural differences. In India, Parsis are generally more affluent and westernised than their neighbours – many Parsis run large Indian companies – and tend to be admired for their honesty and entrepreneurial spirit.

There are Zoroastrians in Iran too, though the situation there is less jolly. In a country where to be a non-Muslim is almost a crime, the Zoroastrians are forced to keep to themselves. As a result, many Iranian Zoroastrians still speak a distinct form of the Persian language known as *Dari*.

Elsewhere, Zoroastrian groups of varying sizes can be found across the Middle East, in Pakistan and the western world. For the most part, they are of Iranian or Parsi Indian descent, though there is a growing number of converts – including the aforementioned Freddie Mercury who received a traditional Zoroastrian funeral after his death in 1991. Well; not *entirely* traditional as there are few places left in the world where traditional Zoroastrian funerals are allowed. But we'll get to that.

First, the science bit: what do Zoroastrians believe? As we've said, the Zoroastrian holy book is called the *Avesta* and is composed of two sections: the *Gathas*, seventeen hymns believed to have been composed by Zoroaster himself, and a number of commentaries which were composed later. As well as the *Avesta*, there are a number of prayer books covering various rituals.

In terms of core beliefs, Zoroastrianism is – surprisingly for a religion thousands of years old – remarkably right-on. Equality, regardless of gender, race or religion, is a basic precept, along with care for animals and the environment: the Zoroastrian calendar contains many festivals which celebrate nature. The equality idea even stretches as far as God: unlike many other beliefs, Zoroastrians don't consider themselves to be God's children or servants, but rather his helpers; doing their bit in the fight against evil.

Loyalty is also encouraged, as well as charity and hard work: Zoroastrianism has little time for the lazy. To get into heaven, it's not enough to simply avoid doing bad things – you have actively to engage in good works.

But basically, it's all about dualism: the idea that God (Ahura Mazda) is the epitome of good and is opposed by evil in the form of Angra Mainya. Again, this is an idea which informs most of the major religions of the world – and came from Zoroastrianism. And while we're at it, here's a few more: the notions of heaven and hell, the idea of judgement at death: it all came from some Iranian bloke three and half thousand years ago.

So like all the Abrahamic religions (Christianity, Judaism, Islam), Zoroastrians believe that Ahura Mazda created the world and everything good, while Angra Mainya is responsible for all the bad stuff. Follow righteousness – *Asha* – and you'll go to heaven. Follow deceit – *Druj* – and you go to Hell. Ultimately, good will defeat evil and a heaven on earth will be established.

However, where this idea differs from The Big Three

Religions is the insinuation that Zoroastrian Devil is the equal of the God. In all the others, God created Lucifer, who later on got stroppy and evil of his own accord and who can't possibly win because, well, he's up against God. In Zoroastrian belief, all good things and *only* good things come from Ahura Mazda – so he couldn't have possibly created the devil. Because of this, academics still debate as to whether Zoroastrianism is a monotheistic belief at all – given that it has a Good God and a Bad one.

There are also six holy immortals, or *Amesha Spentas,* all of whom appeared to Zoroaster one day when he was having a wash in a river. They are a bit like the different attributes of the Christian God in the Holy Trinity and described in Zoroastrianism as light rays emanating from the sun. They are *of* God, but not God; and a bit like angels, they go about spreading positivity in the universe: each of the six having a different aspect of Goodness to look after and promote. There are specific prayers which can be offered to them.

Symbolism plays a big part in Zoroastrian rituals, especially fire, which is regarded as a symbol of the wisdom of the Creator. (It had been previously thought – incorrectly – that Zoroastrians worship fire itself. They do not.) Most of this worshipping takes place in an Agiary – a fire temple. Your typical Zoroastrian will pray several times a day, usually starting with a purification ritual – basically, a quick wash.

Some wear a *kusti*: a cord knotted three times to remind of the Zoroastrian core maxim: 'Good Words, Good Thoughts, Good Deeds'. The *kusti* is usually wrapped around a *sudreh* – a long, white cotton shirt. The *kusti* is ritually tied and untied during prayer. (Children are given a *kusti* at the age of seven as part of initiation into the religion: a tradition that actually pre-dates Zoroaster himself.) Zoroastrianism, however, isn't particularly hung up about how often adherents pray or even where they do it – just as much of it takes place at home. The same applies for the dazzling range of Zoroastrian festivals, most of which are celebratory in nature and mostly celebrate Nature.

One reason why Zoroastrianism has shrunk in numbers is that it does not proselytise or seek converts – while Zoroastrians are generally encouraged to marry within their own community; the Parsis of India being particularly strident against mixed marriages. And if you ever get invited to a Zoroastrian wedding, book some time off work: they can last up to seven days. (And again, the Zoroastrian influence on other beliefs is evident. Islamic wedding ceremonies are distinctly similar to the Zoroastrian rite. Apart from all the Koran stuff, obviously.)

But it is on the treatment of the dead that Zoroastrianism remains distinctly different from most other beliefs. They believe that on the fourth day after death, the soul leaves the body – and after that, the body is simply a useless piece of equipment. As both fire and earth are considered sacred, it was thought inappropriate to desecrate them by cremating or burying a smelly old corpse. Instead, the body was left in an open-topped enclosure called a *Dokhma* or Tower of Silence – to be picked clean by vultures. Once the scavengers had had a good feed, the bones would be placed in clay pot in the *Dokhma*. This practice still goes on in some parts of India, particularly

Mumbai, where it is a rather pungent tourist attraction. Unsurprisingly, most other countries aren't too keen on having dead bodies rot in the open air, so the practice has been replaced by burial or cremation. And since you're probably wondering: Freddie Mercury (who by the time of his death was out of the running for Zoroastrian of the Month – he hadn't practised the religion for years) received a traditional Zoroastrian funeral service, followed by a cremation in London. It was never announced what was done with his ashes.

But if Freddie is camping around heaven and belting out a few tunes for Ahura Mazda, they might both appreciate the historical irony that arguably the most influential religion in history is hardly known in most parts of the world; that the Christian President of the United States can call Iran – or Persia – part of an axis of evil, yet without Persia the President of the United States might not be a Christian: without Persia, and Zoroaster, there might not even have been a United States.

15

Cao Dai

NOW at this stage you may be thinking: a lot of the religions we've looked at so far have quite a lot in common – in fact, they seem, to a greater or lesser degree, to have influenced each other. So what if we're not talking about a load of different religions at all? What if we're really talking about one belief system which, due to various political and cultural forces, has splintered in many different directions?

Well, if you are thinking that, then you're not the first. It's impossible to know who the first person to have this idea was, but what we can say with some certainty is that Ngo Van Chieu was one of the few to do anything about it. Ngo is the founder of Cao Dai, a religion with the explicit aim of bringing all the other religions together, partly through borrowing so heavily from all those other beliefs that pretty much everyone feels at home. There's eastern mysticism, the use of Ouija boards, churches which look like Ikea outlets, a Pope and an eclectic range of saints which includes Victor Hugo, Julius Caesar and Lenin.

Yup, the Cao Daists want to end all the fussing and fighting about religion: a belief they hold so dearly that at one time they, um, had their own army. But that was ages ago. If you haven't heard of them, that's probably because the vast majority of Cao Dai action takes place in Vietnam. If you have heard of them, you're probably Vietnamese. Check your passport.

Once again, there is some dispute over how many adherents there are. Official Cao Dai websites put it at six million, but years of repression by the communist government have almost certainly put a dent in those figures. Some estimates put it as low as two million, but most split the difference and leave it at four million believers.

But give it time: Cao Dai is a relatively new belief system, having been launched only in the 1920s. At the time its founder, Ngo Van Chieu, was, according to the official account, leading a life of 'seclusion and wisdom'. Or, put another way, he was the Governor of Phu Quoc, an island in the Gulf of Siam and a profoundly unimportant French territory. So to pass the time, he read a lot about eastern and western religions and he went to a lot of séances. (Communicating with spirits in China and Asia generally has been a tradition for thousands of years.)

And it was at one of these that he first made contact with a being which introduced itself as Cao Dai – which literally means a tower or some form of high abode, and is a figurative term for God. (Actually, the full name was *Cao Dài Tiên Ông Dai Bo Tát Ma-ha-tát*, but let's be informal.) Cao Dai told Ngo that all religions sprang from one belief system, and that it would be really handy if we could all go back to that basic belief. It was now Ngo's job to let everyone know about it. Of course, this didn't happen all at once: there was a series of conversations during which God filled Ngo in on various aspects of the religion and what its symbols were; the main one being the All-Seeing Eye – which, although not the same, is quite similar to what you'd find on the back on an American dollar note. (The revelation of the All-Seeing Eye, however, didn't happen during a séance: it appeared to Ngo as he was lying on a hammock. Up until then Ngo had considered using a cross as the religion's symbol. But, obviously, that was taken.) All this interaction means that Cao Dai is one of the few religions on earth which claims to have been directly established by God.

Word of Ngo's chats with God and his visions quickly spread, and before long he had a group of around 100 supporters. Ngo gave up the day job and returned to Saigon in 1924, where he started preaching. But God wasn't finished revealing himself. In 1925 and (according to official accounts) completely separate from Ngo Van Chieu, the Supreme Being got in touch with three other civil servants: Cao Quynh Co, Pham Cong Tac and Cao Hoai Sang. They too had been having séance chats with a Being who at first called itself AAA, but on Christmas Eve 1925 revealed that it was in fact the Big Guy, Cao Dai. The timing was significant: Christmas Eve was the anniversary of when God came to the western world; now it was the turn of the East.

Also at the same time, another former civil servant (God obviously felt good office skills would be vital for this new religion) – who had given up the day job to become an opium addict – was told at a séance that he was a reborn holy man. Le Van Trung gave up drugs, drink and meat on the spot, apparently without any withdrawal symptoms.

So: the following year all of the above finally got to meet each other and to establish Cao Dai as a religion proper, the official launch date being September 26. (The full name is *Dai Dao Tam Ky Pho Do*, which means Great Religion of the third period of Revelation and Salvation.) Despite being God's first point of contact, Ngo resigned as Giao Tong, or Pope (yes, they have a pope) after only a few months, preferring to 'study and teach'. (Which is Cao Dai speak for 'the contrary article left after a few months to set up his own branch of the religion'. Cao Dai has developed several offshoots over the decades, but we need not concern ourselves too much with those; the theological differences are not too significant.) The Pope's hat, meanwhile, was taken over by the former junkie Trung.

Now you may be wondering why God chose Vietnam as the launch site for a new religion. Why not more populous countries like China, or powerful ones like the US? The Cao Dai explanation is that Vietnam was the perfect spot because of the general Vietnamese acceptance of other religions – making it ideal for a new one attempting to bring them all together. Which is true, except for the decades of communism which began in 1975, when there was virtually no tolerance for religion at all. You'd think God might have seen that one coming.

Then again, Cao Dao doesn't regard Ngo Van Chieu nattering with God as the start of the story, but as a significant point about two-thirds into it. They split world history into three phases:

1) The Era of Creation or Innocence. God inspires various people to found Judaism in the Middle East, Hinduism in India and Yi King in China

2) The Era of Progress, Wars or Self-Destruction. A few years later and God gets busy inspiring again, this time to produce Buddhism, Taoism, Confucianism and Christianity. However, none of these religions did the trick as God had intended it. Their leaders proved to be weak and began distorting the truth; many of the beliefs didn't spread past the part of the world in which they were founded and became adapted to the needs of those local cultures. Most crucially, limitations on travel and transportation made it difficult for the religions to spread.

3) The Era of Annihilation or Preservation. Ngo Van Chieu gets his message from heaven, probably because God knew that jet travel and the internet were only decades away. The official headquarters for the religion was established in Tây Ninh, in the south of Vietnam, (about 100km from Saigon) and remains the site of the Cao Dai Holy See. (Yes, they have one of them as well).

On the day of the September 26th launch, the religion already had 247 followers, all of them extremely keen to get to work spreading the good word – and spread it they did. The belief quickly found acceptance among the rice farmers on the Mekong Delta and within a few decades had developed into a powerful force in Vietnamese society. This was no doubt due to the enthusiasm of the initial adherents, along with the fact that they used popular spiritualist techniques: Ouija boards and the like. The new religion also was, by its own admission, a mixture of Taoism, Buddhism and Confucianism, Christianity and Islam, so there was something for everyone. (The technical term is a syncretic religion.) And the easy Vietnamese acceptance of new religious ideas probably also had something to do with it; Vietnam already had, for instance, a huge Catholic population.

But it was in the 1940s that Cao Dai became a serious player. A nationalist movement with the aim of freeing itself from French colonial rule had developed, and a number of religious and political groups became involved. Cao Dai had by then millions of adherents, mainly along the Vietnamese-Cambodian border in the south-west of the country. As a home-grown belief system, its religious ideas became enmeshed with nationalist aspirations. So, as you do, Cao Dai established its own army.

Of course, by the time they did it – 1943 – the French weren't in control at all. The Japanese had dropped by as part of their World War II domination plans, and were quite happy to arm a number of local forces in the country, just so long as they were equally keen as them to keep the French at bay. Which is exactly what the Cao Dai did, the combination of religion and machine guns also enabling them to rule parts of south-west Vietnam as their own fiefdom.

It was when the war ended, though, that things got a little messy. At first, the Cao Dai cooperated with other nationalist groups in resisting the return of French colonial rule. But after a couple of years of this, the Cao Dai, along with another armed religious group, the Hoa Hao, had a change of heart. The nationalist movement at this stage was being led by a group called the Vietminh, which had seized control of central government when the Japanese withdrew. The Vietminh were led by fun-loving Commie Ho Chí Minh and funded by China: the religious groups began to realise that if the Vietminh got control of the country, they might not be that keen on indulging religious freedom.

So the Cao Dai and the Hoa Hao switched sides. Now funded by the French (who were in turn funded by the Americans), they became embroiled in a bitter civil war, (or the French Indo-China War), which lasted the best part of a decade and led to the country being divided in two. In 1956, South Vietnamese troops rolled into Tay Ninh, the Cao Dai centre of power, and immediately set about dismantling the Cao Dai army.

Now you might think there's a bit of a contradiction here. Cao Dai claims to be a religion based on 'loving immensely', but seemed to have no ethical problem with establishing an army to kick some ass. The explanation is that, as far as Cao Daists were concerned, this was a legitimate fight for survival against the French and then the Communists. In the broader sense, it was also a struggle for human rights and freedom – something which Cao Dai the religion strongly supports. And in fairness, the Cao Dai army did voluntarily disband as soon as the South Vietnamese troops showed up.

The irony is that perhaps they should have hung on to a few guns. The (mainly catholic) South Vietnamese government weren't too keen on what they viewed as a nutty sect – at one stage, the then Cao Dai Pope, Pham Cong Tac, was forced into exile.

And then things got much, much worse. We all know what happened next: North and South Vietnam glowered at each other for a few years and then launched one of the most infamous wars in history, eventually involving a host of countries from both sides of the Iron Curtain and producing no winners. The US withdrew from the war in 1973 and Ho Chí Minh's armies finally took control of the entire country.

Almost immediately, Cao Dai's activities were restricted. The *Cuu Trung Dai* (executive body) and *Hiep Thien Dai* (legislative body) were abolished and replaced with a Governing Council under the direct control of the government. Various rituals and ceremonies were tolerated, but the steely grip placed by government on the religion's structure meant that it would inevitably shrink in numbers. Still, it was a kinder fate than that experienced in neighbouring Cambodia, where the Khmer Rouge simply killed them all. Any that could fled the country, with Cao Dai centres being established in other parts of south-east Asia, the US and France.

It was a major blow for what, until then, had been a rapidly growing religion. But not a fatal one: despite the decades of oppression, the Communist government was unable to erode the Cao Dai power base in Tay Ninh province, while by the early '90s it showed some signs of resurgence, with an overseas movement, *Cao Dai Giao Hai Ngoai* being founded in California. The Californian city of Riverside is now home to the world's largest Cao Dai temple. Other temples were established in Germany and Australia.

More recently, in a bid to attract some tourist and investment dollars, the Vietnamese government has lightened up on the whole Communist oppression thing and in 1997 gave Cao Dai back its independence. Today, Cao Dai is the third largest religion in Vietnam (after Buddhism and Catholicism), while the Holy See in Tay Ninh is a major tourist attraction.

And with good reason, because by all accounts it has to be seen to be truly believed. Built between 1933 and 1955, it consists of a massive, garishly-coloured nine-storey shrine and many other buildings which combine eastern and western architecture: huge enamel dragons are twisted around bright pink banisters; there is stained glass everywhere, Muslim turrets and Chinese pagodas. Paintings of the vast and eccentric array of Cao Dai saints adorn the walls, along with statues of storks. In the central temple, a giant eye – the symbol of the religion as chosen by God himself – gazes down from between two gigantic box-like structures; monks wearing colourful robes and pointy hats worship to the accompaniment of a string band while hordes of tourists gawk at them. If Timothy Leary had been an architect, this is probably the kind of thing he would have come up with – but apparently, the design was communicated via a medium from God. After visiting here, the British writer Graham Greene actually considered converting to Cao Daism. But then didn't. ("What on my first two visits had seemed gay and bizarre," he later wrote, "was now like a game that had gone on too long".)

All right, so what does your average Cao Daist believe?

Although the religion borrows from many other beliefs, it's fair to say that the main influences are eastern. Indeed, the Buddhist, Taoist and Confucian parts of Cao Daoism are separately represented at the top levels of the hierarchy, though without any major theological differences.

The story goes like this: in the beginning there was Tao, a sort of eternal goo from which everything is formed. At some point the Big Bang happened and from this God was born. But God couldn't create the Universe yet because he controlled only Yang. So he shed part of himself and created the Goddess, who was in charge of Yin. With Yin and Yang now in place, the Universe popped into being. Thus in the same way that all animate and inanimate objects are made of atoms, everything is made by God and is part of God. The aim of all religions, argues Cao Dai, is to achieve 'reunification' with the Supreme Being.

So: Cao Daoists not only worship God the Father, but also a Goddess who they refer to as Mother Buddha. Rather confusingly, Mother Buddha is actually a bloke. Mother Buddha is in charge of Yin, which is female, but isn't part of it. Oh, right.

That's some of the Taoist influence on Cao Dai; now here's the Star Trek bit: the religion teaches that there are 36 levels of heaven and 72 planets which have intelligent life; number one being closest to heaven and 72 being the farthest away. Earth, unfortunately, ain't doing that good, coming in at only 68; and apparently, even the poorest person on planet 67 wouldn't trade places with Bill Gates on this one.

There are three main scriptures which are, as you might expect, a mishmash of the various religions it has borrowed from. However, while these scriptures are presented to adherents as the word of God, they are also not the word of God. Which isn't as confusing as it first sounds. According to a Cao Dai website, "Cao Dai without being Cao Dai is the true Cao Dai" – a fancy-pants way of acknowledging that there are many religious paths to God, and all are equally valid. The main aim of Cao Dai isn't necessarily to convert others to Cao Daism, but simply to get them to acknowledge that all religions are fundamentally the same in this regard: there is no one true religion because they are *all* true religions. Thus to claim that even Cao Dai is the one true religion isn't Cao Dai. Think about it.

Over the years various offshoots of Cao Dai have developed, most of which are esoteric in nature and involve a lot of meditation and development of 'inner divinity'. The esoterics tend to indulge in a lot in séances and spiritually download a lot of instructions and prayers from various famous dead people; usually in verse form. Followers of these branches of Cao Daoism are full-time vegetarians, usually celibate, unshaven and most of the time locked away from the world. In short, they are monks.

However, mainstream Cao Dai (or exoterism) is for those leading ordinary, humdrum lives and involves a simple set of five precepts:

1. Do not kill.
2. Do not steal.
3. Do not commit adultery.
4. Do not get drunk.
5. Do not sin by word.

Apart from that, Cao Daists are expected to fulfil their family and personal responsibilities, to be kind to nature and avoid the unnecessary destruction of any creature. The stress is on spiritual well-being here and a renunciation of materialist values. Support and instruction can be acquired from priests or from attending the odd séance – though this is a rare event for mainstream Cao Daists and takes place only after extensive preparation.

And it is mainly because of spiritualism that Cao Dai has developed its large range of Buddhas, Sages and Saints. An historical A-list of people have turned up in spirit form to give their tuppenceworth, including Joan of Arc, René Descartes, William Shakespeare, Victor Hugo, (author of *Les Misérables*), Louis Pasteur, Lenin. Buddha, Confucius, Jesus Christ, Muhammad, Pericles, Julius Caesar, Sun Yat-sen (the founder of modern China), Napoleon, Thomas Jefferson, Winston Churchill, Chinese poet Li Bo and Rutherford B. Hayes, the nineteenth president of the United states – not to mention a host of people who led quite unremarkable lives when living in this temporal neck of the woods; many of whom are ancestors of the living. (Apart from séances, another method of communication is to leave a piece of paper beside a temple altar, which is then 'read' later on by a medium.)

It is also required that they practise vegetarianism at least ten days per month (as it is believed meat pollutes the body) and participate in prayers and ritual acts of devotion to the Supreme Being. There are four times of the day that this can take place: noon, 6pm, midnight and 6am. However, to worship once a day is usually considered enough.

As with many of the eastern religions from which it borrows, Cao Daists believe in karma and reincarnation: the better you have been in this life, the better your position will be in the next one. And this notion is strongly reinforced in practice: Cao Daists record the birth date of people, but not when they died. Strict limits are also placed on how long a deceased person can be mourned: they have, after all, gone to a better place. (Or a worse one, depending on what kind of life they have led.) The stress is always on the idea that losing the body is no big deal, but losing the soul through living a bad life is a disaster. The ultimate aim of the Cao Daist is to escape the cycle of reincarnation and achieve 'reunification' with God by hopping from planet to planet through the reincarnation process – though the esoteric forms of the religion can by-pass this process slightly through 'astral travelling'.

And when you eventually get to Heaven, it's not quite the Christian concept of sitting on clouds and playing harps; in Cao Daism, Paradise is a vast bureaucracy geared towards running the cosmos smoothly and helping mortals get in – which may be why God was so keen to recruit devout civil servants. Spirits in Heaven can even gain a form of 'promotion' by working hard to help those still in the planetary realms.

But this process does not go on indefinitely. The 'Third Era', which we are currently in, will last just 700,000 years and culminate in a long *hoa*: a sort of judgement day meeting of everyone. So there's still a bit of time.

However, in terms of its' organisational structure, Cao Dai makes the Roman Catholic Church look like a bunch of disorganised hippies.

As we've said, at the top of the structure is the Giao-

Tong, or Pope, who leads an executive body called the Cuu Trung Dai, or college of men. On it sits the Cao Dai *Il Papa* and six cardinals, who have the power to direct adherents both spiritually and temporally – though not without the agreement of the Pope. (Women may reach the rank of cardinal – though not Pope – and sit on a College of Women. In Cao Dai temples, men and women have separate entrances. Barring women from the top job seems odd, given that Cao Dai stresses equality in everything else. The explanation is that Yang is male and Yin is female. Yang created Yin, therefore Yin cannot rule over Yang or there would be chaos.) At the higher levels, the Buddhist, Taoist and Confucian elements of the religion are represented by different clergymen.

Unsurprisingly, selection of the Pope consists of asking God, via a medium, who should get the job. Currently there isn't one, but now that the Vietnamese government has lightened up and there is a chance to expand again, a new appointment is expected soon.

Beneath this there are 36 *Phoi-Su* (Archbishops), three of whom hold the rank of *Chanh Phoi-Su* (Principal Archbishops). There are 72 *Giao-Su* (Bishops), 3000 *Giao-Su* (priests), in charge of temple ceremonies and propagating the religion, and an unlimited number of *Le-Sanh* (Student Priests). These are drawn from the most virtuous of the sub-dignitaries, which come in three varieties: The *Chanh-Tri-Su* (Minor Office-Bearers), who look after followers in the more remote villages; *Pho-Tri-Su* (Sub-dignitaries) and *Thong-Su* (Religious Village Administrators). As with the Catholic Church, all clergy people take vows of poverty, obedience and chastity

And below this multitude of chiefs come the *Tin-Do*, ordinary followers. In parallel there is also a complex system of administrative levels to oversee the more temporal aspects of the religion.

Recently, the Vietnamese Government reaffirmed its commitment to allow the Cao Dai religion to operate independently. The future is brighter than the past has been, yet so far, there have been no signs of major expansion. But they are working on it. In the US, it is still practised largely within Vietnamese communities only, despite a widespread belief within Cao Daism that it is in America that the religion will take off and spread around the world. The only thing stopping it, apparently, is the lack of information about the religion in English. Remember; you read it here first.

14

Shinto

SO it's back to Japan again, and a religion that, in typical Japanese fashion, is difficult to pin down; at least from a western perspective. To put it at its most utilitarian, pretty much all the religions in this book have one aim for adherents: to get into the after-life by worshipping God and being good. Shinto, however, isn't too pushed about that and would rather we make the best of things on earth. Equally, Shinto isn't pushed about attracting new members or the fact that, on paper, most Japanese are Shinto, while in reality, only a small percentage of them could be bothered to claim it as their religion.

Unlike most beliefs, Shinto didn't appear at a definite date during Japanese cultural development. Shinto is as old as Japanese-ness itself, and in many respects it's impossible to disentangle one from the other.

Counting by the official figures, Shinto should be in the Top Ten religions with 100 million adherents – around 75 per cent of the Japanese population. However, this is because of a 300-year-old Japanese law which requires that every birth must be registered with a Shinto Shrine. (This is considered a gesture of welcome rather than an imposition.) But polls tell a radically different story: just over three per cent of the Japanese population name Shinto as their religion. That's not to say that other Japanese don't participate in Shinto festivals or even use Shinto temples for births, marriages and deaths; they do: but in the Japanese mindset, that doesn't *make them* Shinto. It's more like a religious resource which they occasionally use.

Thus to consider the number of adherents as we have in all the other religions, a more realistic figure is around 4.5 million. And your average Shinto wouldn't be too bothered about where they come in a Top Twenty; that's just not their style.

So, rather than ask where Shinto has come from, it's more appropriate to look at how and where the Japanese originated.

And no one knows. At least for sure. There was probably some migration from central Asia and Indonesia, plus some invaders from Korea. But all this happened thousands of years ago, and it's not known what religion they practised. However, it's not unreasonable to assume that it was some form of animism (the worship of various spirits which correspond to wind, rain, mountains, sun etc) which included rites with an agricultural association. (Planting, harvesting etc.) We can assume this because the early Japanese were for the most part farmers, and because the religion described above isn't a million miles away from Shinto. It's worth mentioning at this point that Shinto is one of the few major world religions which doesn't worship a God or even gods in the way westerners would understand it. Instead there is a pantheon of spirits and deities which exist both here and in the spirit world, there being very little division between the two. The Shinto word for what they worship is Kami, which refers to the pantheon of spirits but also various concepts associated with nature and nature itself. So Kami means, er, you know, *stuff*.

Back to the history bit: as we've seen with other cultures, early Japan was carved up between dozens of tribes, all of whom had their own spirits for various bits of nature. But inevitably, someone was bound to take over: the Yamato kingdom was established in or around the third century and not too long afterwards, the Yamato version of animism began to take precedence over the others. As part of this process – and for political reasons as much as any other – various dead Yamato ancestors were given the status of deity while it was claimed that the Royal Family were directly descended from the sun-goddess Amaterasu, arguably the most important figure in the Shinto pantheon. As we already know, (see **Tenrikyo**), claiming to be related to God does wonders for building up loyalty among citizens. And this connection between Shinto and politics continued for centuries afterwards.

At this time, early Shinto didn't have anything by way of temples or centres of worship, at least anything that was built by humans. Being nature-based, worship happened in copses or at 'sacred rocks' called *iwakura*. Similarly, nothing about Shinto was written down nor were there any pictorial representations of the Kami, as they were regarded as formless. In fact, the religion didn't even have a name: making it possibly the most low-effort belief in history.

So it wasn't until the fifth and sixth centuries that the Japanese became a bit more, well, religious about their religion. There were two reasons for this:

1) The introduction of writing. The Japanese seemed to come to writing relatively late (5th century AD), but when they did, they wrote down pretty much everything they could think of. And one of the first tasks was to compile all the various myths into one unified account. This emerged in the form of the *Kojiki* (The Record of Ancient Things) and the *Nihonshoki* (The Chronicles of Japan). Of course these didn't contain *all* the myths – just the ones that were politically acceptable and further bolstered the idea that the Japanese royal family had divine lineage. Even at this stage, there were still areas of Japan which didn't accept the leadership of the Imperial family.

2) The arrival of Buddhism in the 6th century. Although some Chinese Taoist and Confucian elements had already crept into Shinto, it was the arrival of Buddhism which really made the Japanese religion think about its own identity and what its function was. A bit like religion is supposed to do.

Out in the less populous areas, there was some initial resistance to the Chinese religious competitor, but in the towns, and especially the Imperial Court, it was a huge hit: unlike Shinto, it arrived fully formed and with all sorts of sexy ideas like actually building temples at convenient locations, rather than having to traipse out to the forest to find holy rocks.

But its popularity also caused a political problem: the Japanese Royal family were, after all, descended from Shinto gods, not Buddhist ones, so for the first time it became important that Shinto be defined as a separate religion – for the first time, they even bothered to give it a name. Shinto means 'way of the gods': a word with Chinese roots.

Not that there was any particular effort to suppress Buddhism – it was way too popular for that. So instead an attempt was made to explain Shinto as a sort of sister religion: the spirits of Kami are involved in the Karmic cycle and had a special place in protecting Buddhism; or: the Kami were different aspects of the Buddhas. Links were made between the aforementioned sun-goddess Amaterasu and Dainichi Nyorai, an aspect of the Buddha, which means 'Great Sun Buddha'. Comparatively speaking, Shinto was quite a simple doctrine compared to Buddhism or Confucianism, so both the Chinese belief systems were plundered to evolve a Shinto theology. And none of this happened organically: the emperor established a Department for the Affairs of the Deities to oversee the process.

Shinto shrines were built and the two religions settled down to a fairly contented co-existence without the Japanese distinguishing much between the two. And with good reason: Shinto was in fact Shinto-Buddhism.

Over the centuries, occasional attempts were made to separate the two and stress the 'Japanese' aspects of the religion. But they never caught on – mainly because separating the two was virtually impossible.

But not *completely* impossible. We've mentioned this before so there's not that much need to dwell on the details, but in 1868 Shinto was declared the Japanese State religion and the link with Buddhism banned – and for the same old reason: to stress the divine lineage of the Emperor and thus drum up a bit of nationalism within the population. They didn't want the Japanese to worship Shinto so much as worship the Emperor and the Empire.

In 1872, in a classic History-Repeating-Itself Move the Orwellian-sounding Ministry of Religion was founded to manage this transformation. It amalgamated the various strains of the religion into one: State Shinto, and divided Shinto shrines into a hierarchy of twelve levels, with those dedicated to the Emperor's relative, Amaterasu at the top and small village temples at the bottom. In a reverse of previous practice, all family details, (including births – we mentioned this before) were registered with Shinto rather than Buddhist Temples. Priests had to be officially recognised by the State, while children were instructed in a form of theology which (to loosely paraphrase), was called: 'The Emperor. He's great'. Naturally, all traces of Buddhist influence were carefully removed.

By the end of the century, school kids were required to recite an oath of allegiance to the State and the Emperor – portraits of whom were now the main point of worship at most Shinto shrines. The State had managed to engineer a culture where religious worship and political rally became the same thing; where, as far as most Japanese were concerned, they were ruled by a god.

Curiously, it was during this period that Shinto was declared to be 'non-religious'. This neatly sidestepped the apparent contradiction of enforcing Shinto on Japanese society while guaranteeing freedom of religion in the Japanese constitution, but it also catapulted Shinto into a position which, in the Japanese mind, was even better than your ordinary spiritual belief-system: it was so engrained in ordinary Japanese culture and tradition that it was felt to have somehow transcended all the other beliefs; the way the Japanese transcended all other races.

In short, Japanese society became a little introverted and a bit up itself: and remained that way until the end of World War Two.

Interesting fact time: the word 'Kamikaze' doesn't mean crashing your plane into an aircraft carrier. It means Divine Wind – which was what Emperor Hirohito had promised he would use to defeat the Yanks in the Second World War. Divine Winds, it turned out, were no match for nuclear weapons, so shortly after the Japanese surrender, the Emperor resigned his position as a Living God. In the Imperial Rescript of 1946, he wrote: "The ties between Us and Our people have always stood on mutual trust and affection. They do not depend upon mere legends and myths . . . They are not predicated on the false conception that the Emperor is divine, and that the Japanese people are superior to other races and fated to rule the world."

Bummer. Certainly, this recantation of divinity came as much from the fact that the Allied forces had a literal and metaphorical gun to the Emperor's head rather than him actually believing it. Yet the fact they made him do it showed just how important the dismantling of Shinto as a State belief was to re-shaping modern Japan. Today, the constitution forbids any religious belief from having State recognition.

Curiously, this didn't damage Shinto as much as might be expected. Certainly, a certain amount of disillusion set in towards the State and its imperial ambitions, but the Japanese population seemed to realise that Shinto had been used as a propaganda tool rather any great fault lying with the religion itself.

With State Shinto abolished and freed from the literalist requirement to believe in their emperor as a God, the Japanese quickly re-acquired their old habit of a more casual use of the religion. In a 1970s survey, one third of people who professed to have no religion also admitted to having a Shinto or Buddhist altar in their home, while, as already mentioned, only a tiny minority would list Shinto as their religion at all. Yet the decline in Shinto practise has not been proportional to this: festivals are still celebrated, ancestors are worshipped and various other practises still observed – but more, apparently, as a product of culture rather than spiritual belief. Indeed, belief is not a pre-requisite of Shintoism. You just have to turn up.

Some have argued that Shinto is actually not a religion at all, but more a way of looking at the world. After all, it doesn't have many rules, no founder, no major scriptures and no creed. It doesn't differentiate between the physical and spiritual world, doesn't have much of a notion of heaven or an after-life, while a number of completely non-religious customs and practices come from Shinto: flower arranging, garden design, sumo wrestling, the use of wooden chopsticks and the removal of shoes before entering a building. It's not so much a way of believing, but a way of being.

So let's get down to looking at what your average Shinto (if there is such a thing) actually believes.

As we've said, at birth, the local Shinto shrine adds every baby's name to a list, regardless of their family religion. This makes the child an *Ujiko*, or 'named child': it is a gesture of welcome to the child by the local Kami (Shinto is a very local religion), plus it ensures that the child will be added to that pantheon of Kami after death – when they become *Ujigami*, or Named Kami. Children who die before registration (or aborted foetuses) are called *Mizuko* – water children – and are believed to cause plagues and be generally troublesome. There are specific shrines dedicated to *Mizuko*, (there are Shinto shrines dedicated to pretty much everything), with the aim of calming their anger.

As we've said, Shinto has precious few rules, other than a general instruction to live a simple and harmonious life with people and nature. There are, however, four 'affirmations' of the Shinto spirit; in other words, four areas of life which should be paid special attention:

1) Tradition and family. The family is regarded by Shinto as the primary mechanism for passing on traditions and customs. Most of the major Shinto festivals relate to family events, such as births and marriages, while most of the Kami to whom individual adherents would pray tend to be dead relatives. Shinto preserves family life on both sides of the spiritual divide.

2) Love of nature. In keeping with its animist roots, Shinto regards nature itself as sacred – and existing in both the

physical and spiritual worlds. Just like humans, many natural objects have spirits which are part of Kami.

3) Purity. Being clean is a big deal in Shinto, both spiritually and literally: even taking a bath is regarded as fulfilling one of the Four Affirmations. And this applies equally to a person's spirit: Certain actions can cause a sort of spiritual grubbiness, *kegare* (literally, 'dirtiness'), which will need to be cleaned off. These bad actions can range from murder, lack of consideration for others and simple bad manners: ordinary Japanese life is full of ritual phrases to show respect for other people and even for food which is about to be consumed. At meal times, for instance, most Japanese say '*itadakimasu*' (I will humbly receive this food). Additionally, there are some taboos which are more like superstitions than moral directives: women are discouraged from climbing Mount Fuji, while people recently bereaved are discouraged from attending weddings. Certain words are regarded as 'beautiful', and others not. Similarly, organ donation is frowned upon in Shinto, as it would be regarded as giving someone else your Kami. And that's just wrong, man.

However, this emphasis on respect for others and for nature isn't born out of a strict moral code so much as pragmatism: if a person doesn't display the proper respect, they will bring ruin on themselves; if the Kami of the chicken you're eating for dinner feels it has been dissed, then it can hold a grudge *(urami)* and get you back. (Indeed, much of the relationship between Shinto adherents and Kami seems to be more in the nature of mutually beneficial arrangement rather than worship: offerings and rituals are aimed at keeping the Kami sweet or asking them for favours by leaving offerings at shrines such as pictures and small statues. In medieval times, the nobility would even donate live horses to a shrine if they were looking for something big, like victory in battle. Adherents can even ask Kami to 'curse' people they have a dispute with, but only if they have done something wrong and really deserve it. In Shinto, there is no sense that humans are 'fallen' and have to atone for their sins. Shinto regards people and the world as basically good – so its aim is to show adherents how to get the best out of it.)

Thus to placate a narky Kami, Shinto includes a number of purification rituals which mainly involve washing of the body in waterfalls, streams or the sea. Similarly, buildings, buses, planes and cars can be 'cleaned' through blessing.

4) Attendance at Matsuri. In Shinto there is no requirement for regular shrine attendance, but adherents are encouraged to show up for any festival dedicated to the Kami, of which there are many each year, along with festivals celebrating the new year harvests, children and adults. As often as not, these festivals aren't particularly 'holy' in the western sense. They are highly ritualised and will include processions, prayers, offerings and a sermon as you might expect, but also dramatic performances, sumo wrestling, feasting and quite a bit of sake drinking. Drunkenness and loutish behaviour in general are often a central part of Matsuri. This isn't a lack of respect; this is because it is thought that Kami like this sort of thing.

Much of this, of course, takes place at Shinto shrines. Some are large, elaborate structures, but in the main worshipping is done at small local shrines (which have their own local Kami) and even home-shrines: and as often as not, adherents identify more with these local shrines rather than the religion as a whole. Most public shrines are fronted by a *torii*: a gate which separates our world from the world of the Kami. There are well over 100,000 such shrines in Japan today, each with a complement of Shinto priests. Often these shrines are dedicated to particular Kami, with the sun-goddess Amaterasu getting most of the attention. Inside the shrine, she is often represented by a mirror: to remind adherents that everything they see in the physical world is an embodiment of her and all the other Kami.

So let's look at the concept of Kami in a bit more detail. Concentrate now.

As we've said, Kami refers to a pantheon of spirits which created the world. It also can refer to dead ancestors. At the same time, Kami exists in everything, but not everything is referred to as Kami. The word can also be used as an adjective: so say, if a waterfall is particularly impressive, it is Kami because it is showing off its Kami nature particularly well, that being its spiritual or mystical nature. Confused? You should be because even many top Shinto theologians admit to not having a full understanding of exactly what Kami is. While the word is often translated as 'God' or 'spirits', it literally means 'that which is hidden'.

Important to remember here is that Shinto doesn't make much of a division between the spirit and physical worlds: the Kami spirits, even the important ones, don't differ that much from humans; they exist here in the world with us, just in a different way. And they are prone to many of our

faults: they are not omnipotent and can be quite contrary
– some of them are just plain evil. They can even be injured
and die – and death is very much frowned upon in Shinto.
Many are also associated with particular activities, rather
like patron saints in Christianity. So just in case you bump
into any, here are the main players:

Amaterasu. The 'Sun Goddess', and the greatest of the
Kami.

Benten. A female Kami, associated with music and the
arts.

Ebisu. A Kami who brings prosperity.

Hachiman. The 'god' of archery and war.

Izanami and Izanagi. The two Kami who gave birth to
Japan.

Konpira. The Kami of safety at sea.

Susanoo. Brother of Amaterasu, the Kami of the wind,
who both protects from and causes disasters.

Tenjin. The Kami of education, and originally a real
person: a scholar by the name Sugawara no Michizane.

Beyond these there are thousands, if not millions of
Kami: no one knows. The word Kami is actually a shortened
version of *Yaoyorozu no Kami* which means 'eight million
Kami': not because there are eight million of them, but
because at the time the phrase was coined, there was no
concept of infinity. Eight million was the highest anyone
had ever counted up to.

All these Kami – and many others besides – appear in the two aforementioned scriptures, the *Kojiki* and the *Nihon-gi*. And it is in these stories that we can get a real sense of how 'Japanese' a religion Shinto is – and how the Japanese have been tempted at times to think themselves better than everyone else.

The Shinto creation story goes like this: at first there was chaos, but then the universe was created and along with it, a number of Kami came into existence. A few of them got married and had kids: particularly brother-and-sister team, Izanagi (meaning 'he who invites') and Izanami (meaning 'she who invites').

One day Izanagi and Izanami had thrust a jewelled spear into the ocean, and the first piece of land ever formed where the spear touched the water. This was, surprise surprise, the central island of Japan.

These were obviously more liberal times, because to celebrate the creation of Japan, the brother and sister decided to get married. And once they did, they started having loads of sex.

As well as being partial to a bit of incest, Izanagi and Izanami were also not the greatest of parents: their first child, Hiruko, was born deformed (apparently because Izanami had spoken during sex), so they promptly abandoned him.

Happily, this didn't put them off parenting: Izanagi and Izanami continued to get jiggy, in the process producing the other islands of Japan and many other Kami. However, one of the kids was the Kami of fire and so Izanami was badly burned during the birth and eventually died. Izanagi, displaying more bad parenting skills, beheaded the child, though other Kami were born of the blood from the killing.

Grief-stricken, Izanagi went in search of his sister-wife and ended up in Yomi, the land of the dead. But by the time he arrived it was too late: Izanami had eaten the fruit of the dead and was doomed to stay in Yomi. However, she told Izanagi that she would try to do a deal to get out of there if he promised not to search for her again.

Izanagi promised, but soon lost his patience and searched for Izanami again. When he found her, her body had rotted and was full of maggots. And she wasn't feeling too good either. Furious that her husband-brother had broken his promise, she tried to force him to remain in the underworld. But Izanagi fled, and used a boulder to block the entrance to Yomi, thus erecting a permanent barrier between the lands of the living and the dead.

Still angry, Izanami promised to kill 1000 people a day every day in revenge. To balance this, Izanagi vowed to create 1500 new-born babies each day.

But before any baby-making, Izanagi needed time to get over his ordeal: all this contact with death had left him contaminated and as a result he was cursed with bad luck. So Izanagi bathed in the ocean to purify himself: the first time in history a Shinto purification ritual had been performed. As a result of his historic bath Amaterasu and her brother Susanoo were created.

So Daddy gave them some jobs. Amaterasu was given authority to rule the land: obviously the plum gig, because almost immediately Susanoo had a tantrum; one so bad that Daddy banished him. But Amaterasu didn't handle the crisis too well either: upset by her brother's wobbly, she had a bit of a sulk and hid herself in a cave. And because she was the sun-goddess, this wasn't great news for the earth: everywhere was plunged into darkness.

So, a bit like how parents try to coax huffing teenage kids out of their bedrooms, other Kami gathered outside the cave to convince her to come out. Amaterasu refused, so one of the Kami performed a comical – and sexual – dance which made the others laugh. When Amaterasu heard all this jollity, she emerged from the cave. The others grabbed her and finally managed to make her see sense.

Amaterasu settled down to the humdrum life of your average sun-goddess. She had children and grandchildren, and one of these, Ninigi, was dispatched to rule Japan. He took with him a mirror (the symbol of Amaterasu) and a sword. His grandson, Jemmu, is regarded as the first Emperor of Japan from whom all the Emperors right up to the present day have been descended.

As we've mentioned, this story is not just religious, but also political: it established the predominance of the Yamamoto clan as rulers of Japan and other clans of the time as less important. For instance, the rival Izumo clan were said to be descended from Susanoo. And it also explains why Japan is known as the land of the rising sun, and why there is a sun on the Japanese flag; because the Japanese are all, more or less, related to Amaterasu. And in Japan this notion hasn't entirely gone away: in 2000, the Japanese Prime Minister, Yoshiro Mori, described Japan as a 'divine country centred on the emperor,' which caused something of a stir. It's tough falling from heaven.

13

Jainism

SO FAR, our religions have given us a fairly rosy view of humanity's state in the cosmos: we are all redeemable, God loves us and, perhaps surprisingly, ain't that pushed about how we practise our various beliefs. Well, not any more. Jainism won't let you off the hook so easily, because if there's one way of summing up the Jainist philosophy, it's that well-worn adage: life is crap, and then you die.

Over and over and over again.

OK, Jainists don't use words like crap, but they do view life as pain: a deeply unpleasant section of our eternal existence that we'd be as well getting over with as soon as possible. They believe this life has virtually nothing to recommend it: certainly not fancy holidays, soft-top sports cars or any material possessions; even books and clothes are suspect. And yes: some of them take this view so literally, they go naked.

Luckily, the vast majority of Jainists live in India, where

it's not that chilly, and where there have been adherents for three or four thousand years. Jainism is one of the oldest surviving religions in the world. In numerical terms, Jainism has seen better days, though its influence on Indian society and some of the other religions there has been profound. Together with Jainists in India and other countries, (there are small pockets of Jainism all around the world), there's somewhere between 4.5 and five million of them.

Some, however, might dispute the right of Jainism to appear in this list at all, arguing that it is a philosophy rather than a religion: Jainists don't believe in God; at least not an all-powerful deity who created the universe. Technically, that makes them atheists. Some academics have argued that to describe what Jainists believe requires a new word: transtheistic – meaning 'inaccessible by arguments as to whether or not a God exists'. Obvious, really.

Yes, it is complicated, so take a deep breath. Jainism teaches that the Universe has always existed and always will exist; that it is governed by the interaction of natural forces and substances. So because the Universe has always been there, there was no need for anyone to create it. Indeed, they argue that the Christian/Muslim/Jewish notion of a God creating the world is silly, and here's why: in the Abrahamic religions, God is eternal and perfect, which means that everything He does is perfect. Obviously, you can't improve on or change perfection, so why would God have bothered creating the universe at all? That would imply that what was there before needed some improvement – which is a contradiction. Think about it.

However, Jainists do believe in a spirit world. Humans

and animals have souls which are eternal and experience reincarnation. They also believe in a range of deities, some good, and some bad. And while they do pray to the (good) gods, Jainists don't believe that those gods can help us in any way while we struggle through the misery of the mortal plane. We're on our own on this earth, and it's up to us to make the best of it. Life is crap, and then you die. Jainism is derived from the Sanskrit word *jinah*, meaning saint, which in turn comes from *jayati*, meaning 'he conquers': Jainists are conquerors of mortal existence.

This eternal universe idea also creates a few problems when it comes to describing the history of Jainism. Because they reckon that their religion has also been around forever. This is the way it works: time goes through cycles which endlessly repeat themselves. Each of these cycles is divided into six ages or *yugas*, which last thousands of years.

At the start of each cycle, or *Utsarpini*, things are pretty good. There is no evil; people get everything they need from Wishing Trees. Outsize clothes shops are presumably also doing well because the size of the average man is six miles tall. But by the third age, evil has arrived and people are shrinking, so a Tirthankara appears: the word literally means 'crossing maker' and is a holy man (or woman – though this is disputed within the religion), who has attained such a high level of spiritual purity that they can teach others how to beat the endless reincarnation trap and get into heaven. Their mission, generally speaking, is to remind people about Jainism and to encourage them to practise their faith more rigorously. Throughout the entire cycle, twenty-four Tirthankaras will pop up at irregular intervals and go about preaching Jainism. But despite their work, when we get into the fifth and sixth ages of the cycle, people become more selfish and less religious; to the point that even Jainism itself is lost.

And then the process starts all over again, with the first age of a new cycle and a new crop of twenty-four Tirthankaras.

In this cycle, we're in the fifth age and we've had our twenty-four, so things aren't looking good. According to Jain scripture, this age is wholly evil, and people will rarely live longer than 125 years. In the sixth age, that lifespan will be reduced to twenty years and we'll all be the size of dwarves. Bad news for the insurance industry and the owners of basketball teams.

The first Tirthankara of this cycle was, Bhagava, otherwise known as Lord Rishabha, (they are all called 'Lord'), who was, the story goes, born before civilisation developed, and apart from religion, also taught agriculture and is said to have had one hundred sons. Busy guy. He is mentioned in the ancient Hindu scriptures, the Vedas, though we don't know if this is the same bloke. (The Jains don't regard the Vedas as scripture.) Certainly, Jainism, or some version of it existed when Hinduism was in its formative years. Some believe it pre-dates Hinduism or may have come about as a protest against the Vedic (early Hindu) practices of the time: the Vedic religion then involved animal sacrifice, which for Jainists would be a huge no-no. Buddhists readily accept that Jainism was an established religion when Buddha popped up, and that Buddhism has been influenced by the Jainists. Then again, Jainism is influenced by Hinduism and vice versa: not surprising really because, back when this all started, it was just 'religion' with some local variations; but free of the modern distinctions we draw. And we are talking about a long time ago here – probably about 2000 BC when the Aryans came to India from southern Russia and their religious ideas mixed with those of the people already living there.

Anyway, Rishabha was followed by Ajita, Sambhava, Abhinandana, Sumati, Padmaprabha, Suparshva, Chandraprabha, Suvidhi, Shital, Shreyansa, Vasupujya, Vimala, Ananta, Dharma, Shanti, Kunthu, Ara, Malli, Muni Suvrata, Nami, Nemi, Parshva and Mahavira.

Alas, there isn't a shred of historical evidence that any but Rishabha and the last two actually existed, so we'll have to start with them. Parshva, about whom little is known, did his stint as Tirthankara some time around 850 BC, during which time he introduced four basic Jainist principles: non-violence, truthfulness, not stealing and not owning things. (Jainists, of course, reject this thesis, arguing that these ideas had always existed.) The twenty-fourth Tirthankara, Mahavira, popped up two hundred and fifty years later and added a fifth principle: chastity. Mahavira was born as Vardhamana in north-east India and was a prince: the son (obviously) of a king and queen who already followed the teachings of Parshva. Mahavira comes in for mention in some Buddhist texts as he was a contemporary of Siddhartha Gautama – the Buddha

When he reached thirty years of age, Vardhamana renounced his royal lifestyle and went to live the life of a *Sadhana*: an ascetic who has given up all worldly goods. He spent over twelve years meditating and fasting,

(Jainists love fasting), and eventually achieved *Kevalnyan*, or enlightenment. As you do, he changed his name to Mahavira, (which modestly translates as 'great hero'), and began teaching. And he was good at it, establishing a community of 14,000 monks and 36,000 priests. He died at the age of 72, but just before that he embarked on a particularly intense period of fasting which brought him to *moksha*: a spiritual state which freed him from reincarnation. The religion spread to central and western India, but began to suffer when the somewhat more jolly Hindu belief arrived about 1000 years later. However, in the 19th and 20th centuries, Jainism has experienced a bit of a revival. But as any Jainist will tell you, this has all happened before.

So: Jains might not believe in an all-powerful God, but they do believe in the soul. They call it a Jiva and believe that all living things have one: from humans right down to single-cell organisms. And Jains have a number of categories for these different types of Jiva, predicated on how many sense organs they possess.

The hierarchy is:

Panchendriya – Beings with five senses: touch, taste, smell, sight and hearing. (*Panchendriya* are divided into four sub-classes. **Infernal beings**: souls living in hell, or the Jain form of it which is located at the bottom of the Universe. This variety of Jiva experiences the greatest suffering. **Higher animals**. This includes all non-human animals above insects. **Human beings**. This is the only form of Jiva which is able to obtain liberation directly. **Heavenly beings**. These are the Jiva who have escaped earthly life and the only ones who can claim to be happy.)

Chaurindriya – Beings with four senses, they being touch, taste, smell and sight. This category includes wasps, locusts and scorpions.

Treindriya – Beings with three senses: touch, taste and smell. This category includes insects like ants, beetles and moths.

Beindriya – Beings with two senses: touch and taste. This category includes things like worms and termites.

Ekendriya – Beings with one sense, that of touch. This includes some plants, such as trees, flowers and vegetables, but other elements that the rest of us might regard as, well, not alive at all. Again, they come in a number of categories: **Earth-bodied,** such as clay, sand and metal. **Water-bodied,** such as fog, rain and ice. **Fire-bodied,** such as fire and lightning. **Air-bodied,** such as wind and gas. The Jiva of these one-sense beings are called *nigoda.* Jainism teaches that there is an indefinite number of them, and they are in intense pain. Cheery.

Listing all parts of the physical world that Jains believe have a soul is the only way to give a sense of how much respect for the environment they have to exercise: build a sandcastle and you could be torturing a poor soul. The earth may be considered a place of torment, but it is also sacred.

So obviously, compassion and non-violence towards all these souls is a central Jain teaching – and which is why all Jains are required to be strict vegetarians, while also avoiding certain vegetables considered to have a Jiva. Many are also vegans. In India, Jains run animal shelters, while many adherents also wear face masks – to avoid accidentally swallowing any insects.

This consideration extends to other religions too. One of the central pillars of Jain philosophy is *Anekantavada*, which means – awkwardly translated – 'non-one-endedness', and deals with the idea that any point of view has within it an inherent bias: true wisdom consists of being able to study ideas from a multiplicity of viewpoints; in short, to be able to see through the eyes of other people. Thus Jainism actively seeks out links with other beliefs and has even, on occasion, donated money for the building of churches and mosques.

Yet with all this gentleness and generosity (Mahatma Gandhi was deeply influenced by some aspects of Jainism) goes a rather grim view of this world.

Firstly, this is how Jainists reckon everything has been put together. As we've said, the Universe, (including earth) is infinite and was always here. However, the Universe is part of space, rather than space being part of the Universe. Thus in Jain cosmology, space is divided into the space of the Universe (*lokakasa*) and that of the non-Universe (*a-lokakasa*), which has no substance to it.

Space is infinite, but the Universe is not. It is divided into five levels:

*The supreme abode, or heaven. The region where liberated beings live for ever.

*The upper world. The region where celestial beings live, but not forever.

*The middle world. The region where human beings live. This, lucky for us, is the only part of the universe from which a being can achieve enlightenment.

*The lower world. This region consists of seven hells where beings are tormented by demons and by each other. Happily, this torment does not last forever.

*The base. The region where the lowest forms of life live.

Let's go back to the Jiva thing: Jainism teaches that there is an infinite number of these Jivas – or spirits – in the Universe, though each one is unique. But there is also Ajiva – the physical universe. A lot (but not all) of these Jiva are trapped in Ajiva: in plants, animals and humans, gusts of wind etc. But unlike the Christian soul, these aren't too thrilled about being trapped: according to Jain theology, contact between Jiva and Ajiva causes the Jiva nothing but suffering.

Thus for the Jainist, life on this earth is suffering. You could bring about a world of peace and harmony where everyone lives in big houses and wears gold hats, but still the Jiva would suffer. The only way to escape this torment is the rigorous practice of Jainism, which eventually leads to permanent escape from reincarnation in physical form. In Jainism, reincarnation can go on forever and can go up or down the evolutionary scale depending on the spiritual condition of the person at the point of death: they can return as an animal, a bit of earth or a *nigoda* in the lowest level of Hell.

And the way to dodge such a fate is to avoid karma.

Now the concept of karma in Jainism is somewhat different to that of other religions; in Jainism, it is an actual, physical substance, albeit invisible and undetectable. Every human action attracts karma and this karma sticks to the Jiva, weighing it down and anchoring it more in the physical world. Bad deeds attract heavy karma; and the more karma you carry, the more likely you are to think bad thoughts and perform even more bad deeds. Bad karma comes in four varieties: one which deludes the Ajiva, one which interferes with the intellect, one which distorts the senses and one which obstructs energy. However, good deeds attract a lighter form of karma, (again in four types, but this time controlling duration of life and the circumstances of reincarnation), which at least gives the Jiva a chance of graduating to a higher form of physical existence with the next reincarnation – where there might be a wee bit less suffering.

But that's not too say *no* suffering: the only way to escape from eternal reincarnation and eternal suffering is to achieve *moksha* – and the only way to do that is by completely withdrawing from the world. That way, you can avoid karma altogether.

And as we've said before, with no karma, the Jiva will, at the point of death, float to the top of the Universe or *Siddhashila*. There, the Jiva will mix with all the other escaped Jivas and experience its own true nature free of any suffering, in eternal stillness and 'non-involvement' and with the added benefit of infinite knowledge: making you the equal of everyone there, including the Tirthankaras. It sounds kinda boring, but it's probably better than being reincarnated as some gas. And in fairness, while Jainism is a tough religion to practise, what it promises is not just life after death, but that you get to be a sort of god. Cool.

In practical terms there are two ways to achieve *moksha*: you can become a monk, which involves extreme asceticism and the hope that at death they won't have to come back here at all. Option two is to live as a lay person, with the hope that you will be reincarnated as something better each time. Both have to live their lives by the five vows of Non-violence, Truth, Non-stealing, Chastity (which for lay people means no sex outside marriage) and Non-materialism, as well as the three guiding principles of Jainism or 'three jewels': right belief, right knowledge and right conduct. Lay people are expected to engage in good works and not to choose a job that involves any sort of violence.

Jainism is also big not just on doing good things but on thinking good thoughts. To be seen to be doing the Right Thing simply isn't sufficient; you gotta *believe*. Vengeful or angry thoughts are verboten because for the Jainist, redemption can come only from within. As in Christianity, you don't just say you love your enemy; you really have to love them. In many respects, the whole aim of the religion for the Jain is the accumulation of wisdom to bring about this attitude; which is probably why a lay Jain is referred to as a *shravaka*: listener.

This aspect of controlling the mind is particularly apparent in the Jain tradition of fasting. And Jains love to fast: there is a dizzy range of types of fast in Jainism, from giving up favourite foods to starving oneself to death. Even on a regular day, most Jains don't eat or drink after sunset or before sunrise. This is all a form of penance and a way of getting rid of some of that pesky karma. However, the most important point of fasting is not just abstinence from food; the faster is aiming to reach a state where they *do not want the food*. Now, that's impressive.

But they do have a powerful set of examples to live up to: Mahavira is said to have fasted for over six months, and many Jain monks have equalled that achievement; some have fasted for a whole year. There is even a type of fast called a *santhara*, which is, in effect, a fast to the death. It is not, however, suicide, as a decision to end one's life is usually taken when, well, the person is a bit upset. The decision to go for *santhara* is always taken coolly, and only when it's beyond doubt that the body is heading for death anyway. The aim is to purify mind and body before the demise; not just of a desire for food, but of a desire for anything.

Because Jainism is so engrained in the daily life of adherents, there are no strict rules about temple worship. Jainists do much of their praying at home. (All Jain prayers, by the way, are in Ardha Magadhi, a language at least as old as Aramaic, the language of Christ.) However, there are elaborate Jain temple rituals where various Tirthankaras are venerated and given offerings – though not asked for anything. Remember, Jains don't believe beings in the spirit world can help anyone here. (Even the celestial beings known as devas – a kind of angel – are of no use. In fact, for devas to experience eternal bliss, they too have to come to earth and get rid of karma, just like the rest of us.) Temples are, naturally, used for marriage and various family rites, and in these there is a striking similarity to the Hindu versions. All Jainist rituals usually begin with a ceremonial wash and changing into clothes which are used only for temple attendance.

Some of the temples contain rich imagery – including swastikas -and depictions of figures from Jain history. But others have no adornment at all, believing idol worship to be wrong. This is because there are two main strands of Jain: the Digambar and Shvetambar traditions. The story goes that about two hundred years after Mahavira floated to the top of the universe, a monk called Bhadrabahu had a vision that famine was coming and so led a group of around 12,000 people to southern India. Twelve years later they returned to discover that the folks they left behind had established their own and (slightly) more liberal interpretation of Jainism. Bhadrabahu's bunch, which became known as the Digambar, (which means 'sky-clad' or naked) were so against the idea of possessions that their monks went naked, while they also believed that women couldn't achieve *moksha*. But in a flush of crazed liberalism, the Shvetambar had decided that there was nothing in Jain scripture preventing monks from wearing clothes or from the ladies getting into heaven. There are other, relatively minor theological differences between the two strains, and over the years a number of sub-sects have also developed. In the last few decades some efforts have been made to reunite Jainism, though with little success so far. And yes, the Digambar monks still don't have a stitch on, though seeing as they spend most of their time in remote locations praying and fasting, there are no legal issues. Nuns of both sects wear white clothes.

Jainists also like a bit of a pilgrimage, though again, there is no requirement to do this. They usually involve a trip to a shrine or temple, and during the course of the trip, the adherent takes on the lifestyle of the ascetic; which means, yes, lots of fasting.

The Jainist sacred literature is known as the *Svetambaras*. It was passed down orally until the fourth century BC and arranged into its current form some 800 years later, when it was first written down. (Some strains of Jainism, remember, eschew possessions to such an extent they refuse to own even holy books.) The scriptures consist of 45 texts, outlining pretty much everything you need to know about karma, how the universe is constructed and how you should live your life. But because of the insistence on memorising everything over eight centuries, large chunks of it have, understandably, simply been forgotten, while a famine in around 350BC killed many monks, and with them, more of the scriptures. There is some dispute as to how much of what survives is genuine.

Now let's meet some of the Jain gods: with many of these there is a Hindu influence, or perhaps both traditions have drawn from a common Indian history. Jain gods fall into four main groups: *bhavanavasis* (gods of the house), *vyantaras* (intermediaries), *jyotiskas* (luminaries), and *vaimanikas* (astral gods). However, all these 'gods' would be viewed as inferior to Tirthankaras and anyone else who has managed to liberate their souls and more importantly, control their passions. Indeed, the job of many of these deities is to serve the Tirthankaras – a job they don't always manage to do.

The worship of any of these gods is non-mandatory, (they are more of an example for the adherent); as is, as we've said, attendance at Temple or doing anything outside the five basic rules. (Jain Temples are administered by lay people – many of whom are not even Jains: monks and nuns lead strictly ascetic lives.) It is up to the person themselves to decide if they are working hard enough to get rid of the karma – and to make this decision requires developing the mind to a point where it is free of attachment and desire.

Indeed, it could be argued that all praying and worshipping in Jainism is utterly pointless, as the Jain deities cannot and will not do anything to help people, or Jiva, on earth. In Jainism, the point of worship – the point of everything – is to instil discipline by example or action into believers so they can edge closer to a state where they care absolutely nothing for the physical world: clearing the way for their Jiva to enter a part of the universe where they will have no cares at all. Which is why, even though they don't have to, so many Jains go to Temple every day.

12

Baha'i

ONCE again, you'd wonder why folks fight about religious divisions when they have so much in common. Baha'i believes that *all* religions are divinely inspired; it's simply a matter of bringing them together. We've heard that one before, yes, but in fairness to Baha'i, it has put its theological money where its mouth is: it counts Adam (of Adam and Eve fame), Abraham, Moses, Buddha, Noah (of the Ark fame), Krishna, Jesus, and Muhammad among its many prophets. It was founded in Iran and it developed out of Shia Islam, but the Baha'i headquarters are located in Israel. This would be a religion with Issues were it not for its utter self-belief and the fact that, for such a relatively new religion, it has been enormously successful. There may be only 6.5 – 7 million Baha'is around the world, but they can be found in close to 250 different countries and over 2000 ethnic and tribal groups: a massive geographic spread comparable with the Big Two beliefs, Islam and Christianity.

Not that you'll find many Muslims hanging out with Baha'is: in Iran, at least, Baha'i is regarded as an heretical belief, and over the last 150 years or so the religion has been actively suppressed. Their shrines have been destroyed and their leaders imprisoned and executed.

Yet despite this, Baha'i still has great time for Islam, believing that all religions come from God – are in fact manifestations of God which have come at different stages in history and in different parts of the world. The Baha'i believe that because God is eternal, all-powerful, omniscient etc, it is impossible for the limited human brain to fully understand what God is and what's going on in his mind. (Baha'i don't actually think God is a bloke: to ascribe God a sex would be to limit a limitless being, i.e. to say God is a man would mean God is not a woman. But God cannot *not* be anything.) Indeed, that parenthetical sentence demonstrates the limits of human language in even describing God.

Er, yeah, right.

According to Baha'i, all we can know for sure is that God exists: so when we give God attributes such as 'Goodness', this is a false analogy based on human ideas. Yet this is all we can do. The closest we can get to 'knowing' God is to study the teachings of God's messengers, (the prophets mentioned above – plus many more – who are described as manifestations of God), and the world around us which God created.

Thus all religions, while divinely inspired, give only part of the story of God, while also reflecting the historical and cultural mores of the time and place the religion was revealed. Baha'is believe that more and more of God will be revealed through different religions as time goes on: it's just that Baha'i is the latest expression of this; they don't even believe that Baha'i is the end of the story. More religious revelation is to come, though probably not soon. Seeing that Baha'i just got here, relatively speaking, there's enough to be going on with. Thus when each previous religion referred to a 'judgement day' in its scriptures, what was meant was the arrival of the next manifestation of God. Indeed, the Baha'i don't believe the world will end, but will evolve into a new era of universal peace and justice. Something to look forward to.

So here's the story: as we've said, Baha'i started in 19th century Iran, then Persia. As now, it was a mainly Muslim country, though back then Christians, Jews and Zoroastrians were treated a bit more tolerantly – and adherents from all those religions as well as Islam joined Baha'i when it got up and running.

It is, however, the Islamic component of the religion which is the most important: specifically the Shia tradition. We'll go into all of this in much more detail later on, but suffice it to say it was the belief of Shias that the descendants of Mohammed would take on the spiritual and temporal leadership of the Muslim faith. These men, (naturally, this is Islam), would be called Imams ('teachers'). There were eleven of them in a line, with the eleventh, Hasan al-Askari, dying in 873. According to the Shia account, his son, – and twelfth imam – Muhammad al-Mahdi, although only five years old, officiated at the funeral. But then he disappeared and hasn't been seen since. For the first few years, the 12th imam communicated through intermediaries known as Babs ('gates'). But the last Bab died in 941, and since then there hasn't been word from the 12th imam.

It's not known exactly why the Imam disappeared – it's believed that God is keeping part of the reason secret – though Shias believe it is a test of their faith and that before he returns pretty much everything has to go belly up: governments, religion, society. The world will be engulfed in calamity and injustice before the 12th imam reappears, bringing order and justice. As such, he is a sort of messiah, and therefore a pretty big deal in Shia Islam. (Sunni Islam doesn't accept this account, believing the 11th imam died without leaving behind any heirs.)

Every now and again – including right up to the present day – various people have claimed to be either the Imam himself (otherwise known as Mahdi – the Guided one) or one of the Babs who would speak on his behalf. Shias believe that before the 12th imam starts his comeback gig, a Bab will be appointed first by God.

So, considering the fashion in those days for executing heretics, you'd want to be pretty sure of your facts before you start making any claims about the imminent arrival of anyone. But in the late 18th century in Persia, a man by the name of Shaykh Ahmad al Ahsai did exactly that. He set up a sect called Shaykhi which claimed that the return of the Bab was imminent, and that Muslims should prepare for this. Shaykh Ahmad al Ahsai claimed to have got his information from various visionary experiences, which, while insistent that the Bab was on the way, were somewhat short on specifics: al Ahsai died in 1826 without getting to meet the Big Guy.

The visionary baton was then passed on to Siyyid Kázim-i-Rashtí, who was, apparently, the only man to fully understand the teachings of al Ahsai. Siyyid went one further than his old boss, telling his followers that the Bab had actually arrived on earth and it was only a matter of finding him: something which Siyyid singularly failed to do, dropping dead in 1843.

But before his death, Siyyid did urge his followers to hit the road and start searching, which they did. Not too long after, one of the sect members, Mulla Husayn, travelled to the city of Shiraz in the south of Persia. There he met a young man wearing a green turban: a sign, apparently, that he was descended from the Prophet Mohammed. The young man, whose name was Siyyid Ali Muhammad, brought Mulla back to his home, engaged in some impressive religious discourse and, despite Mulla's initial scepticism, eventually convinced Mulla that he was in fact the Bab, the gate of God.

This happened two hours and eleven minutes after sunset on May 22, 1884. Luckily, someone must have had a watch handy. Especially so for the Baha'i religion, as it regards this as a pretty significant date in human history.

Mulla declared his allegiance, and with him in tow the newly discovered Bab went about collecting some more converts: eighteen, including Mulla, who were named the Letters of the Living and instructed to travel throughout Persia and announce that the Bab was back.

But not everyone was too thrilled with this announcement. Part of this would be political: a new Bab would obviously be a threat to the status quo; part of it was plain scepticism, and part of it was theological: this guy was acting like a prophet, and the orthodox Muslim view was that there was only one prophet, him being Mohammed. Indeed, the belief that Mohammed was the greatest and final prophet before the end of the world is a fundamental of Islamic belief.

It was bound not to go well.

The Bab himself went to Mecca and Medina to preach, but was largely ignored. However, things went better back in Shiraz where he was building up something of a following and even had his name mentioned during the Muslim call to prayer. So he was arrested. The authorities said they would let him go if he recanted his claim, but the Bab refused, so he was dispatched to the prison of Mah-Ku in the north of the country. Once there, the Bab set about converting the other prisoners and the guards, so he was moved to a more remote slammer in Chihriq, where he had even more success: to such an extent that soon he was allowed visitors.

At the time, it was probably the better deal compared to that of the eighteen Letters: still free to preach the Bab's word, many of them were tortured and killed.

But even the Bab couldn't get away with it forever, so in 1850, having been moved to another prison in Tabriz, he was sentenced to death. The story goes that a crowd of 10,000 people collected to see the execution, which was to be carried out by a regiment led by a Christian named Sam Khan. Khan apologised to the Bab in advance, and then ordered that the Bab be suspended against a wall by a rope and shot. It could be that the regiment all shared Khan's reservations, or it could be that they were really rubbish soldiers, or it could be a miracle, but of the 750 guns aimed at the Bab, not one of them managed to hit him with a bullet: only the rope holding him aloft was frayed. Khan refused to have anything more to do with the execution, and so on July 9th 1850, a regiment of soldiers with a better aim finished the job. Some time later, the Bab's remains were smuggled to Haifa in Israel.

For the followers of the Bab, known as Babis, this was a severe blow. Yet his achievements had been considerable: he had built up a huge following, to such an extent that the Babis even had their own army to defend themselves against government forces. The year before the Bab's execution, the guy who 'discovered' him, Mulla Husayn, had died in one such battle.

But this wasn't the end of the story; or even the official launch of Baha'i. Don't forget: the Bab was only the warm-up guy for an even more important figure: someone whom 'God shall make manifest' and whose coming had been foretold in the scriptures of all the great world religions. And like most of founders of world religions, he was in prison. In 1852, someone had a go at assassinating the Shah of Persia, Nasser-al-Din Shah. We're not exactly sure who did it, but the Shah reckoned the Babis were the culprits, so many more were chucked into prison or executed. Among those was one Husayn Alí who did some time in a dungeon in Siyah-Chal prison in Teheran. Shortly afterwards he was expelled to Baghdad, but while in prison he got the notion that he might be the One the Bab had spoken about. This came as something of a surprise to Subh-i-Azal, then the leader of the Babis, and surprisingly, led to some tension between the two men. Husayn even retreated to the mountains in Kurdistan for a while, just to calm things down.

But the belief that he was the One wouldn't go away, so Husayn emerged again and continued with his claim and in 1866 publicly declared himself to be Bahá'u'lláh, a messenger of God. He wrote to several world leaders of the time telling them about his new job, yet none of them seemed to share his excitement at this news: at least one of the messengers he dispatched was executed, while Bahá'u'lláh himself was arrested again (this time by the Ottoman Empire) and sent to a penal colony in Akka, in present day Israel.

And there he remained for decades. Towards the end of his life his confinement was relaxed somewhat – he was allowed to live outside the prison while technically remaining an inmate – but Bahá'u'lláh never actually got to preach as the Bab had done. Instead, Bahá'u'lláh converted people – and established himself as the head of the religion – through his writings. He left behind a large body of work, including the *Kitáb-i-Aqdas*, (the most holy book), the Book of Certitude, the Hidden Words and the Seven Valleys, which mixed theology and esoterics. He died in Akka in 1892 and Baha'is turn towards this place when they make their daily prayer.

It was a tough job to inherit, and that particular task fell to Bahá'u'lláh's eldest son, Abdu'l-Bahá, who wasted no time in fulfilling what seemed to be the first condition of the position: getting thrown in jail. There he remained until 1908 when the Young Turk revolution led to his being sprung.

Until the end of his life in 1921, Abdu'l-Bahá travelled the world preaching. He penned a document called the Divine Plan, was knighted by the British for humanitarian work during World War I and is buried in Haifa, Israel – close to the body of the Bab.

The work was passed on to Abdu'l-Bahá's eldest grandson, Shogi Effendi, who arguably has done more than any Baha'i in spreading the religion – though he did have the advantage of not having to spend any time in jail. Apart from all the theological work one might expect from the head of a religion, Shogi also built up the administrative side, even launching a Seven-Year Plan, (the first of many such plans since then), which outlined his vision of how Baha'i would spread around the world.

The structures which Shogi built up were based on writings from his grandfather and great-grandfather, Abdu'l-Bahá and Bahá'u'lláh, and were a bit like the governments of many western countries: there was an Hereditary Guardian, who would be named by the previous Guardian, along with an elected Universal House of Justice. Under this would be all the national spiritual assemblies.

Obviously, you can't organise all this overnight, so by the 1950s, the House of Justice was yet to have an election, and much of the power remained with Shoghi and agents directly appointed by him: known as Hands of the Cause of God.

But in late 1957, Shoghi dropped dead, leaving no will and no named heir – and thus a power vacuum. The 27 Hands of the Cause of God (let's call them HCGs for short) met and decided that, as Shoghi had not named a successor, one could not be appointed. They declared their intention to lead the religion in a caretaker capacity until elections to the Universal House of Justice could he held.

Well: 27 put their name to this announcement, but one

may already have had his doubts. In 1960, a HCG by the name Mason Remey declared that he was in fact the next Guardian of the Faith and Shoghi had appointed him. Understandably, most of the other HCGs wondered why he hadn't mentioned this sooner and were somewhat sceptical: so Mason left altogether to establish Orthodox Baha'i. (Or more correctly, he was kicked out as a 'covenant breaker'.) It has attracted relatively small numbers and since then has split into various sub-sects, some of which have lost the plot somewhat: in 1980, one of Remey's followers, Leland Jensen, predicted a nuclear disaster that year followed by two decades of conflict and ending in the establishment of God's Kingdom on earth. Must have missed that one.

In April 1963 the first election of the Universal House of Justice took place and it remains the supreme governing body of the Baha'i faith. Anyone over 21 is eligible for election to the House of Justice; well, as long as they are a man.

Which is a wee bit of an inconsistency in the religion because if there's one thing Baha'i is big on it's equality: between all races, classes, religions and yes, even the sexes. (Although men and women are 'The two wings on which the bird of human kind is able to soar', Abdu'l-Bahá instructed that only men can belong to the house of Justice. The reason for this, apparently, will be revealed by God at some later date.) Everyone is equal before God, and all religions are equal: we might call the Supreme Being by different names, but it's the same deity we're all talking about.

And this fundamental belief in equality translates into a

number of practical measures which Baha'i would like to see eventually instituted. Apart, obviously, from the eradication of all prejudice, they would like to see the introduction of a universal auxiliary language, the abolition of extremes of wealth and poverty, the setting up of a world tribunal to sort out disputes between nations and free education for everyone.

So as you might expect, the Baha'i are big supporters of the United Nations. It has consultative status with a number of UN organisations, along with permanent offices in New York and Geneva and has undertaken a number of joint development programmes.

Similarly, Baha'i adherents also work as a sort of UN for religions, working actively to solve disputes between religious groups. Inter-faith dialogue is a major component for Baha'i because, as we've said, they regard all religions as being divinely inspired. And by establishing such links, they do not seek to convert people from other religions; there isn't even a compulsion on Baha'is to bring up their own children within the Baha'i faith

Thus Baha'i is a very practical religion; there is a fair amount of study and prayer, (study circles are very popular), but any sort of monasticism is forbidden: Baha'is are expected to be out in the world, working to improve themselves and the societies they live in. Indeed, Baha'i considers work to be *a form* of prayer: especially if that work is in the service of others.

On the personal level, it's all about self-improvement rather than self-interest. Baha'i don't believe in heaven and hell in the more literal, Christian sense. As with God, Baha'i theology teaches that we can't really know what the after-life is like, no more than a child in a womb can imagine life in the outside world. Thus Heaven and Hell are not physical places but rather how the individual will perceive the after-life: if they are full of sin, they will conceive it as Hell; if they are full of virtue, it will seem more like Heaven. However, there's still a chance even there for improvement: the soul (which is eternal) can make progress towards God and start to have more 'heavenly' experiences or move away from God and start growing cloven hooves. How exactly all this happens after death isn't clear from Baha'i writing because, well, we simply don't know.

Now Baha'i is – relatively speaking – not a particularly censorious religion in a fire-and-brimstone type of way. It is up to the individual to decide if they want to develop in this life (which influences how far they end up from God in the next). A big part of Baha'i is not to be too judgemental of others and not to 'rate' some sins as being worse than others.

However, there are rules, most of which derive from the *Kitáb-i-Aqdas*. There are no specific punishments for breaking the rules, though occasionally Baha'i are banished from their communities for activities which may damage the standing of the religion. The idea is that the individual will voluntarily submit and that over time, when entire countries become influenced by Baha'i (oh yes, these guys are ambitious), the Baha'i 'rules' will become the social norm.

And given that this is a religion which developed out of Islam, Baha'i is relatively conservative. Alcohol, gambling and drugs, (except when prescribed by a doctor) are all on the No List, along with all the usual sins: gossiping, murder, tax evasion. Sex has to be within marriage and homosexuality is banned. There are gay Baha'is, but they are expected to remain celibate or try to get 'cured'.

However, it's worth repeating that while Baha'i counts such things as sins, they don't go on about it: there's no name-calling in Baha'i.

There are eleven holy days a year, which commemorate important dates in the history of the faith. On nine of these, adherents are expected not to work: what dates these fall on is too complicated to explain, because the Baha'i calendar, as devised by the Bab, consists of 19 months in the year, each month being 19 days long. Four or five days are also chucked in make it a solar year. New Year's Day, known as Naw Ruz, comes on March 21st, the vernal equinox and also the Persian New Year.

Marriage is a big deal in Baha'i, especially interracial unions. Divorce, while not explicitly banned, isn't exactly encouraged: in Baha'i, folks don't just marry for life, but for all eternity. So, as the religion advises, you should choose carefully – and clear it with the parents. Marriage ceremonies usually take place in homes and are fairly simple, the only requirement being to read short wedding vows.

Indeed, most Baha'i worship takes place in the home, and is regarded as a private matter. Adherents are required to recite one of three obligatory prayers and to meditate each day. Prayer is seen as a form of 'conversation' with God; in effect, another form of meditation. Apart from the official prayers, Baha'is can make up their own. From March 2nd to March 20th each year, (the last 19 days of the Baha'i year), they are required to undertake a sunrise-to-sunset fast.

Not that Baha'is don't get together: it happens in each other's homes or local Baha'i centres, mostly to have study groups and communal prayers. Unusually for a major religion, Baha'i has hardly any rituals apart from marriage, a prayer for the dead and the Morning Prayer. This stems from a belief that rituals can quickly become a habit and lose their meaning, while imposing the same rites across different countries can turn into a form of 'cultural imperialism' which erodes the diversity of different cultures. Even when Baha'i meet to pray together, one person prays aloud on behalf of the group. The Baha'i faith has no professional clergy.

There are actually only seven official Baha'i centres of worship on the planet, though scripture envisions a place called *Mashriqu'l-Adhkar*, (Dawning place of the mention of God), which would incorporate a House of Worship, a university, hospital and other buildings. One does exist, but, bizarrely, it's located in Turkmenistan: not a country recommended for the casual visitor.

It's an unusual choice not just because Turkmenistan is a one-party state run by a man with only a passing acquaintance with sanity, (and who fancies himself to be God-like), but because Turkmenistan is a predominantly Muslim country. And in Islam, Baha'i is regarded by many as an offensive heresy. The more hardline Islamist States routinely suppress the religion; especially, as we've said, Iran. Hundreds of Baha'is have been arrested or executed, have had their homes and shrines and cemeteries bulldozed and are forbidden from entering third-level education or having government jobs. Iranian newspapers routinely run articles rubbishing the religion and the Iranian secret police keep a constant eye on them. And by all accounts, there is no sign of this pressure letting up: because Baha'i has its headquarters in Israel, the ever-hysterical Iranian government accuses them of being Zionists.

Nonetheless, Baha'i continues to expand and develop around the globe. Various ten-year, seven-year and five-year plans have been launched and successfully completed with the aim of translating scripture into other languages, (now available in 800 tongues), sending 'pioneers' into new territories and building new national spiritual assemblies. The next big year for Baha'i will be 2021: the completion of the first century of the 'Formative Age' of the Baha'i faith.

And the work spreading Baha'i will continue: very deliberately, Baha'i has grown from the Middle East into Asia, Africa and both American continents. So far, there isn't a country yet with a Baha'i majority. (Guyana is the highest with seven per cent.) But give them time.

11

Judaism

OK, NOW we're into one of the big ones, but already there's confusion: Judaism occupies a unique position in the religions of the world because it can be regarded as both a religion *and* as an ethnicity. Obviously, Jews have been hugely influential in the development of both western and eastern societies, as well as on many of the world's major religions, and today Jewish people live in virtually all parts of the globe; however, there are millions of Jews who regard themselves as either non-religious or have converted to another faith. Similarly, there are Jews whose ethnic background is not Jewish.

So let's be clear: in this chapter we are looking at Judaism *solely as a religion*. The words 'Jew' or 'Jewish' are *not* synonyms for 'Israeli' or as a description of ethnic background.

So it would be really handy at this point to come up with the number of people in the world who regard themselves as Jewish by religion. Handy, but impossible, because no such worldwide estimate has been done. In studies carried out in the US, only 51 per cent of Jews count Judaism as their religion, but that's the Yanks for you: making a worldwide extrapolation based on that probably wouldn't be too accurate.

Instead, a wild guess will have to do. Estimates for the numbers of Jews in the world range from 12 to 17 million, so let's settle on 14 million who count Judaism as their belief.

And having said all that, let's contradict it almost immediately by stating that you can't look at the roots of Judaism without looking at the roots of the Jews. Who are an ethnic group. Ah, you'll get the hang of it.

Let's go back: way, way back to the Semitic Tribes who probably originated in southern Arabia more than 5,000 years ago. Now when you read the word 'Semitic', you probably think of the phrase 'anti-Semitic', meaning anti-Jew. In fact, the Semites were a group of nomads which included Arabs, Aramaeans, Carthaginians, Ethiopians, Abyssinians, Phoenicians – and the people who later became known as the Jews. They were united by a common language and their descendants constitute the vast majority of the inhabitants of the modern Middle East: pretty much everyone there is a Semite. This is one of the reasons why, so many centuries later, both Islam and Judaism can regard Abraham as a major prophet – and still argue over whether he was an Arab or a Jew.

The Semites were nomads, though they also did a bit of farming and are credited with the invention of the first alphabet. They wandered around Arabia, Sinai and Syria and eventually established their own great dynasty by conquering Mesopotamia. It was ruled by a guy called Sargon whose reign lasted fifty years and who established his capital at Akkad. But Sargon also conquered the Mesopotamian city of Ur, located (many, but not all historians think) in modern-day Iraq.

Ur is the birthplace of Abraham, and the point where the history of the Hebrews start. The story goes that Abraham was a good age (99) when God instructed him to head out of town and into Canaan, (Palestine). God knew this was a pain, but made a deal (or covenant) with Abraham that if he embarked on the trip and upheld God's law, then Abraham's descendants would inherit the lands there. This was good news for a number of reasons: apart from the chance to finally get a foot on the ancient Middle Eastern property ladder, Abraham was childless and his wife, Sarah, was 90. So one can assume they'd given up on having kids. Abraham went for the deal and set out, had a rake of children and lived to a ripe (even) old(er) age.

Now, of course, it's difficult to be certain, but it's unlikely Abraham was a wimp: he probably had a good-sized tribe with him of which he was the Patriarch and General; occasional ass-kicking was probably necessary as they made their way to Canaan, both in self-defence and possibly as mercenaries to some of the kingdoms they passed through. It's reckoned the Hebrews (as they were called then), arrived in Canaan around 1800 BC, give or take a few hundred years.

The journey taken by Abraham and his followers was not an unusual one for the time; what makes it unique is the idea that God told him to make it – and that Abraham believed that there was only one God. As we've said, there is some dispute over who was the first monotheist, (see Zoroastrianism), but it's likely that this belief developed out of existing practices.

The religious culture Abraham grew up in would have come about as a result of mixing Mesopotamian, Semite and other beliefs, but essentially involved worshipping a pantheon of gods. Abraham's father, Terach, had made his living selling idols of the gods, some of whom were dead Mesopotamian rulers: one of their stories was that the aforementioned Sargon was, as a child, placed in a basket of reeds and sailed down a river. Sound familiar?

The religion also contended that creation took place in Mesopotamia, making it the centre of the Universe – in turn making Mesopotamians special; in other words, a Chosen People.

The Hebrew name for God was Yahweh – which was also the name of a Mesopotamian war god: Yahweh of the hosts. Indeed, early sections of the Jewish scripture, the Torah, quote God as telling the Jews to worship him and no other Gods; and it's the phrasing that's interesting here. Yahweh doesn't seem to be denying the existence of other deities, but rather instructing the Hebrews to ignore them: which is why the accounts of God's early relationship with the Hebrews is so tempestuous. God wasn't above throwing a strop or sending down the odd disaster if he felt he wasn't getting enough attention: just like many of the other gods of the time.

Thus many academics believe that while the Hebrews would have accepted Yahweh as their main deity, they may have also worshipped others such as Baal, a fertility god.

It may have been centuries before the notion became implanted that there was only one God – and that this is the God for everyone.

But back to the story: Abraham buys land in Hebron, settles down, has children and grandchildren. His children include Ishmael and Isaac, who have a spat which leads to the creation of Islam. (See **Islam**.)

One of the grandkids is Jacob, who takes over the job as patriarch and thus regularly chats with the Almighty. One day, as part of renewing the covenant. God gives Jacob a new name: Israel. Israel (Jacob) had twelve sons, each of whom had their own extended families, or tribes: and it is from this we get The Twelve Tribes of Israel.

But things didn't go that well in Canaan. Because, mainly, of famine, the twelve tribes had to up sticks and move south to Egypt: then, the local superpower. However, it's not entirely certain if *all* the Hebrews headed south; it's quite possible that some of them remained behind – certainly the Bible says that when the Hebrews returned from Egypt, there were relations of theirs waiting for them.

So perhaps they shouldn't have gone at all, because the experience in Egypt was a less than happy one. Eventually, most of the Jews became slaves. But in and around the 13th century BC, with Egyptian power waning in the area, the Hebrews decided to move back to Canaan, which they still regarded as the Promised Land. Some reckon that at this stage relatively few Hebrews were escaping slavery: many of them had moved up the social ladder and were doing quite well. There is speculation that King Tutankhamen was of Hebrew origin on his mother's side and that he knew Moses.

Whatever the truth, the loose confederation of tribes which made up the Hebrews set out for the Promised Land under the leadership of Moses. But it wasn't easy; nor was this a bunch of peace-loving hippies wandering around the desert: the Hebrews were, in effect, an invading force which fought prolonged battles with the Canaanites, the original inhabitants of Canaan who, understandably, weren't too sympathetic to the 'God promised us this land' argument.

And it was early into this process – apparently three months after the Hebrews left Egypt – that Judaism had its first major event. God brought Moses up Mount Sinai and gave him the Ten Commandments: for the first time, the religion had a moral framework. Not that the Hebrews instantly adopted this set of rules; when Moses came back down the mountain, he found the Hebrews worshipping a golden calf: a pagan idol. So five hundred years after Abraham came up with the idea that there was only one God, the Hebrews were still something of a polytheistic society.

Nonetheless, God didn't get entirely fed up with the Jews. The descendants of Aaron, Moses' brother, were designated as the priest class, and put in charge of the tabernacle, a sort of portable house of prayer. This was later situated in the city of Shiloh for over 300 years.

Moses died and his chosen successor, Joshua, carried on the fight, largely defeating the Canaanites, but having altogether more trouble with the Philistines, originally an Aegean people. Indeed, the fighting continued over the next few hundred years and included several setbacks, such as the capture of the tabernacle at Shiloh. These defeats are interpreted in the Torah as evidence of God's displeasure with the Jews, rather than evidence that the Philistines were handy in a scrap.

Eventually the Hebrews – or Israelites as they now called themselves – defeated the Philistines under the leadership of their first proper King, David. In part due to the weakness of the neighbouring countries, David was able to establish an independent state with its capital in Jerusalem.

David's achievement was not just in winning the war, but in uniting the twelve tribes into statehood – a process which continued with his son, Solomon, who built the first permanent Temple in Jerusalem and which was looked after by the priestly class. But following Solomon's death, things went belly-up again. The next king, Rehoboam, brought in a heavy taxation system, causing a revolt and eventually a split in the country. Ten tribes in the north became Israel, while the two in the south, remaining loyal to the House of David, became Judah, (from which we get the word Jew – though this wasn't to be coined for several hundred years).

The two states existed side by side, sometimes cooperating, something fighting with each other, for over 200 years, until 721 BC when the Assyrians invaded the northern state, Israel. In them days, they didn't do invasion in half measures: pretty much the entire population were removed and replaced with foreign captives, who became later known as the Samaritans; at least one of whom later turned out to be good. (And today they exist as a tiny sub-sect of Judaism.)

But as soon as one invading power had invented the

steal-an-entire-population concept, there were lots of copies. Some 130 years later, the Babylonians rode into the southern state, Judah, destroyed Jerusalem and the Temple and brought the Hebrews back to Babylon, where they remained for somewhere in the region of 70 years. (In truth it was the Hebrew elite who were brought to Babylon, during which time some of them composed the 'Babylonian Talmud': which is used to this day.)

But then the Babylonians were conquered by the Persians led by Cyrus the Great.

Now as we've mentioned already (see **Zoroastrianism**), the Jews would, during this time, almost certainly have come into contact with the Persian Zoroastrian religion and may well have absorbed some of its influences in the composition of the Torah and in relation to ideas like Heaven, Hell and resurrection. Certainly when Cyrus allowed the Jews to go back to Judah, (also under Persian control), it was to 'build a house for God' – which would seem to imply that he felt that his God and the Israelite God were the same person.

Back in Judah, the Jews were granted considerable autonomy, rebuilding the walls of Jerusalem, and the Temple which had been destroyed by the Babylonians: now known as the Second Temple. And thanks to the Babylonian captivity, they also had the Torah, the Jewish set of rules for living life and for religious observance. At this stage, all shreds of polytheism had vanished and it was probably during this period that the term 'Jew' came into use: deriving, as we've said, from the word Judea.

As for the ten Israelite tribes which had inhabited the northern state, Israel, they never returned and are referred to as the Lost Tribes. All sorts of Da-Vinci-Code-type conspiracy theories exist as to what happened to them, though most likely they migrated through Asia and even Europe, mixing in with local populations and eventually dissolving into them. The Jews who returned to Judea are the forebears of most Jews today – yet they represent only a small proportion of the Hebrews, the Chosen People.

Persian rule in the area was replaced by the Greeks and everything remained pretty much the way it had for about 300 years. The Greeks liked the Jews, regarding them as a 'philosophical' people. But in 141 BC, following attempts by local proxies to suppress Judaism, the Jews revolted and established an independent kingdom once again: one that lasted a little over 100 years until the Romans rolled into town in 63BC. A chap by the name of Herod was appointed King. You may have heard of him.

During this period, the Jewish priestly class didn't exactly cover themselves with glory: they were widely regarded as the puppets of the Roman-appointed puppet leaders. So increasingly, the Jews turned to the Pharisees or Scribes – who were at that time only a small Jewish sect – also known as Rabbis, meaning teachers. In effect, this was the birth of what is known as Rabbinic Judaism or Judaism as it is practised today: with no full-time clergy to preach or tell adherents what the Bible means. Instead there are Rabbis – teachers – there to encourage study and personal exploration.

Now we don't need to dwell too much on what happened next: the arrival of Jesus has, let's say, been extensively reported elsewhere. (See **Christianity**.) Anyway, that was just one of the convulsions taking place in the Jewish world. Another was that Judaism was becoming a victim of its own success: the Jewish population was now far too large for everything to revolve around the Temple in Jerusalem. Those who lived too far away, both in Palestine and other countries, (the Jewish tradition of emigrating had been established since Babylonian exile), had set up their own synagogues, which forced something of a re-think as to how the religion should be organised. This led to the establishment of a number of teaching academies, where Judaism was debated.

There was also considerable friction with the Romans, which led to two revolts, one in 70AD and a second in 132 AD. The first resulted in the destruction of the Temple: a catastrophic event for Judaism. All that is left of that building is what is now known as the Western Wall – a major place of pilgrimage for Jews. Jewish belief is that the Temple will remain in ruins until a descendant of David re-establishes the glory of Israel and re-builds the Temple.

The second revolt resulted in Jews being banned from Jerusalem altogether. The teaching academies survived, but now there was a sense that Judaism was under threat and needed to be preserved. This resulted in the Talmud: a collection of writings and sayings from the early prophets, (including the Babylonian Talmud), and a strengthening of the role of the rabbi within Judaism. From now on, with no Temple and not even access to its remains, Judaism would be organised locally, around the rabbi and the synagogue. In effect, Judaism became a religion for a people in exile.

Just as well too, because the sense of threat was well-founded: in the third century, the Roman Empire became Christianised, turning Jerusalem into a major centre for Christian pilgrimage. Eventually, Jews were barred from building synagogues. Over the next 1,000 years these were followed by Muslim invaders, (who built their own mosque, the Dome of the Rock, more or less on the site of the Jewish temple – see **Islam**), then the Crusades, then the Turkish Ottoman Empire, then the Egyptians, then the British. With each invasion, more Jews left to live abroad: by the middle of the 1800s, some estimates have it that there were as few as 12,000 Jews left living in Palestine.

Indeed, over time Jews even began to evolve into distinct ethnic groups outside Israel: Ashkenazi Jews (of Central and Eastern Europe with Russia); the Sephardi Jews (of Spain, Portugal, and North Africa) and the Yemenite Jews, from the southern tip of the Arabian peninsula. These differences, however, are mostly cultural.

Yet in few places did they have an easy time of it. Ironically, given modern events, the Jewish 'Golden Age' abroad took place around 1,000AD in Spain – under a benign Islamic regime. But in most parts of Europe, Jews were subjected to oppression, pogroms, forced conversions and ghettoisation: one thousand years of Christian prejudice which had its ultimate expression in the Nazi holocaust.

More recent events in Jewish history, particularly the founding of the state of Israel, are well known and more a political than a religious story, so instead let's look at what Jews actually believe and the various versions of Judaism: of which there are many. Judaism is not a monolithic religion in the sense of there being one central authority (such as a pope); it is the Holy Books which form the centre of the belief, and like anything written down years ago, it is open to different interpretations.

Now, obviously, one of the factors which made Judaism unusual back in the dawn of time was this idea that there might be only one God: and that this God is concerned with the fate of humanity. Indeed, in modern Judaism, the idea of a blessed trinity or of addressing prayers to anyone other than God – such as saints – is viewed as heretical. Jews also disapprove of icons or symbols, such as crosses

Another unique feature was the moral aspect of Judaism: all the other religions were concerned with making sacrifices to the gods, not because they particularly liked these deities, but because it was in the adherents' interest to keep them sweet. For the first time in history, God wasn't looking for sacrifices (though Jews did make them in the early years of the religion), but for his followers to lead a good life: this was the main form of worship to the Hebrew God.

Thus the Jewish Bible, the Torah, is big on instructions on how to do this. Apart from the Ten Commandments, there is the 613 *mitzvot* – hundreds of handy laws for leading the moral life; though many of them apply to living in the desert a few thousand years ago and only about half of them have a practical application today. It is by living this life well that adherents get to heaven, which in Hebrew is called *gan eden* – the Garden of Eden. Jewish teaching on the after-life is a little vague and tends to vary among different strains of Judaism. But don't forget that for the Jews, the Messiah is yet to come and establish a new kingdom on earth. Jews also refer to heaven as *olam haba*: the World to Come.

Parallel to the Torah is what's known as the oral tradition: interpretations and commentaries on the Torah which originally were passed down orally (mostly by the Pharisee sect) but processed into book form in the Mishnah not long after the time of Christ. However, further debate went on for centuries afterwards in Jewish centres of learning, to be eventually put together in the form of the two Talmuds (Palestinian and Babylonian). There is a lot of Jewish law, and a lot of interpretation of that law. There have, however, been Jewish groups which based themselves on what was written in the Torah alone. But they're in a tiny minority. It's complicated.

So in describing the rules of Judaism, it should be kept in mind that the various versions of the religion practise and interpret them in different ways. However, the general concept that worshipping God is not just about what happens in the synagogue, but how the adherent lives their life applies to all of them. Don't forget: the Jews still regard themselves as a people specially chosen by God, so it is up to them to set examples of holiness for the rest of the world and to work to increase the levels of holiness on the planet. Now, that's pressure.

What's contained in the Ten Commandments is pretty well known, so we don't need to dwell too much on the no-swearing/murder/adultery aspects of Judaic theology. Just as important as what is forbidden is what the average Jew is expected to do.

The Sabbath or *Shabbat* is extremely important in Judaism, it being the day when God took a break from creating the world and also being a commemoration of the Exodus from Egypt. It begins at sunset on Friday night and lasts until sunset the following day. Just like God, Jews are expected to relax with their families and forbidden from working (there is actually a list specifying what constitutes work), while many even forgo driving, preferring to walk to synagogue for Shabbat services. A religion where God expressly tells you to chill out must have something going for it.

The Jewish *kashrut* regulations (which means 'keeping kosher') are based on the idea that some foods are 'pure' and others not. This means avoiding animals which eat other animals or which live on the sea floor consuming the excretions of other animals: which means no birds or beasts of prey and no seafood other than fish, and no food which comes from 'dirty' animals – such as pork. Vegetables should be thoroughly cleaned, while consuming meat with milk is also frowned upon. Although these rules have a spiritual basis, there is an element of practicality here: a kosher diet is a healthy one. Again, different strands of the religion observe different kosher laws.

Among the stricter forms of Judaism there are also a number of rules which dictate modesty of dress for men and women and when they are and are not allowed to have sexual intercourse: during menstruation, for instance, is considered a major no-no. Wearing of a skullcap is more generally observed by male Jews.

And, of course, there's prayer. Judaism contends that it is possible to have a personal relationship with God – God is interested in every single one of us, and works invisibly in the world. However, that's not the same as saying we can know God: in Judaism, because God exists outside our physical and intellectual boundaries, it's impossible for us to know what God is actually like – even in the Torah God tells Moses that it is impossible to look at God's face and live. Instead Jews must investigate God's nature based on what's written in the holy books, and through prayer. Jews are required to pray three times a day, and can do so in different ways: in thanksgiving, praise or simply to ask for help: Judaism teaches that the more you ask for help, the more God will help you. Blessings are also an integral part of the Jewish day: anything eaten or drunk invariably has a blessing to go with it, as do a range of natural phenomena, like weather; it's part of a constant recognition of God's role in the physical world.

But while personal prayer is important, equally so is communal worship: Judaism is all about the family and – understandably, given its history – all about the community, both local and world-wide.

This all takes place in the synagogue, which, apart from being a place of worship, is usually also a place of study and a community centre. Depending on the variety of Judaism practised, women and men sit separately; the service is performed in Hebrew or a mixture or Hebrew and the local language. Everyone keeps their head covered, except for young or unmarried girls. All synagogues contain an Ark: a cupboard within which the Torah scrolls are kept and above which burns a *Ner Tamid*, an eternal light. (And yes: the Ark of the Covenant, the container which held the ten commandment tablets as carved by God was what they were looking for in *Raiders of the Lost Ark*.) Central to any Jewish service is the reading of the Torah. During the course of a year, a full Torah is read aloud. As we've said, the Rabbi is the most important figure in a synagogue, though priests – known as *Kohen* – still exists but have a limited role. When a rabbi is not available, others can be appointed to lead the community in prayer or call up others to read sections from the Torah. These are voluntary roles and considered an honour.

However, there are many different other sorts of Jewish clergy, in the main experts in various aspects of Jewish Law, in circumcision or the preparation of kosher food. These would visit synagogues or be called in for a specific reason, such as overseeing a divorce case. (Yes, divorce is permissible in Judaism, and under Jewish law, it's the 'no-fault' kind.)

The importance of family is also reflected in the number of family-related rituals; from *Brit milah*, where baby boys are circumcised, to *Bar mitzvah*, the passage from childhood to adulthood for 12 or 13 years old Jews; Marriage with the traditional breaking of a glass underfoot, (another reminder of the destruction of the Temple) and the funeral rite. For the death of the parent, the mourning period lasts for a year.

Judaism is also rich in holy days and festivals, most of which take place during autumn: a time of the year, according to Judaism, when adherents can reflect on the previous twelve months and how they can improve their relationship with God. All festivals start in the evening – because this is when God started creating the world. The exact dates vary from year to year because the Jewish calendar is based on movement of the sun and moon, but many of the festivals themselves are familiar to western ears: *Rosh Hashanah*, the Jewish New Year; *Yom Kippur*, the annual Jewish period of repentance; Passover, or *Pesach*, which marks the escape from captivity in Egypt; *Shavuot*: when the Jews received God's laws at Mount Sinai. And that's just a few of them.

But as we've said, because of the study-based nature of Judaism, the religion has fractured into many strands of belief, some which regard each other with a degree of hostility, but most of which have good relationships. Given the troubled history of the Jews, unity is, understandably, a fundamental principle.

Some of the major varieties of Judaism are:

Modern Orthodox. A common traditional form of Judaism, which has a broad adherence to historic traditions and practices. However, it makes some allowances for modernity

Traditional Orthodox or *Haredi Judaism* is a more conservative form of Judaism. It is sometimes called Ultra-Orthodox Judaism, though this is considered offensive. It differs from modern orthodox mainly in how stringently some practices are observed.

Hasidic Judaism is a subset of Haredi and arguably the most conservative form of Judaism. Yes, they are the guys with the beards and ringlets. Founded in Europe, it was a reaction to a perception that Judaism was too 'academic' and explored more esoteric forms of worship.

Conservative Judaism, or *Masorti Judaism*. It developed in

Europe and the United States in the 1800s in reaction to a lessening of oppression towards Jews in many parts of the world. It adopts a less fundamentalist teaching of Judaism and argues that Jewish law is not static but has responded to different eras. It maintains that the Torah was inspired by God rather than dictated to Moses by God, as the Orthodox version believe

Reform Judaism. Originally formed in Germany, it takes a more individualistic approach to the laws of Judaism, arguing that it is up to the person to decide what rituals to observe. Reform also sees Jewishness as a religion rather than a race.

Reconstructionist Judaism. Like reform, believes Jewish law is up for interpretation, but believes this decision should be in the hands of the community, not the individual.

Karaite Judaism. This is not a result of rabbinical Judaism. The followers of Karaism believe they are the inheritors of the Second Temple period, before rabbinical Judaism fully took hold. Others contend they were a sect which began in the 8th and 9th centuries. The Karaites, believe in *Peshat*, (Plain or Simple Meaning): a more literal interpretation of the Torah with no commentaries. They are semi-detached from the rest of Judaism.

Samaritans. Although Jewish, they maintain a separate cultural and religious identity. Very small in numbers, they live entirely in Holon in Israel and Mount Gerizim on the West Bank.

Judao-paganism. (See Paganism)

Humanistic Judaism. A form of the religion which, while not quite being atheistic, basically takes the attitude that God isn't that important. (See **Humanism.**)

There are a few other movements associated with Judaism, but which are not Judaic denominations, most notably the Kabbalah movement, thanks to Madonna. Kabbalah is a form of Jewish mysticism, the word itself referring to the Jewish oral law. Most branches of Judaism, other than Hassidic Jews, tend to disapprove of it.

All these denominations exist in Israel, though Israelis tend to classify themselves in different ways to Jews overseas. Most Jewish Israelis classify themselves as 'secular' (*hiloni*), 'traditional' (*masorti*), 'religious' (*dati*) or *Haredi.* These classifications (very) roughly correspond to how rigorously they practise the religion (many secular do not practise Judaism at all), but may also be an indication of ethnic background, (whether from western or eastern Europe, north Africa etc), how politically active they are and what political views they hold. These general classifications are in fact so subtle and laden with meaning that for the casual visitor to Israel, it's best not to ask.

And not just because it's complicated and controversial, but because, for the non-Jew, it's probably impossible to fully understand what it's like to be born into the Judaic tradition: because of the unyielding tragedy, because of their huge influence on world history; because your average Jew has had to deal with *so much history*. If you want proof of God, look at the Jews: their very survival is a miracle.

10

Spiritism

SPIRITISM? 15 million adherents around the world? Perhaps 50 million with an interest in it?

No, me neither. But you know what your problem is: you haven't been to South America on your holidays recently. Although the religion was founded by a Frenchman and at one stage was doing great business around Europe, World War Two effectively killed it stone-dead. But in South America, particularly Brazil, Spiritism has been swooped up and embraced warmly, both as a belief in itself, (Kardecian Spiritism, it's called), as a shot in the arm to some (sort of) traditional beliefs like Umbanda and as an influence for a crop of new Spiritist religions with cool names like Christian Rationalism, Union of the Vegetal and Valley of Dawn.

Of course we need to be precise about our terms here: you may think Spiritism is merely séances and furniture-moving. Well, it is, but with lots more added: Spiritism claims to be the message of Jesus, but updated by visiting spirits; a sort of Christianity 2.

Which, in turn, may bring you to ask: isn't that Spiritualism? Well, no it isn't: you try calling a Spiritist a Spiritualist and see the reaction you get.

Spiritualism was a religious movement, popular in many English-speaking countries from the mid-1800s to the early twentieth century. Most spiritualists were also Christians, but believed that they could communicate with angels, dead people and perhaps even God. One influence on the spiritualists was Franz Mesmer – from whom we get the term Mesmerism. We'll come back to him.

The movement failed to make any significant mark on Christianity, mainly due to its own predilection for flashy, special-effects-type séances, most of which were proved to be fake. Today, people who practise spiritualism are either members of other religions or part of a small group called Survivalists.

So now that we know what Spiritism is not, let's find out what it is: and the first thing you should know about Spiritism is that it was influenced by Spiritualism. Well, of course.

The first seriously big box-office event in Spiritualism was the emergence of the Fox Sisters in Hydesville, New York. In 1848, the Fox family began to hear unexplained rapping noises in the house. Convinced that this was some sort of ghost, (the house already had a reputation for being haunted), the two daughters, Kate and Margaretta tried to figure out how to communicate with the spirit. In front of other family members and neighbours, they devised a sort of Morse-code system of knocks and bangs which revealed that the 'spirit' belonged to one Charles B. Rosma: a peddler (or more correctly, former peddler) who claimed he had been murdered and buried in their basement. An extensive dig in the basement did produce a skeleton, though it could never be proven that it was Charles B. Rosma, or that Charles B. Rosma ever existed.

It was enough to catapult the Fox sisters to fame on both sides of the Atlantic – including France. (Much later, it all went horribly wrong for Kate and Margaretta. They slipped into alcoholism and mutual recrimination and eventually Margaretta demonstrated how she could produce the knocking sounds at will – by cracking her toe joints.)

But anyway: the Fox sisters were famous in France; that's the important thing. Equally popular in France during the middle 1800s was the introduction of the 'Talking Board' – an early form of Ouija Board; the design of which was suggested, apparently, by some spirits themselves. Whether the spirits had any design qualification is unlikely, because they were big awkward yokes with a centre board which would spin around to various letters, slowly spelling out a message.

And thirdly, (bear with it, we are nearly there), there was also great interest in the work of the aforementioned Franz Mesmer. A German-born physician, Mesmer had arrived in Paris with an already mixed reputation: Mesmer had developed a technique for healing people which he ascribed to 'animal magnetism'. No, not sexual attractiveness, but the original meaning of the phrase as coined by Mesmer: a sort of invisible substance which flowed between creatures, increasing or decreasing their store of health.

Mesmer had come to believe that he was a powerful 'channeller' of this stuff.

The channelling would typically take place with Mesmer staring into the patients' eyes until they became, well, mesmerised. In truth, he was hypnotising them, though at the time no one realised this. And few scientists accepted Mesmer's 'animal magnetism' explanation, saying there was no proof of his invisible substance existing.

One of the scientists to come to this conclusion was Hippolyte Léon Denizard Rivail.

Born in 1804, Hippolyte came from a family with a legal tradition and even as a teenager had given a great deal of thought to how to bring the various Christian sects together. (Although born Catholic, he was educated in Protestant Switzerland.) However it was in science and education that Hippolyte excelled: a major Big-Brain, he spoke several languages and taught mathematics, physics, chemistry, astronomy, physiology, comparative anatomy and French and over the years gained a reputation as one of France's major educators.

So it was from genuine scientific interest that Hippolyte began studying the various phenomena connected with the work of Franz Mesmer. At the time, he was by no means alone in this: many scientists were studying mesmerism and people like the Fox sisters; the subtext being that science might be about to make a breakthrough in explaining the supernatural – that science, not religion, might find a way to describe God.

So it was in this context that Hippolyte – then still completely sceptical – took the next logical step. He got himself a Talking Board and hired a medium. Well, two mediums actually. The details are somewhat sketchy, but it's believed that they were sisters, though later he drafted in a third medium named Celina Bequet. The sisters were young, flighty things and in their previous chats with the otherworld had tended to deal with light, frivolous subjects: the French nineteenth-century equivalent of talking about *Big Brother*. However, whenever Hippolyte was in the room, the two young women became grave and intellectual – apparently because they were 'channelling' some higher order of spirits who wished to speak specifically with Hippolyte. To test this, Hippolyte devised a long list of questions to put to the Spirit World. A very long list: 1,018 of them, which took two years to answer, mainly through 'automatic writing'.

So extensive was the picture of the next world as described by the spirits that Hippolyte (now thoroughly convinced), asked the spirits could he publish their conversations in book form. The spirits, naturally, announced that this had been their intention all the time – and that it was they who had planted the idea in his head. (Could they not have given the man *some* credit?.) They further announced that the book should be titled *Le Livre des Esprits* (The Spirits Book.) Through Celina Bequet, Hippolyte also discovered that he, (Hippolyte) had had a number of previous incarnations – one as a man named Allen, another as a Gaul Druid named Kardec.

So he published under the name Allen Kardec: partly because he liked it, but mostly because he knew what reaction he would get from his fellow scientists if he published under his own name. Studying such phenomena was one thing; believing them was another.

Published in 1857, *The Spirits Book* did exactly what it said on the tin: provided a pretty exhaustive account of everything that goes on in the spirit world. A lot of what it contained was compatible with Christianity: one God, the source of all creation and the source of all good. However, other bits of it were downright heresy: although Kardec wrote that God in the spirit world is the Judaeo-Christian God, he expressly denied that Christ was his Son – merely one of his messengers. He also claimed that there is no such thing as the Holy Spirit; merely manifestations of various spirits. Humans, apparently, are made up of spirit, body and the stuff that binds the two together: known as perispirit. The book also suggested that there were many inhabited worlds in the universe and that we would all be reincarnated many times, with our spirits improving with each life lived.

For the first time someone had used spiritualist techniques not just to chat with dead Uncle Johnny but also to provide a theological basis to talking with spirits. Naturally, this completely scandalised the Catholic Church, which condemned the book and in one case even organised a book-burning. (This happened in 1861 and was ordered by the Bishop of Barcelona. The Bishop died nine months later and through mediums, later asked Kardec's forgiveness; which he was big enough to give.)

And don't forget (see **neopaganism**): this was an age when around Europe, people were hugely interested in this sort of thing. *Le Livre des Esprits* went on to sell millions of copies and was read in all the best company: even Emperor Napoleon III had Kardec over for a few chats.

The book also marked a major departure away from

Spiritualism. As we've said before, it had operated as a disapproved-of adjunct to Christianity: spiritualists were never going to contradict Christian theology. But Kardec had done just that, with a brand-new picture of the after-life and especially with his contention that the soul goes through a number of compulsory reincarnations. To underline this difference, Kardec began calling what he was doing Spiritism.

Later on, Kardec also became rather hostile to the table-knocking variety of mediums, preferring to rely only on those capable of 'automatic writing' (where there was less chance of the medium being affected by preconceived ideas, he felt).

Now completely convinced that he had hit on something which could transform the world, Kardec established the Parisian Society of Psychologic Studies, of which he remained president until he died, as well as a monthly magazine, *La Revue Spirite*. With similar societies springing up all over the world, Kardec set about collating communications which came via his own research and from other Spiritists.

There was a corpus of work which had to be completed: the basis for a new set of religious truths which had yet to be revealed. In 1861 he published *Le Livre des Médiums*, (The Book on Mediums), a practical account of how mediums go about their business.

But in 1864 came the work which, understandably, got the most negative reaction from the Church. *L'Évangile Selon le Spiritisme*, (The Gospels according to Spiritism), sought to expand and clarify the teachings of Jesus from conversations Kardec had had with loads of dead people.

The intention was to show that Spiritism was not in conflict with Christianity; the result was the exact opposite. The *Gospels* still banged on about reincarnation, arguing that all souls will be saved; it simply takes longer for some than others. It also claimed that Christianity was not the last word on revealing God: this was a process which was ongoing, with Spiritism only the latest instalment. Oh, and just to really annoy Catholics, the book maintained that God approved of divorce.

However, there was much which didn't conflict with Christian beliefs: particularly a stress on the importance of helping others through charity work.

This was followed by *Le Ciel et l'Enfer, (Heaven and Hell)* a fleshing out of the reincarnation thesis. It stated that there is no heaven or hell, just various states of reincarnation.

The final book was *La Genése, les Miracles et les Preditions selon le Spiritisme (The Genesis, Miracles and Premonitions according to Spiritism)*, an attempt to meld Spiritist ideas with those of science. It maintained that the creation of the universe was a sort of 'intelligent design', that there are no such things as miracles – spirits being natural, not supernatural – and that the prophecies in the Bible were more like intelligent guesswork.

These five books formed the foundation of Spiritism, right up to the present day.

But Kardec died in 1869 and with his departure there opened up something of a void in the organisation: he, after all, was the president of the society and the editor of *La Revue Spirite*. Yet this alone does not explain why the Spiritist cause went into something of a nosedive both in

France and around Europe after his death. Indeed, no one seems to know exactly why it happened. Most likely, it was a combination of factors: some pressure from the Church; scientific advances, particularly the discovery that what Franz Mesmer was doing was simple hypnotism; a loss of interest in, what for some, was a simple fad; the rise of several totalitarian regimes in Europe; the onset of two world wars.

The wars probably had the most devastating effect. When WWII came to an end, there was no Spiritist movement left. Today, Kardec's grave in the cemetery of Montmartre is still a place of pilgrimage, yet the number of followers in Europe is, relatively speaking, tiny. If you want the real action, you gotta get to South America.

In 1873, just four years after Kardec's death, the Society of Spiritist Studies was formed in Rio de Janeiro, mostly by the sons and daughters of wealthy Brazilian families who had sent the kids to study in France.

Now like France, Brazil is a Catholic country, so you'd imagine that a new Spiritist organisation would receive an equally chilly reception. But not so: not that the Catholic Church there gave the thumbs-up to Spiritism; it was more of an acceptance that there was little they could do about it. Religions quite like Spiritism had been operating in Brazil for some time; though in a clever, quiet way.

Today, about 45 per cent of the Brazilian population can claim African ancestry – due to the huge amount of slaves who were imported into the country. Naturally, the first order of business was to save their heathen souls and convert them to Christianity (specifically Catholicism), which the slaves were apparently quite happy to do. But only *apparently*: in effect, they continued to practise their old religions, but simply substituted Catholic religious figures for their traditional deities. It looked like Catholicism, it sounded like Catholicism, but it was actually a number of African beliefs – most of which involved rituals where adherents could speak to the spirits of the dead.

As a result, Brazil was (and still is) a society where people can be involved in several religions without any contradiction, and where Christian and 'heretical' ideas could co-exist with a relative degree of comfort. (For instance: a survey conducted in 1971 found that 70% of Brazilians considered themselves Catholic and only 11% Spiritists. However, 68% said they believed Spiritism to be valid, and 49% had visited a Spiritist centre.) Nonetheless, back in the late 1800s, the Spiritist beliefs were given the warmest welcome in the poorer sections of Brazil, where the populations tended to be of African origin.

So in 1874 The Brazilian Spiritist Federation was launched, with the express aim of spreading the Kardecian good word. Today it's still in the business and the principle organiser of Spiritism in Brazil. Much of this success is due to a receptive population but also to Francisco Candido ('Chico') Xavier, a minor-level civil servant, who, between 1932 and his retirement in 1961, produced on average three books a year on various Spiritist subjects, making Chico a household name in Brazil. However, because Chico claimed that the books were 'dictated' to him, he never made a cent out of his prodigious output – that's all gone to the Spiritist Federation.

And just as Allen Kardec would have wanted it, most of this money has gone to the poor in the shape of schools, job-training centres, orphanages, nurseries, hospitals and hospices. In some of the hospitals, especially psychiatric hospitals, a certain amount of 'Spiritist medicine' is practised, which has generated no little controversy. In recent times some evangelical groups have preached against the belief, but so far with little effect: Spiritism has such mainstream acceptance in Brazil that politicians admit to be followers; and there have been three Brazilian postage stamps commemorating Kardec. It's spread to Mexico and other Latin American countries and is now making progress in the US.

The arrival of Spiritism in the region also influenced the creation of other belief systems, particularly Umbanda, which is a mixture of some old central African religions, particularly Quimbanda, a dollop of Catholicism and Spiritism. Other Spiritist-influenced newcomers include Christian rationalism, which claims not to be a religion but believes in reincarnation; Union of the Vegetal, which combines an old Inca belief with drinking hallucinogenic tea; Valley of Dawn, a religious community which mixes Christianity, mysticism, Afro-Brazilian religions, ancient Egyptian beliefs and flying saucers.

Because of the plethora of Spiritist-influenced beliefs, and because ordinary Brazilians don't have much of a problem floating between one group or another, the Spiritists now tend to call themselves Kardecist Spiritists. Thus the figures quoted earlier: there are probably ten million or so Kardecist Spiritists around the world, but possibly up to 50 million who may dabble occasionally in Spiritism.

So let's do the usual look at what these people believe. Probably the most significant change which came about since its arrival in Brazil is a movement away from science and back towards faith: Kardec's intention in writing his books was to describe what he was seeing like any scientist, and in the process create a new paradigm for looking at the universe which combined both science and religion. In South America, his scientific journals have become more like scripture: Spiritism has changed from a religious movement and into a religion.

So: Kardecist Spiritism is based on the teachings of Jesus, but with a few new twists. In the Bible Jesus said: "If you love me, keep my commandments; and I will ask the Father, and He will send you another Comforter."

This 'comforter' or 'consoler' is Kardecist Spiritism, which is in fact a truer form of Christianity: the unnecessary elaborations have been taken out, while the religion has also been freed from the problems of it being mediated through human institutions. This is because the tenets of Kardecist Spiritism have been communicated directly by enlightened spirits.

Because of this the ritual aspects of the religion are not that important – they can take place in any church or house of worship. What's crucial is the guiding spirit behind them. However, because, over the years, many Kardecists have been expelled from the religions they previously practised, Kardecist Spiritism has developed its own rituals. Well, sort of. We'll get to that

But as you might expect, not all Kardecists see it this way: there is a small offshoot who call themselves Scientific Spiritists and who stick to Kardec's original intention that it remain a method of philosophical enquiry only.

As we've said, reincarnation is a major part of Kardecist

belief, the idea being that we are reincarnated again and again until we achieve perfection. Christ was incarnated in this world as an example to us to show how we should go about trying to achieve that perfection. On many other planets there are spirits in material form which are further along in this process: their societies are more developed and the people more advanced. The reason we are unaware of these places is because they exist on a slightly different plane to ours: analogous to how we can't see the spiritual plane, even though it is all around us.

Well, obviously some of us *can* see it, and they are called mediums. However, they are just more developed than the rest of us rather than completely different: we are all communicating at some level with the spirit world; we just might not be aware of it.

However, it's unlikely that any spirits will be nagging you to go to Kardecist Mass because, well, there isn't such a thing. There are no religious rituals within the belief system, nor is there any requirement on you to do anything. What there are, though, are mediumic meetings; or good old fashioned séances. These take place in Spiritist Centres, (which are all over Latin America), and a distinguishing feature of them is how plain they are: no crosses or pictures or idols of any kind. As *The Spirits Book* states: spirits have no recognisable form; therefore they should not be represented.

Thus the meetings take place in dark, windowless rooms around square or rectangular tables. Normally adherents will sit around the walls, while a 'President' and 'Workers' (gifted mediums) will sit at the table. The room is dark to make it easier for the spirits to materialise in physical form.

At a typical meeting, a huge range of spirits will be communicated with: from a recently departed relative of one of the adherents, to spirits with 'unfinished business' in the material world: often the adherents will advise the spirits, rather than the other way around. Sometimes the spirits are mischievous or angry or lie about who they are. Some of them just talk guff.

There are, however, a few more traditionally 'religious' features: a Book of Prayers in which adherents can list the names of people – alive or dead – whom they wish to pray for. Spiritist blessings can also be administered and 'energised water' can be drunk.

There are no priests or ministers in Kardecist Spiritism. Obviously, mediums do get a lot of work – though there are strict rules that they should never use their skills for fame, money or self-interest. In fact, Kardecists find it quite acceptable to receive visitors from other religions; just so long as they accept the Judaeo-Christian Ten Commandments.

So not much in the way of ritual, but Kardecists are very big on prayer, regarding it as a method of clearing bad feelings from the mind and for preparing for higher spiritual achievements. There are no set Kardecist prayers – just an encouragement to express how one feels at any given time to God, and to ask for guidance. Reading and study of Spiritist tracts is also a central part of the religion, and most Spiritist centres double as reference libraries and lecture centres.

But that's not to say that Kardecist Spiritism is without any opinions: capital punishment, suicide and abortion are all frowned upon, as they regard abortion as murder and believe the other two only create problems for future

incarnations. They are also big on pacifism and inter-
nationalism. To that end, the International Spiritist Council
(with its headquarters in Paris) was founded in 1992. As to
how much progress the Council can make in spreading the
word remains to be seen: as a movement, it claims to be
unique in that it has 'scientific evidence' of the after-life.
The problem is that, in the modern world, many people
regard this evidence as no more than a parlour trick.

9

Sikhism

GO ON, admit it: you've heard of Sikhism but about all you know is that it's got something to do with India and that they probably wear funny hats. Or is that the other ones? You know, Hindus? Muslims?

Well, relax; chances are that you've never actually met a Sikh or even been near one: because the vast, vast majority of them – 90 per cent – live in India; the Punjab to be exact. The largest group of overseas Sikhs is 500,000 in the UK – but compare to that over twenty million of them back home in India. Indeed, the connection between Sikhism and the Punjab is so acute (all scriptures are written in a variant of the Punjabi language), that it borders on the Jewish phenomena of Sikhs being both a religious and ethnic group: except that not everyone from the Punjab is a Sikh, and there were other religions there long before Sikhism came along, most notably Islam and Hinduism.

Sikhism is actually something of a whippersnapper compared to those two belief systems, only popping up in the sixteenth century.

Then again, some maintain that Sikhism is a syncretic religion which has borrowed from much older beliefs, such as Hinduism and Sufism (which is the local Indian brand of Islam). Just don't suggest this idea to any Sikhs, who believe that their religion was directly revealed by God. They might get angry – and Sikhism is a belief which has done its share of ass-kicking in the past. Even today, many of them carry knives. Really.

Traced back through its Punjabi and Sanskrit roots, Sikhism means 'disciple', 'learner' or 'instruction'. Sikhs are on this earth to learn and improve themselves. They worship one God, Waheguru, which means 'The Wonderful Lord'. However, God has many names in Sikhism; Waheguru is just the most important of them. Others words include: Ek Onkar, (One God) Satguru (true teacher) Satnaam (true name), Hari, (meaning, yellow, or sun) and loads more.

Pretty much everything the Sikhs know about Waheguru was taught to them by ten gurus (a teacher or master), who lived from 1469 to 1708. Each added their own bit to the theology or contributed to the development of the religion, but obviously the most important was the first, Gurû Nânak Dev.

Nânak was born in 1469 in a small town near the city of Lahore, now in present-day Pakistan. His folks were Hindus, of the Khatri clan, one of the many ethnic sub-divisions in that part of the world, and the Kshatriya caste: which was a pretty good one; most of Nânak's ancestors had been administrators or high-ranking government officials. Nânak's Dad was an accountant. So they were doing OK.

Nânak also had a sister, Bibi Nanki, who, it is said, recognised his Guru potential from early on. Mom and Pop, unfortunately, seem not to have noticed. In Hindu tradition, a major rite of passage for boys is the presentation of the Sacred Thread: literally, three strands woven together which can be worn from one of the shoulders or around the neck, depending on the situation. Getting the Sacred Thread was a big deal in India in those days, because it was available only to the higher castes: without the sacred thread, you were effectively barred from education or a range of the nicer jobs. And there's no way you would get a wife.

This last point probably wasn't foremost in Nânak's mind at the time – he was only nine – but the story goes that during the ceremony he refused to put on the strand, debating the matter back and forth with the Hindu priest. The thrust of Nânak's argument was that a piece of material can be destroyed: all he needed was the true name of God in his heart.

Material can be destroyed; and so too can all your future employment prospects. It's not recorded how his parents reacted to this, though one imagines they weren't too pleased. But that was only the start for Nânak's poor tormented parents: while still a boy, he pursued his interest in religion by going on journeys and eventually leaving home altogether.

And it is during this period that many believe that Nânak met Kabîr. Kabîr was a mystic who is still revered in both the Hindu and Sufi Islamic traditions, (indeed, there's a story they fought over his body at the funeral), mainly due to his teaching of God seeing all humanity as one. Later on in life, Kabîr even took the rather bold step of eschewing any religious affiliation at all: to make the point that God may have different names, but it's still God. It's not known what religion Kabîr was born into: which is no more than he would want. As we shall see, Kabîr's ideas about religion obviously had an effect on young Nânak.

But then it appeared that he settled down for a while. He got married, had two sons, while his brother-in-law – married to the aforementioned sister, Bibi Nanki, even got him a job as manager of a government granary. No doubt, Granny and Granddad heaved a sigh of relief.

It didn't last long though. Before work, it was Nânak's habit to go to the local stream, the *Kali Bein* to bathe and meditate. One morning, when he was twenty-eight, he went to the stream as usual, but then disappeared. He was gone for three days and when he returned, he was 'filled with the spirit of God'. And rather than say to his family, "You'll never guess where I've been," his first words on return were, "There is no Hindu; there is no Muslim." – a direct echo of Kabîr's ideas about how God sees people, not religions.

Nânak said much more than this, obviously, but 'There is no Hindu; there is no Muslim' formed the basis for much of his teaching for the rest of his life.

At this stage even Mum and Dad probably realised that Nânak was more cut out for Guru work than Granary Management, so he embarked on his new career – which involved some travelling. The exact routes are disputed, but it is widely accepted that Nânak set out on four huge (for the time) journeys: the first east into Bengal and Assam, the second south into Ceylon via Tamil Nadu, the third north towards Kashmir, Ladakh and Tibet, and the final tour west into Baghdad and Mecca. In all these locations he preached and debated, speaking out particularly against what he regarded as empty religious rituals, pilgrimages, the caste system, and the sacrifice of widows (at the time it was the tradition for widows to throw themselves on their husbands' funeral pyres). He taught that true religion cannot be found in books, but in the heart. One of his most famous sayings was to ask Muslims to be true Muslims and the Hindus to be true Hindus: in other words, to adhere to the spirit of their religions rather than to focus on partisan differences.

When the journeys were over, Nânak settled in the Punjabi town of Kartapur where he taught for a further fifteen years. (While making a living as a farm-hand).And although Nânak never asked anyone to follow him, it was here that he did start to collect a band of disciples. They began referring to him as Guru, or teacher. Although the followers at this time were still Muslim or Hindu, they began to refer to themselves as Sikhs – disciples.

A typical day for Nânak was to rise at dawn, say his prayers, preach to the faithful, work in the free kitchen and then go out to the fields for the day job.

The free kitchen was a central, and practical, part of Nânak's teaching: that the true path to God was not through fasting or pilgrimage, asceticism or any showy religiosity, but through living an ordinary life as well as possible. And just as religious ritual is unimportant, so too are the indicators of social status. Thus the free kitchen, where people of all religions, castes and social backgrounds could come together and share a simple meal – which they get for free. This tradition continues today, in what are known as Langars.

It's fair to say that at this stage Sikhism wasn't regarded as a religion proper. However, Nânak had established the 'Three Pillars' of Sikhism:

1. Meditation on God and reciting and chanting of God's Name.

2. A requirement on Sikhs to live as householders (i.e. not to be priests or ascetics), to make an honest living while appreciating God's blessings.

3. To share wealth within the community – as represented by the communal meal.

Guru Nânak died on 22 September, 1539, aged 70, leaving a new body of religious thought, lots of disciples and a new Guru to take his place.

Now we do have nine more Gurus to go through. All contributed to the development of Sikhism in their own way, though in all fairness, some had more time than others: one died when he was only seven years of age. So in a totally non-judgemental-everyone-is-equally-good way, here are the next nine gurus:

Angad Dev. A disciple of Nânak, he was hand-picked by the big man for the job. But he didn't last that long in it (13 years), as he died when just 48.

Amar Das. Could be credited with turning Sikhism into a religion proper. The Sikhs were still a loose amalgam of disciples when he took over, but during his tenure he introduced specific ceremonies for births, marriages and death as well as a diocesan system of organisation. He also gave Sikhism three festivals, all based on existing Hindu holy days, while the Guru's residence in the town of Gôvindvâl became a centre of pilgrimage. He was also notable for vigorously preaching the principle of equality for women and for banning purdah (the practice where women have to completely cover their bodies) and suttee (that whole widow-setting-herself-on-fire thing). A big champion of the Langar, he refused to meet with anyone until they had visited the Langar first and sat with ordinary people. This included the Moghul Emperor Akbar, who did what he was told. Amar had a good long run at the job and lived until he was 95.

Râm Dâs. Râm was Amar's son-in-law, and despite having only a seven-year tenure and dying when he was but 46, displayed the family gift for organisation. He founded the city of Amritsar, which is the holiest city for all Sikhs, but went on to be the site of some of the greatest tragedies in Indian and Sikh history. We'll come back to it.

Arjun Dev. The son of Râm Dâs. All the remaining gurus would be descendants of this line. Arjun was responsible for compiling the Sikh scriptures, the *Âdi Granth* (first book: it contained all the writings of the first five gurus); a job which literally killed him. At which point it's time for a word on the political situation. Between 1526 and 1707

189

most of India and many places beyond were part of The Moghul Empire: the guys who built the Taj Mahal. Now the Moghuls were interesting for many reasons, but what sets them apart from many historical dynasties was their religious liberalism. They were Muslim and most of the Indians they ruled were Hindu, yet there were no attempts at conversion and even the traditional tax on non-Muslims was not applied. One or two even started to develop their own makey-uppy belief systems combining Hindu, Muslim, Zoroastrian, (there were a few of them in India back then) and Christian ideas; one even declared his infallibility. In short, many of the Moghul Emperors were quite mad and loved dabbling with other religions. So when the Emperor Jahangir heard that Arjun was compiling the Sikh scripture, he couldn't resist sticking his oar in with a few suggestions. Arjun refused, and was tortured and executed at the age of 43. There were, of course, other reasons for this: Arjun had been quite pally with Prince Khusro, who made no secret of his ambition to seize Jahangir's throne.

Har Gobind. The torture and death of the previous guru brought about a distinct change of attitude within Sikhism, and a change of direction from its new leader. Har essentially militarised the religion, introducing martial arts training and weapons – and fought four battles with the Moghuls. Har always carried two swords with him: one for spiritual use *(piri)*, and one for killing people *(miri)*. He built the second holiest Sikh shrine, the Akal Takht, and founded the city of Kiratpur. He was imprisoned for a year by the authorities but on his release demanded that his fellow Sikhs be let out also. This event is now commemorated as a Sikh holy day.

Har Rai. The grandson of Har Gobind. He basically kept everything going in the old man's tradition: maintaining a military force but avoiding any major conflicts with the Moghuls. His eldest son was Ram Rai, and you might expect a shoe-in for the next Guru job. But during a case in a Moghul court, Ram (with the best of intentions), distorted the meaning of some Sikh scripture. Har Rai banished his son and named his younger brother, Hari Krisan, as his successor.

Hari Krisan. Unfortunately, Hari was just five years of age when he got the job and died less than three years later. He nominated his grand-uncle as the next guru.

Teg Bahadur. Teg toured extensively and composed hundreds of hymns to Sikh scripture (unlike his three predecessors who contributed none). But he is best remembered for his valiant defence of the Kashmiri Pandits, who were Hindus. In another classic bonkers move, the then Moghul ruler Aurangzeb departed from the centuries-old policy of religious tolerance and tried a few enforced conversions. When the Pandits refused to convert, Aurangzeb threatened to kill them all and Teg deployed his forces to protect them. For his trouble, Teg was executed by Aurangzeb. Teg could have saved his own life by performing a miracle for the Emperor, but he refused to do this.

Gobind Râ'i (Singh). The tenth and final of the Gurus, who combined many of the qualities of his predecessors. Following the execution of his father and Aurangzeb's crazed attempts to convert everyone to Islam, he basically began his tenure during a war – during which his mother and four sons were also killed. Gobind composed many prayers and compiled another Sikh holy book, the Dasam Granth Sâhib. He introduced various administrative systems, but probably his largest contribution to Sikh culture was the creation of *Khalsa*.

Khalsa (pure) was a new level of commitment within Sikhism. It was still religious, but with an added political and military dimension: in short, it was a direct response to the threat posed to Sikhism by the Moghul Emperor. By undergoing *Amrit*, a new baptism ceremony, all Sikhs made an even deeper commitment to defend their religion and uphold the values of Sikhism. All men were given the surname Singh (Lion) and women Kaur (Princess) – a move which completely repudiated the caste system and partially explains why so many Indian people have the surname Singh: this tradition carries on today. It turned the Sikhs into an even more lethal fighting force.

However, most significantly, Gobind Singh did not name a successor. He proclaimed that the Granth Sâhib, the Holy Scripture, would be the guru from now on. And since then it has been known in Sikhism as the Gurû Granth Sâhib.

Gobind Singh died in 1708, but left the Sikhs in pretty good shape. Over the next few decades the Sikhs developed into a powerful regional force, eventually helping to drive the Moghuls from India and establishing their own kingdom in the Punjab, in 1801, with its capital in Lahore.

But then came the British, and Sikh independence ended after just fifty years. And it wasn't that bad: many Sikhs joined the British Indian army and in general, Sikhs in

India remained pretty prosperous – until 1919, when things suddenly turned sour. A burgeoning independence movement in India had led to martial law in certain parts of the country, so when thousands of Sikhs turned up at the holy city of Amritsar to celebrate Baisakhi, a religious day, the British interpreted this as a breach of the rules and fired. Anywhere between 300 and 1,000 unarmed Sikhs were massacred.

As a result, most Sikhs, who had up until then enjoyed fairly convivial relations with the British, joined the pro-independence movement.

An independent India, however, didn't do the Sikhs any favours, as almost immediately it transformed into India and Pakistan – which now owned most of western Punjab. (There weren't enough Sikhs to claim Punjab as their own state.) Millions of Sikhs crossed the border back into India, which in turn gave birth to a movement demanding an independent Sikh state. In 1966, the Indian Punjab was carved up to create a state with a Sikh majority, yet there was still discontent at what some regarded as continuing Indian oppression. A particularly militant Sikh group finally had a showdown in 1984 with the Indian government in the Harimandir Sâhib shrine – again in Amritsar. This time, thousands died. Four months later, Indian Prime Minister Indira Gandhi was assassinated by two of her Sikh bodyguards. Communal violence between Sikhs and Hindus left thousands more dead.

Things have calmed down in more recent times, with the two religions re-building relations. Because the Punjab is one of India's most prosperous states, Sikhs have done well economically and maintain their military traditions within the Indian armed forces. However, despite Sikhism's stress on equality, some Sikh 'castes' have developed

Yup, just like the Jews, the Sikhs have an awful lot of history. But now that we've dealt with it, let's look at their beliefs, because, despite the often-bloody past, it is a peaceful and generous religion.

As we've said, Sikhism maintains that it is a religion directly revealed by God. But it is fair to say that there were probably some influences. Kabir we have mentioned already, but there was also the *Sant Mat* movement: a load of Hindu philosopher poets who also preached against the caste system and religious bigotry. The *Bhakti* strand of Hinduism with its monotheism and intense devotion to God has elements in common with Sikhism, while there are some bits of Islamic Sufism in there as well. However, what's unique to Sikhism is its rejection of idol worship and avatars: an avatar being a mortal incarnation of a God.

Sikhs believe in one transcendent God who is without a sex and whom it is impossible to know in his/her totality. However, this doesn't mean God is totally unknowable. You can get to know God a bit, and the way to do this is through meditation and striving for enlightenment: through the heart or the 'inward eye'.

There is no heaven or hell in Sikhism: the choice is endless reincarnation or a final spiritual union with God. To beat the reincarnation trap, you must work to solve social conflicts and end your attachment to worldly goods. Sikhs also believe in karma: that bad and good actions will have an effect in the form of future incarnations as well as how long it takes to achieve union with God.

Classical Sikh teaching is that asceticism or pilgrimages, (even though Sikhs do do some pilgrimages), won't get you there; what will is a life which balances work, worship, family life, charity and defending the rights of all creatures and human beings. Sikhs are encouraged to have an attitude of *caldî kalâ*, (buoyant hope).

As well as that, Sikhs are encouraged not to do bad things: particularly to avoid the Five Evils: *ahankâr*(pride), *krôdh* (anger), *lôbh* (greed), *môh* (attachment) and *kâm* (lust). Alcohol, tobacco and drugs are also forbidden, as well as eating meat that is not humanely slaughtered. Divorce is also a no-no, and most marriages in Sikhism are arranged. But let's be clear about what that means: it does not mean forcing anyone into a marriage they don't want, but rather that the man, woman and their respective families all agree about the union. So if it goes wrong, it's everyone's fault. Sikh women do not have to take their husbands' names.

As we've mentioned, there are two main Sikh scriptures, the Gurû Granth Sâhib and the Dasam Granth. Much of it was written in verse and is intended to be sung. Everything in the Gurû Granth is referred to as *Gurbani* – meaning it was revealed directly by God to the Guru, who wrote it down. (This is similar to aforementioned *Sant* tradition: they also had gurus who had the same experiences.) However, the Dasam Granth, which most scholars believe is wholly the work of the final Guru, Gobind Singh, does not have the imprimatur of guruship and sections of it are still debated. There's also the *Janamsâkhîs* (birth stories) which contains tales from the life of Guru Nânak. However, due to inconsistencies, they are not as well regarded as the other books.

In terms of observance, the biggest form of worship is termed *nâm simran,* or remembrance of the Divine name. This can mean a number of things, but can range from literally repeating the name of God over and over to quite high levels of meditation. And this should be pursued, if possible, all day, every day. However, there are set prayers to be recited every morning and evening, along with a prescribed morning regime which involves rising before dawn, washing and reciting God's name. Families also recite passages of the scripture together, while most Sikhs regularly attend the Gurdwara (doorway to God), or Temple. Many do this on Sunday, but only because it's the most convenient day of the week. Generally speaking, men and women sit on different sides of the temple (though Sikhism is a religion which has always stressed equality of the sexes: in the temple and even on the battlefield), and are required to remove their shoes and cover their heads. On entering, all must approach the throne containing the Gurû Granth Sâhib, the Sikh scripture which is treated like a Guru. Everyone sits on the floor, to emphasize their equality before God. Gurdwaras always have four doors, to demonstrate the idea that everyone, including other faiths, are welcome to enter, while all Sikh temples contain a Langar: the hall where food is served. Sikhs are not required to be vegetarian, but vegetarian food is always served, so as to accommodate everyone. Outside, the Sikh flag is always flown.

Sikh temples do not have priests – any Sikh can lead the prayers and most volunteer for various tasks. However, there is a Granthi: a custodian of the shrine and the scripture who organises the daily services. Each temple is independent: Sikhism is not a centrally organised religion.

But the most important and defining Sikh ritual is the baptism rite where adherents become *Khalsa*. Baptised Sikhs are required to wear the Five Ks at all times: articles of faith which have different meanings. They are:

1. *Kesh* (uncut hair). Hair is a gift from God; therefore there is no need to cut it. For men, this includes growing beards, and all this hairiness is a symbol of God's perfection.

2. *Kangha* (comb). Sikhs might not cut their hair, but that's not the same as being dirty. They are required to comb their hair at least twice a day and to wear the *Kangha* in the hair to keep it in place.

3. *Karra* (circular bracelet). A steel bracelet, it was originally used for protecting the arm in battle. Today it is a symbol of Sikh unity with the Gurus, each other and with God.

4. *Kachera* (shorts). They are sort of knee-length breeches, but not underwear. They are worn to symbolise morality.

5. *Kirpan* (small sword). They are about six to nine inches long and symbolise the Sikh independence of spirit. But they are real swords, and can be used in self-defence or in the defence of others. Some Sikhs also learn *Gatka*, the Sikh form of martial arts.

Sikhs are required to carry the five Ks at all times – which in the paranoid times we live in has caused some problems. In most western countries, however, they have been protected by legislation guaranteeing freedom of religious expression.

Sikhs have a number of annual festivals: some, as we have said, which have a Hindu origin, but most of which commemorate the birth or death of various gurus and other significant dates in Sikh history. The dates, though, are the problem: as Sikhs traditionally use a lunar calendar, the holy days don't fall on the same western dates each year. A new calendar was recently introduced to solve this problem, but as not all Sikh groups approve of it, the problem remains.

A more worrying problem still festers in Punjab, where some Hindu nationalist groups are starting to voice discontent – and claiming that Sikhism is no more than a Hindu sect. If the trouble escalates again, almost inevitably it will lead to more bloodshed. Religions preaching peace can often be dangerous things.

8

African Traditional and Diasporic

NOW THIS all seems tremendously unfair: we've featured religions from every other part of the world, but the African religions all get lumped in together. And you're right, it is unfair. The problem is that there are so many of them that, to give them all equal airtime, would require another book in itself. The other problem is that the majority of Africans nowadays consider themselves to be Muslim or Christian.

The other oddity about African religion is that, thanks to slavery, it is probably more vibrant outside the continent where it has merged with other belief systems. We'll come to that, and we'll also tell you about one or two African religions. But first let's make some recklessly sweeping statements: although we are talking about a continent's worth of belief, yet there are some common features of African traditional religions. Most of them are monotheistic to the extent that they believe in one God who created the world. However, below God there is pantheon of lesser spirits. The gods are usually worshipped with song, dance, animal sacrifice, and (in some extremely rare cases) human sacrifice or a thing called *trokosi*: a living human sacrifice. In *trokosi*, girls generally as young as ten are given as sexual slaves or 'wives of the gods' to priests in compensation for some crime committed by a family member or in return for some favour from the gods. The practice still goes on in Ghana, Togo, and Benin and various human rights groups are working vigorously to stop it altogether.

However, it should be stressed that in Africa as a whole, such practices are extremely rare. The other common factors in African religions are a stress on honouring the spirits of ancestors and a large degree of syncretism: as we've said, most Africans are Christian or Muslim, but in Africa both these religions have been influenced by Traditional African beliefs: especially in their reverence for various saints and angels – some of whom bear more than a passing resemblance to old African deities. In one case, that of the extremely scary paramilitary group, the Lord's Resistance Army in Northern Uganda, they use rosaries and have a communion rite, but also pray facing Mecca and communicate with spirits through mediums. But they're probably confused.

Now this is a bit weird, but probably the best way to learn more about African traditional beliefs is to look at how those beliefs have travelled overseas – where they have probably made more of an impact than they currently do in Africa.

The bad news is that we're not talking about one religion here and that it's impossible to list them all. The good news is that we've actually mentioned one of them already. Remember Umbanda? (It was in the **Spiritism** chapter.) If you do, you can skip the next paragraph; if you don't, here's what was said:

"Today, about 45 per cent of the Brazilian population can claim African ancestry – due to the huge number of slaves who were imported into the country. Naturally, the first order of business was to save their heathen souls and convert them to Christianity (specifically Catholicism), which the slaves were apparently quite happy to do. But only *apparently*: in effect, they continued to practise their old religions, but simply substituted Catholic religious figures for their traditional deities. It looked like Catholicism, it sounded like Catholicism, but it was actually a number of African beliefs – most of which involved rituals where adherents could speak to the spirits of the dead. The arrival of Spiritism in the region also influenced the creation of other belief systems, particularly Umbanda, which is a mixture of some old central African religions particularly Quimbanda, a dollop of Catholicism and Spiritism."

Yeah, of course you remember. The thing is that Umbanda isn't unique in this regard. Over hundreds of years, African slaves were transported to the 'modern' world and brought their belief systems with them. Few of those religions survived unchanged; many morphed and combined with other religions to create new faiths: which puts them into a distinct category of religion. Not quite African Traditional, not quite Primal-indigenous (the next chapter), not quite western (for the most part, they have mixed with European ideas); African Diasporic faiths have spread all over the Americas and the Caribbean. Some are organised, some shambolic, but there is an awful lot of them: by most estimates *100 million people* practise some form of this religion.

Which really shouldn't be that surprising; Africa is an awfully big place and there are an awful lot of Africans. We just don't get to hear about them much.

And let's say it again: it is impossible to list all such religions because, well, Africa is an awfully big place. But we can tell you about some of the main players. And to do that, we need our history fix, and, by way of example, the origins of a people called the Yoruba.

The Yoruba are a large ethnic group in West Africa with a distinct culture and language that's probably around 5,000 years old. There are 40 million of them, with the bulk resident in south-west Nigeria, but also in Benin and Togo. Happily, we don't have to say where the Yoruba came from. This is Africa: where we all come from.

Nonetheless, the Yoruba do have various creation myths, most of which involve a chap called Oduduwa, the first ancestor of the Yoruba Kings. One version has it that Oduduwa came with an invading army from the East, (which could mean Mecca, Sudan or simply eastern Nigeria). However, the oral traditions in the still-existing town of Ife in Nigeria, (the capital of the Yoruba kingdom), say that he descended from Heaven on a chain, carrying with him some soil and a chicken. The soil he scattered on the waves. Then he put the chicken on the soil which scattered it around, forming the earth. Where Oduduwa first set foot on the soil was Ife, where he fashioned the first human beings from the clay.

Over time, Yoruba developed into a large kingdom:

well, not kingdom exactly, but a loose confederation of city-states, usually ruled by a King who usually claimed lineage from Oduduwa, (Ife being regarded as a Holy Site rather than a capital). There was, however, a sort of democracy in these places, with locals councils balanced against the king – who could be forced to abdicate if he got too up himself.

The Yoruba had pretty sophisticated societies, with a pretty sophisticated belief system which they called Orisha, referring to all Yoruba culture but also to heavenly messengers who helped in human affairs. There was a pantheon of hundreds of gods, but the main one was Olodumare, who created the universe. There was also a concept called Ori, which literally means 'head', but could also, very roughly, mean soul: by working with Orishas and the spirits of dead ancestors, one could balance one's Ori and achieve physical and psychic healing: and come to know oneself. Yoruba shrines are today a major tourist attraction in Nigeria.

But like they all do, the Yoruba Empire finally fell apart, partly due to invaders, partly due to civil war. And it was at this point – mostly in the 19th century – that Atlantic slave-traders began scooping up Yoruba and dragging them off to Cuba, Puerto Rico, Brazil, Trinidad and other parts of the New World. There are two cruel ironies in this: (1) just a few decades later, slavery was banned in most parts of the world; (2) as we've mentioned, today most Yoruba, like many Africans, are Christian. By kidnapping large numbers of Yoruba, Europeans actually helped their native traditions to survive.

Not that they meant to, obviously: the millions of

people taken from Africa during the years of slavery weren't regarded as people at all but subhuman brutes, only fit for digging holes and working on banana plantations – which is why so many Yoruba were taken to Cuba. At the time Cuba was still a Spanish colonial possession and for the most part was treated as a huge factory: there was a Spanish-descended elite who were doing very nicely, thanks very much, and everyone else; small farmers, workers and slaves. Which is why, in modern-day Cuba one of the major religions practised is **Lukumí**: a belief system combining Yoruba beliefs and Catholicism. The religion is actively suppressed in Cuba, and as a result many adherents officially classify themselves as Catholics, (the trick they have always used), but by the most conservative estimates, there are three million of them in Cuba alone.

(At this point, though, we should issue an official Confusion Warning: virtually all of the religions we will be talking about have several names. The Yoruba-based beliefs in different countries are considered by some (but not all) to be the same religion. For our purposes, we'll be treating them as cousins. In all cases, they vary from country to country, while in some instances they are a mixture of Yoruba and Catholicism, or Yoruba, variants of Christianity and some other African belief systems. Or Yoruba, variants of Christianity, other African belief systems and some European religions. You've been warned.)

With that in mind, let's go back to Cuba. Lukumí is also known as Regla de Ocha, (Rule of Orishas) or Santeria (way of the saints): though the last term is a disparaging one applied by the Cuban ruling class. Lukumí means 'friends', (and, it is believed, what the Yoruba originally called themselves). Now in Cuba at the time, it wasn't just Yoruba who had been kidnapped to be slaves: other African ethnic groups were there as well, and as a deliberate policy the slave-masters broke up families and intermixed the various groups so as to maintain control.

However, since as early as the seventeenth century, the Spanish government had allowed the Catholic Church to organise *cabildos*: essentially a sort of early sports and social club for slaves. The idea was that to have a place where the slaves could get together and talk about the old country would be a good way to reduce tension. For the slaves, however, it was a way to maintain their old cultural traditions, communicate with each other and pool resources; they sang, they danced, they played the drums. Pretty soon cabildos were being organised for specific ethnic groups – and pretty soon after that, some of the residents of Havana started complaining about the terrible racket they were making. Poor dears. Still regarding the cabildos as a necessary evil, the government decided to move them out of town: giving the slaves even more privacy to practise their old religions. By the time the bulk of the Yoruba arrived in the early 19th century, the cabildos system was well established – and so effective that it was banned a few decades later. But by then it was too late. When slavery officially ended, the cabildos were simply replaced by 'societies'.

Another major advantage the cabildos provided was that it gave the Yoruba slaves time to devise a 'code' for practising their religion in broad daylight. There are well over 400 Orisha deities, so they hit on the idea of choosing a Catholic saint to correspond to each Orisha god. Thus even when working, the slaves could openly pray to a different 'saint' every day. And the slave-masters never realised what was going on: their assumption was that the slaves were practising Christianity, but that they didn't quite 'get' the idea that it was God they should be praying to, not the saints. Thus the disparaging term Santeria, Way of the Saints.

The slave-masters may have thought the slaves were a bit thick, but the slaves must have been chewing off their own arms to stop laughing. Here's a few of the people they were praying to:

Shango, known as the Sky Father or god of thunder. An ancient Yoruba king who was deified after his death. Cover name: **Saint Barbara,** an Asian saint who secretly converted to Christianity

Eleggua, otherwise known as **Eshu,** and an Orisha who should be treated with respect. He is the protector of travellers and god of roads, with the power over fortune and misfortune. He is also the personification of death. Depending in the situation, his cover name was **Saint Anthony** or **Saint Michael.**

Obatala, the god who made the world and humans, (though not all creation). Otherwise known as **Our Lady of Mercy.**

Ochun/Oshun, the goddess who reigns over love and diplomacy. Cover name: **Our Lady of Charity,** Cuba's patron saint.

Ogun, a god of war and fire. Cover name: **Saint Peter**

Oya, a warrior goddess of wind, lightning and fertility. Cover name: **Our Lady of the Presentation** or **St. Theresa.**

Yemaya, a mother goddess. Patron deity of women, especially pregnant women. Cover name: **Our Lady of Regla.**

As a result of all this, the words Saint and Orisha are interchangeable in modern-day Cuba – and the connections between the Christian and African saints remain. Christian religious imagery is common in Lukumí.

As you might expect, given its history, other aspects of Lukumí are pretty secretive and a lot of the religion is still only transmitted orally. However, it is known that animal sacrifice does play a part in rituals. Mainly it's chickens, a staple diet of many of the African-descended communities. The blood is offered to Orisha, while the meat is cooked and consumed by the adherents. (The US Supreme Court ruled in 1993 that this is not animal cruelty.) Fruit is also offered, and during the course of the rituals there is much drumming and dancing: to such an extent that some reach a trance state, where various Orisha speak through them.

As with the original Yoruba religion, the spirits of dead ancestors are held in high esteem. And in Lukumí, no one goes to Hell: there is no devil.

A similar story in Cuba is that of **Palo,** or Regla de Palo which comes mainly from the Bantu, Bantu means 'People' and more correctly refers to a group of related languages spoken by over 300 million Africans across the bottom half of Africa. Palo means 'stick' in Spanish and seems to have derived from the use of wooden sticks in the preparation of the altar.

The belief has two basic ideas: that the natural is sacred. A bit like Shinto in Japan, they believe natural objects have spirits or powers. The second idea is the veneration of dead ancestors, though, as with a lot of other African religions, there is one supreme God with a pantheon of lesser gods below. Again, Palo has melded this with much Christian imagery, though this time not as a way of protecting the original belief. The kingdom of Congo converted to Catholicism in the 14th century, so it seems as if African and western beliefs came together in Africa, not Cuba.

Most of Palo worship is around a kind of altar called a *Nganga* which typically contains sacred earth, sticks and, er, human remains. Yuk. Each altar is dedicated to a specific spirit. Adherents can also get to talk to these spirits, mainly by the spirit taking possession of individual adherents. However, it's believed this idea is not African but came about through the influence of our old friend, Kardecian Spiritism. It's not known how many people in Cuba practise Palo, though it is thought to be most popular in Havana.

Over to Brazil now, where the African Diasporic religions have huge numbers. **Candomble** arrived in Brazil as early as the mid-1500s, and, despite being banned by the Catholic Church and some adjoining countries, thrived in the slave population and later on in wider Brazilian society, where today it has at least two million adherents. However, because it developed in several parts of Brazil without much cross-fertilisation, Candomble has several 'nations' within it, the main differences being what deities are worshipped and what African languages and music are used in the rituals. In some areas the religion is called Macumba, and involves some additional witchcraft-like practices.

Now unlike in Cuba, Candomble has evolved from a wide range of African ethnic groups: the Yoruba, of course, but also the Ewe (from Ghana, Togo and Benin), the Fon (from Nigeria and Benin; they speak a related language to the Ewe) and the Bantu. Like Cuba, the formation of the religion was helped by the establishment of *irmandades* (brotherhoods) in the 18th and 19th century by the Catholic Church. The Church set them up to enable (Catholic) preaching in the slaves' native languages; but almost certainly they were used for a wide range of other purposes.

Candomble has a pantheon of gods, with each nation opting for gods worshipped by their ethnic group in Africa. However, within the religion as a whole, the various deities are roughly equivalent to each other, (such as hunter gods, fertility gods etc) and gods from one nation can make guest appearances at the rituals of another. At birth, every adherent is 'chosen' by some patron spirits which are revealed by a priest.

As in Cuba, Candomble used Christianity as a 'cover', but over time, some of those elements did become combined into the religion. Crucifixes often appear in Candomble temples and, as in Cuba, the connection with Christian saints remains. Some Native American spirits have also crept in: an indicator that the syncretic nature of Candomble was not simply about hiding the true nature of the religion from the white slavers. As with many pantheistic religions, new gods can be incorporated fairly easily.

The main Candomble ritual, known as a *toque,* divides into two parts, the first being the preparation, which can be attended only by priests and initiates (a sort of altar boy). Most of it is domestic chores: getting costumes ready and decorating the venue in the colours of whatever gods are to be honoured. Various animals are slaughtered and prepared for the feast. On the day of the ceremony, divinations are carried out, in which the priests contact the god of wisdom, (the name varies depending on the 'nation') to ask for guidance for particular adherents.

The second part involves all the adherents and priests known as *children-of-saint:* basically, mediums. As in Cuba they enter a trance-like state and then perform a dance exhibiting the traits of whatever spirit is inhabiting their bodies. There then follows a large feast. Again, African music plays a large part in the ceremony – which has gone on to influence many secular Brazilian musical styles.

Temples in Candomble are known as houses and are usually in the charge of a female High Priest with a male second-in-command. The High Priest is usually succeeded by one of her daughters.

And just down the road from a Candomble House you are just as likely to find a house for the **Umbanda** religion. Younger than Candomble, it really only developed in the early 20th century and combines bits of the Yoruba pantheon, (as usual, connected with Christian saints), some Angolan spirits, some native Brazilian gods and Kardecist Spiritualism; about which, of course, we know already. Because it has borrowed from so many religions,

Umbanda has a huge pantheon of gods which are sub-divided into various legions or 'falanges'. Each of the falanges has different areas of expertise or represents different aspects of the universe – and as a result Umbanda seems to have a larger variety of rituals that other Diasporic Brazilian beliefs.

Umbanda is also an almost exclusively urban phenomenon, with Umbanda houses on every street corner, amongst the poorer and middle-class areas. Just like Candomble, the religion features divination and animal sacrifice, though the larger Umbanda houses look more like western churches.

And that's enough of Brazil. Instead let's travel to some neighbouring countries to examine the religion which probably has the coolest name out of any of them: **Voodoo**.

Or Vodou, Vodou, Voudou, or Vudu, depending on what part of the world you are in. Voodoo started back in God-knows-when in West Africa amongst various peoples. The basic story is that Nana Buluku, the god-creator of everything, had twins: Mawu, goddess of the moon, and Lisa, the sun god. (And yes, Lisa is a bloke.) The kids, and their kids, and their kids, kids are known as voduns – spirits who interact with the world, the god-creator being above that sort of thing. And that's not to mention the spirits of millions of dead ancestors floating around the place. Today in West Africa something like 30 million people still practise Vodun, as it's called there; though often in parallel with Christianity or Islam.

In Africa, there are many variants of Vodun, and these mixed together when slaves from the Guinea coast of West Africa were brought to Haiti. Again, it went through the pretending-to-be-Catholic phase, and also mixed in with some beliefs from the native Haitian inhabitants, the Taíno and Arawak. As a result, Voodoo rituals include images of Christians saints, both as representations of African gods and as spirits in their own right, (or *mistè* – mysteries), as well as pieces of Christian liturgy: and this degree of syncretism has influenced the other religions in Haiti also: it's been said that Haiti is 80% Roman Catholic, 20% Protestant and 100% voodoo. Indeed, it was a voodoo ceremony which kicked off the Haitian revolution.

Voodoo believes in one God, Bondyè (from the French *Bon Dieu* or 'Good God'), and many adherents today regard Bondyè as the same as the Judaeo-Christian God. However, Bondyè, as in the old African belief, is remote from his creation, so adherents turn to vast legions of spirits for help. These include ancestors, saints and angels divided into twenty-one 'nations' and sub-divided into families with their own surnames, (many of which correspond to ethnic groups in Africa).

And these spirits are everywhere: everyone has their own personal spirit, though other spirits may routinely affect a person on a day-to-day business. Roughly speaking, spirits are divided between 'cool' and 'hot'. And in Voodoo, as in life, it's always better to be cool. The aim of the adherent, or Vodouisant, is to achieve harmony with the physical world around them and other people, as well as with all the spirits. To find out what spirits are interfering with the Vodouisant is the job of the priests and priestess, who do this via various ceremonies, mediumistic readings and dream interpretation.

In terms of ritual, most Vodouisants have a small altar

set up in the home; mostly devoted to the spirits of their ancestors and various other spirits whom they have chosen to serve. They say the Our Father and Hail Mary prayers on a daily basis. Voodoo public rituals, however, are exhausting affairs: involving days of preparation. A Voodoo service starts in the morning and ends late at night and involves music, hymns, various Catholic prayers and most importantly, name-checking vast arrays of spirits. In Voodoo, everyone gets a mention: which is at the basis of its moral code also. It is a participatory religion, based on the importance of family, and beyond that, community and the idea that what you give, you get back.

All of which is only the build-up to what you really want to know: do Vodouisants make dolls and stick pins in them? Nope. Never did. And no one knows exactly how this idea became a staple of so many horror films. It may have grown out of what was known as 'New Orleans Voodoo': which isn't Voodoo at all. It's an African-American form of folk magic called Hoodoo, which is based on some remnants of original African slave culture. One theory is that it could have been a method used by slaves to scare their American owners.

And that's just some of the African Traditional and Diasporic beliefs. Unsurprisingly, they bear many resemblances to each other. But more remarkably, they have striking similarities to some of the other religions we've looked at in distant parts of the world where there is no possibility they could have influenced each other. Perhaps God does work in mysterious ways.

7

Primal-indigenous

YES, THIS isn't a religion either, but a collection of various beliefs; and, unlike the last chapter, there isn't even much of a unifying factor. 'Primal-indigenous' is a catch-all term which includes a range of small religions across the world which are particular to various ethnic groups or have survived despite encroachment from the major world religions. Many are extremely old, (though there are a few newish beliefs which fit into the category), and although they often exist in places thousands of miles apart, they do share some traits in common: particularly a history of shamanism or animism.

Oh yeah, and it's reckoned there are three hundred million people in this religious category – and that *excludes* the African beliefs we dealt with in the last chapter.

Best to start, though, by explaining shamanism and animism.

And let's be clear: Shamanism is not a religion, nor does

it refer to people in weird capes chanting in front of Stonehenge. (Neo-pagans; you gotta love 'em.) Shamanism is simply a practice which has popped up in many religions in many different forms. It is a generalisation; possibly an unfair one.

Nonetheless, we'll stick with it. Shamanistic practices predate many organised religions – possibly all of them. Certainly it goes back as far as the Stone Age.

The word Shaman comes from Turkic-Mongol areas such as Siberia and Mongolia, and simply means 'He (or she) who knows'; which in the days before proper doctors and scientists is a pretty good description: the Shaman (though, of course, in different cultures they have different names) could cure diseases, sometimes cause diseases, provide counselling, see the future and explain everything – all by an ability to communicate with the spiritual world.

Now we've already seen how forms of Shamanism have survived in many of the African and African diasporic religions. Elsewhere it has had more mixed fortunes. In Europe, unsurprisingly, it has been virtually extinguished, thanks to Christianity which regarded such practices as at best paganism and at worst a form of devil worship. However, tiny pockets of it do survive in the European section of Russia: in Mari-El, a tiny Russian Republic populated by a Volga-Finnic people known as the Mari. Most of them converted to Christianity in the 16th century, but their native religion, Marla, does survive in small numbers – mostly in rural areas. Marla also has a strong animist element, with adherents believing most parts of nature have a spirit. Before crossing a river, a Mari will greet it.

Not far away from them is the Udmurt Republic, also

part of Russia. The Udmurts speak a similar language to the Mari and similarly, some of their original religious practices survive, though not much: just one village, Varklet-Bodja, adheres to the old belief and still has a *tuno,* whose job it is to locate prayer sites favoured by the spirits, cure illnesses and find missing cattle.

In Asia, many shamanistic beliefs survive, the most notable being the spacey Kulunge Rai and the Limbus, two peoples who live deep in the forests of eastern Nepal and for whom the Shaman is an extremely powerful and sometimes feared figure. As we've seen elsewhere, some of the practices have amalgamated with large religions, most notably Tibetan Buddhism: such as Bon, which despite apparently developing in a different way, is to all practical extents a branch of Tibetan Buddhism. (Most Buddhists, however, regard it as a different religion and Bon has been oppressed for centuries.)

In North America, Native American shaman, are best known thanks to the movies, and their practices still exist today. However, the Native American shamans are not 'medicine men': these are respected figures in the community, but, as the name implies, they are healers. The shaman, on the other hand, communicates with spirits, often by his spirit leaving the body and flying through the heavens and the underworld. Shaman can only get the job if they are 'called' to do it. Native American Shaman would also be regarded as the guardians of the tribe and the living repository of stories and lore.

This 'calling' to be a Shaman – which often exhibits itself in a manner of acting we in the West might call 'crazy', is common in many cultures, such as the Chukchi people of

Siberia. The Chukchi believe that all objects, animate or inanimate, have a spirit. (Chukchi are the butt of many Russian jokes, mainly for their rural lifestyle and a now defunct practice where Chukchi travellers could 'borrow' each other's wives.) Among the Tapirape, a tribe who live in the Amazon forests of Brazil and had little contact with the outside world until 1950, Shamans are called to their jobs by dreams. In the Shuar tribes of Ecuador and Peru, Shamanism is a skill which can be learned by 'apprenticing' oneself.

Being a Shaman isn't an easy job: in most shamanistic societies it's the job of the shaman to sometimes battle with malevolent spirits in order to protect people; often to achieve the trance-like state necessary to do their job, the shaman has to ingest large quantities of various psychotropic drugs. And those things can mess with your head, man.

It can also be a job where you have to be fairly secure in your gender identity. In some societies, the shaman becomes especially powerful if he takes on the attributes of the opposite sex. In other words, a man, for instance, would start dressing as a woman. Among native American tribes this is known as 'two-spirit' i.e. two spirits inhabiting the same body, though the practice is found in other parts of the world: the aforementioned much-maligned wife-swapping Chukchi do it, as do many groups in South America. In Korea, however, all the shamans or Mudang, are women.

Many primal indigenous beliefs are also, as we've said, animist in nature, which means, in its simplest form, that 'everything is alive': animals, natural phenomena such as storms, the sea the sky, even rocks, mud and houses can have a spirit which must be communicated with; though obviously, what bits of the world have 'souls' varies from belief to belief.

Naturally, people also have spirits, which must also be venerated after death. For the people of Nias, a tiny island off the coast of Sumatra, the body has four souls: two which die with the body. The Dakotas of the US also believe in four souls: one stays in the body, one hangs around the village, one goes into the air and one travels to the land of souls. Things must get crowded.

But enough of all this generalising. Let's go visit with some living, breathing examples of primal-indigenous religions in the world today. First, it's South America and the **Mapuche**.

The name literally means People of the Land, though not so many of them live up to that description any more: thanks to centuries of war, colonialism and government oppression, most live in slums on the outskirts of the larger cities in Chile and Argentina. But in their day, the Mapuche were definitely a force to be reckoned with: they resisted incorporation into the Inca Empire and after that successfully fought the Spanish to a standstill from the 1500s to the 19th century –until the Chilean army got their hands on a load of repeating rifles. Many of the Mapuche were subsequently interned and placed on tiny reservations, where disease did more to reduce their numbers than centuries of war ever could.

Today about 600,000 Mapuche descendants live in Chile, with a further 300,000 in Argentina, some of which still try to maintain their agricultural traditions and have been engaged in battles with logging companies who, as they are in the habit of doing in them parts, are trying to destroy the world's eco-system for a few bucks. Around 200,000 of them still speak the Mapuche language.

Most of the Mapuche are Christian, but their Shamanistic culture survives intact. The *Machi* is usually an older woman whose job it is to ward off evil, attract some rain for the crops and cure diseases. The Machi would have an extensive knowledge of herb lore which takes years to accumulate. Many non-Mapuche would make use of the Machi's skills.

Many of the primal-indigenous religions, however, have survived pretty much intact. Tengriism was once the dominant belief of all the Turkic-speaking peoples and in Mongolia, and replaced a previous polytheistic belief. It even travelled as far as Europe, where it survived until the Middle Ages. A lot of that business was taken by the major world religions, but **Tengriism** still survives in Mongolia.

They worship Tengri, which means Sky-father, and back in his day, Gengis Khan claimed to have a direct mandate from Tengri himself. Tengri is not seen as a person but literally as the sky itself, though he did have a couple of sons, their mother being, of course, Mother Earth. The religion was established by a chap named Geser, or Bukhe Beligte, who although born a man, had many god-like powers. There is a Tengri epic poem which relates this story, but takes many days to perform and requires a fiddle-like instrument called a morin khuur. Their religious symbols include the sun, the skies and a cross – though not the Christian variety.

Most important in Tengriism is living in harmony with

the world. They believe that everything a person needs is provided by Father Sky, Mother Earth, the spirits of nature and of dead ancestors: and this balance must be maintained by leading an upright and respectful life. However, if things do get a little out of balance, the Shaman is brought in to restore order.

Other primal-indigenous beliefs clearly have some syncretic elements, but are distinctive enough to remain religions in their own right. One example is **Yazidism**. Although the belief definitely has Middle Eastern roots, it is today exclusively practised by ethnic Kurds. There are around 500,000 of them, scattered around Iraq, Syria, Turkey, Iran, Georgia and Armenia. Two related beliefs, Alevism and Yarsanism, are more Islamic in nature, but Yazidism remains distinctly different.

Where the religion came from is a question still largely unanswered. The best guess is that a group of Sufi Muslims came into contact with a religious belief, possibly with ancient Iranian roots, and the two intermingled. Foundation of the religion is credited to Sheikh Adî Ibn Mustafa, a Persian, who settled in a village just north of Mosul, Iraq. Today, Mosul remains the spiritual capital of Yazidism. He died in 1162, and his tomb is still a place of pilgrimage. However, Yaizidis themselves claim to have been around at least since 2000 BC.

The interesting thing about Yazidism is, well, that we don't know what's interesting about it: your average Yazidi won't tell you. For centuries, the Yazidis have hidden the details of their theology from the dominant Muslim culture and today only initiated Yazidis have any idea what the religion is all about. Indeed, much of what the religion appears to be about might be little more than obfuscation to hide the real truth. All that is known is what the Yazidis have chosen to reveal.

They believe that God created the world but that all the day-to-day business is taken care of by seven angels, the chief one being Malak Ta'us or the Peacock Angel. (Though why he is called the Peacock Angel is unclear: peacocks were not native to Iraq and Iran at the time, leading to speculation that the faith was in fact imported from India, or that the peacock is in fact a chicken.) Yazidis believe that Sheikh Adî Ibn Mustafa was an avatar (or human incarnation) of the Peacock (or Chicken) Angel. Another name for him is Shaytan, which bears an unfortunate resemblance to the Islamic name for Satan – so Yazidis have been accused of devil worship: a misconception which has fuelled religious tensions and sometimes been exploited by Dan Brown-type novelists.

The Yazidi version is that Shaytan is the head of the archangels, not a fallen angel, and most certainly is not evil. They claim evil comes exclusively from the human spirit, and not any outside agency. Good and bad luck can come from God or his angels, they believe, but it's not up to the likes of us to question this.

The Yazidi God is obviously the same one as the Judaeo-Christian deity, and in their holy books there are copious references to Abraham and Adam. But their version of creation differs quite a bit from the usual accounts.

This is what they reckon happened. God made Malak Ta'us from his own 'illumination' and taught him never to bow down to other beings. God then made the other six archangels and ordered them to bring him dust from the earth. With the dust he created Adam and breathed life into him. He then ordered the archangels to bow down before Adam. Six of them did, but not Malak Ta'us, who said: "How can I submit to another being? I am from your illumination while Adam is made of dust."

This, it turned out, was just the answer God wanted to hear, so he made Malak Ta'us the head of the angels and His representative on earth. Yazidis believe that Malak Ta'us returns to earth on the first Wednesday of Nisan: a month which occurs in the Hebrew calendar around March/April. Yazidis regard this as the start of the year.

The choice that Malak Ta'us made is central to Yazidi belief: since evil exists only in human hearts, it is up to each human to choose the good, just as Malak Ta'us did.

Eventually Eve came along, though at this stage the various roles of the sexes had to be decided. Adam and Eve had a bit of a row as which of them would provide children. So to settle it, each put their seed in a jar and left it for a while. When Eve's jar was opened, it was full of creepy-crawlies and the like, but in Adam's jar was a beautiful boy child. This child became known, rather unimaginatively, as Son of Jar – but it is from Son of Jar that the Yazidis believe they are descended. The rest of us came from Adam and Eve, but the Yazidis came from Adam alone

Thus the Yazidis are big on religious purity, which in practical terms expresses itself as a caste system within the community, as well as a raft of laws on how to live and what foods to eat: it's a bit Islamic, a bit Indian. There is a taboo on eating lettuce and wearing the colour blue, either at the same time or separately.

Yazidis never marry non-Yazidis and usually take a

partner from within their own caste. (There are three of them.) Indeed, they believe that mixing with outsiders too much is polluting, and so traditionally most Yazidi men avoid such things as military service. They also believe in reincarnation: the seven archangels regularly take human form, and occasional some lesser souls as well.

They pray five times a day and if they can, make an annual six-day pilgrimage to Mosul and have a number of festivals, many of which last several days. Today, their position in Iraq is an interesting one: although ethnically Kurdish, they don't regard themselves as so and would have little to do with Kurdish claims for independence in the region.

But while the Yazidis would be very picky about what goes into their bodies, other religions have slightly different views. As we've mentioned already, many shamanistic religions involve the use of drugs: and a very active example of this are the Native Americans of the US and Canada.

The drug, or plant, in question is peyote, which contains some natural antibiotics and therefore has some genuine healing qualities, but which also has a good dollop of mescaline: a drug which can, well, get you completely off your face. It's been associated with religious and 'mystical' experiences for centuries, and there is some evidence that the Native Americans in the southern US and Latin America have been gobbling it down since pre-history, though it seems they had been keeping a lot of this good stuff to themselves: the current peyote practices only became widespread among North American tribes in the last two centuries.

Different tribes use the plant in different ways and have

varying beliefs. However, one man credited with bringing it into more general use is Quanah Parker. Quanah was a Comanche, the son of a chief and white woman, Cynthia Ann Parker, who had been captured during a battle and kept for a few years. Quanah fought many battles with federal troops, and after one near-fatal shooting, was treated by an Ute medicine man, (the Ute have an Aztec lineage), during which he was given peyote.

As you do when you've taken a load of drugs, Quanah had a vision of Jesus, who told him to give up his violent life, atone for his sins and teach the peyote religion to his fellow Native Americans. Which he did. He established the **Native American Church Movement** which taught that peyote was a sacrament given to them by Jesus.

Combined with traditional Native American medicine ceremonies, it spread rapidly through the various tribes, most of which were now squeezed into reservations. Quanah went on to become extremely wealthy and to have five wives and twenty-five children.

Despite resistance from within some Native Americans and without, (a court ruling eventually allowed the Indians to legally use peyote within their religion), the belief now has around 250,000 adherents. The Peyote Road, as it is sometimes called, stresses family life, the importance of work and the avoidance of alcohol and recreational drug use. Hmm. Although all believe in a link between Jesus and peyote use, not all believe Jesus is God, but rather a spirit sent by God, otherwise known as the Great Spirit.

Quanah Parker is credited with saying: "The White Man goes into his church and talks about Jesus. The Indian goes into his Tipi and talks with Jesus." And this is, broadly, how the religion is practised today. A group will gather, either in a tipi or a sweat lodge, (a sort of sauna) take the peyote, sing songs, engage in various rituals. Sometimes this lasts a few hours, sometimes, all night.

As you've probably noticed, a lot of primal-indigenous beliefs contain some degree of syncretism and many are quite recent. **Modekngei** emerged in 1915 on the tiny island of Palau, which is located about 300 miles east of the Philippines. Before that date Palauans had a belief system which involved a pantheon of gods known as the *bladek,* whose main job would be to protect and help adherents. The second group, the *deleb,* were made of up of the spirits of the dead. But unlike many other religions which involved ancestor worship, the deleb were feared: they were more like ghosts in western mythology, and would usually have some sort of gripe or issue about how they died. They were also believed to inhabit the bodies of certain animals, which wouldn't be eaten.

Now to negotiate with all these spiritual forces, the Palauans had shamans who would communicate with the various gods, place curses, lift curses and generally help out any way they could.

But then in 1915, a resident of the island named Temedad announced to the island that the night before he had had a visit from the Supreme Being *Ngirchomkuuk* who had called in to say that, well, there was only one Supreme Being.

It took the Palauans a little time to accept this, but eventually they did, whilst maintaining their traditional methods of worship, which involve chants called *keskes.* However, as Modekngei remains as a solely oral religion, not that much is known about the details of their belief or where Temedad got his ideas from. Some say Ngirchomkuuk is like Jesus Christ, but that's not the same as saying the Palauans believe that he is the Judaeo-Christian God. Certainly, the introduction of Modekngei was timely as it helped unite the Palauans while having to suffer repeated invasions during two world wars. The religion was suppressed, but today about one third of the islanders still practise.

Speaking of wars, some belief systems have been created by such conflicts. They are relatively recent and distinctly weird, yet still fit the criteria of a primal-indigenous belief. They are known by the collective term of **Cargo Cults**. They've been around since the 19th century, though there was a distinct growth in them during the two world wars.

In very broad terms, cargo cults have arisen when native peoples – with very little knowledge of the outside world – have come in contact with western culture and wildly misinterpreted what it means: especially when western goods suddenly arrive in their area.

World War Two is the best example of this, and it happened mostly in Melanesia in the south-west Pacific. White soldiers arrived on some of these islands and their supplies would be parachuted in. The native inhabitants construed this to mean that goods created by ancestral spirits and the gods were being supplied to the white people. The whites shared some of the goods with the indigenous peoples, but when the war ended, the soldiers left and so too did the goodies. So the natives began aping the white practices: they built airstrips, radio sets out of coconuts, headphones and even life-size mock-ups of airplanes in the hope that the ancestral spirits would re-continue the supply.

Bizarrely, this kind of activity has been replicated in many parts of the world. Some Native Americans believed that their ancestors would arrive on the railway, while the Hmong people of Southeast Asia believed (due to the Vietnam War), that Jesus would one day arrive in a Jeep and dressed in military fatigues to bring them to the Promised Land. Some Amazonian Indians have carved copies of cassette players in the belief they would enable them to communicate with spirits.

But given that the supplies never arrived, many of the cargo cults have faded away. Yet in some parts they still persist. In Vanuatu, also in the south Pacific, the **Jon Frum Cargo Cult** is still active, it is believed to have started when a local man, Mancheri, claimed to be a local god, Kerapenmun, but he also described himself as Jon Frum. He promised the people that he would supply houses, clothes, food and transport, which they believed and still do: they think he will return with these goodies on February 15, though they don't know which year.

It is suspected that the name 'Jon Frum' is another misinterpretation of western culture, and probably derives from US soldiers describing themselves as '*John from* America'.

And if you think that's unfortunate, Vanuatu also plays host to a cargo cult known as the **Prince Philip Movement**. The Yaohnanen believe that Queen Liz's hubby is the head of all cargo suppliers.

The general pattern with primal-indigenous beliefs is that those which survive unchanged do so owing to geographic remoteness or a suspicion of outsiders. The others absorb other beliefs, while some ancient belief systems are just about hanging on. On the tiny island of Naurun in Micronesia, just north of Australia, the religion is maintained only by a handful of people, mostly due to being swamped by western (Australian) culture. On what is the smallest island nation in the world, the Nauruans once believed in a female deity called Eijebong, and that the world was created by a mythological spider called Areop-Enap. The spider created the moon, sky and the earth from a mussel shell, the sun from a worm and men from stones. And who's to say that's not the truth of it?

6

Buddhism

IT'S FAIR to say that Buddhism is a religion much concerned with the nature of truth. And do you know what that means? That means it's hard work. That means there's a gob-smacking array of versions of that truth and contradictions and some difficult conclusions and loads of impossible-to-pronounce words. Still, if 376 million people can get their heads around it, we should be able to as well.

Yet the thing about Buddhism – which has influenced many of the religions we've seen already – is that it is a belief system set far outside the traditional western notions of what a religion should be. Buddhism provides as many questions as answers. It's not centred on a personal relationship with God, because there's not really a creator God at all. There's no Heaven or Hell, no saviour or even any need for you to believe any of this: in Buddhism, you have to make up your own mind, every step of the way.

Which is one reason why there are three main strands

of the belief and almost countless subsets. For a religion that's all about meditating and peace, Buddhists aren't too shy about fighting their own corner or even dissing each other over theology.

But before we get to the gossipy bits, let's meet the man himself: Siddhartha Gautama – The Buddha. It's not known exactly when he was born, but most guess it was about 580 BC in the village of Lumbini in Nepal, (though there's some dispute about this also). This makes Buddhism a relatively young religion for India: some of the other religious players had already been there for some time, particularly early or Vedic Hinduism. So Buddhism, while a distinctly different religion, did grow out of Hinduism. However, Hinduism owes something of the form it has now to Buddhism.

The Hinduism practised at the time is sometimes called (and it's a wee bit derogatory) Brahmanism, because the Brahmins were the priests of the religion and extremely powerful figures: and you only got to be a Brahmin if you were of the right caste. There was a lot of chanting and animal sacrifices and a big stress on asceticism. Apart from the Brahmins, there were also *Samanas,* who did a lot of fasting and sometimes walked around naked, the idea being that if you spent most of this life thin and naked, your karma would be improved for your next reincarnation.

Another point worth mentioning now: although Siddhartha Gautama is referred to as *The* Buddha, he wasn't the only one. The word Buddha basically means one who has discovered the true nature of life through meditation, study and leading a virtuous life. Eventually, through a process called *Bodhi,* they achieve *Nirvana,* which means 'awakening'. Buddhism teaches that Siddhartha was only the latest in a long line of such people – and that more will follow him.

So back to the Buddha, who, luckily for him, wasn't born to naked skinny parents, but well-fed and well-dressed ones: young Siddhartha was of a royal family, his father being Suddhodana, a local chieftain of a people called the Sakyas. But it wasn't all fabulous holidays and bling: Siddhartha's mother died shortly after he was born, and he was raised by his sister, Mahapajapati.

Buddhist texts have many, and fancier versions of Siddhartha's birth story, one being that he descended directly from one of the Buddhist heavens and into his mother's womb. From that point on she was incapable of doing wrong while the young fella was gestating; which was just as well because pregnancy lasted ten months. (No wonder his poor mother expired.) The Buddha, apparently, arrived without having to mix with the bodily fluids usually associated with childbirth, and was an impressively early developer: within seconds of being born, he stood up, took seven steps to the north, looked around and declared: "I am the highest in the world; I am the best in the world; I am the foremost in the world. This is my last birth." Not short on self-confidence either.

This was obviously one seriously gifted kid, so it's not entirely surprising that not long after, a local seer predicted that Siddhartha would either become a great king or a great Holy Man. Given that Kinging was the family business, Dad preferred Option A, and certainly didn't fancy his beloved son becoming one of those skinny naked guys. So as rich people will do, he threw money at the problem: young Siddhartha wanted for nothing. He had three palaces, one for winter, summer and the rainy season. Dad's idea was to keep his son from having any dissatisfaction with his life – because that might prompt him to take the religious path.

You could see the logic. Then again, having everything his own way probably caused discontent anyway. The official account claims that the Buddha always felt some unease. Siddhartha was married at sixteen to a local princess, Yashodhara, and had a kid. Things remained pretty normal until, at the age of 29, Siddhartha finally came into contact with the outside world.

One day, he sneaked out of one of his three palaces, and encountered what became known as the Four Passing Sights: an old crippled man, a sick man, a rotting corpse and a wandering ascetic. Suddenly, he realised that birth, sickness, old age and death come to everyone: that these were problems to which he must find answers. He gave up the palace, the riches, the wife and child and went off to become a Holy Man.

And yes, he was going off for a life of self-sacrifice and to found one of the great religions of the world, but this wasn't a mission the wife and child signed up for: the Buddhist accounts say Siddhartha left quietly at night, kissing his wife gently so she would not wake up, and that he did have some qualms about what he was doing. But then that's it: no more wife. She appears in the story of the Buddha only one more time, about two years later when Siddhartha visits one of the palaces. Understandably, she was a bit miffed about being deserted and instructed their son, Rahula, to ask Dad for his inheritance – meaning the

Kingdom. All Siddhartha offered was to sign the kid up as a monk.

The depiction of Yashodhara as the gold-digging-bitch-type seems necessary to justify the Buddha's departure, and today is much discussed by Buddhists. Interestingly, the name Rahula, their son, translates as 'chain' or 'obstacle'. According to some versions, Rahula did go on to become a monk, and Yashodhara eventually became a nun.

So with the family out of the way, Buddha joined a couple of Brahmin hermits and started the whole naked skinny guy thing. As you would expect, he soon achieved high levels of meditation but wasn't entirely happy with the results. So he tried asceticism and was soon able to push his body further than his teachers could. Basically, he nearly starved himself to death.

Yet still it didn't do the trick for him. He abandoned asceticism and went back to meditation; the process discovered what is known as the Middle Way: a path in between the extremes of self-indulgence and self-mortification. It's also known as the Noble Eightfold Path: "And what is that middle way? It is simply the noble eightfold path, that is to say, right view, right intention; right speech, right action, right livelihood, right effort, right mindfulness, right concentration. That is the middle way discovered by a Perfect One, which gives vision, which gives knowledge, and which leads to peace, to direct acquaintance, to discovery, to Nirvana."

Armed with this new knowledge, the Buddha accepted a little buttermilk from a passing shepherd and decided to sit under a tree until he found the truth. At the age of 35 he attained enlightenment and properly became a Buddha.

For the remaining 45 years of his life, the Buddha criss-crossed the Ganges plain preaching and building up a considerable following among all castes. He also founded two monastic communities which continued his work. The Buddha, however, refused to name a successor or to formalise his teaching – leading to many schisms and variants of the religion in later years.

So not long after, the first Buddhist Council was staged to put some sort of shape on everything. The idea was to formalise the theology (though none of it was written down until centuries later), and establish some sort of rules for monastic life. This became known as the Pali Canon, Pali being one of the main languages spoken at the time.

Back then, Buddhism was fairly small religious beer, relatively speaking, but a hundred years later it had grown considerably and was already facing its first split. On one side were the traditionalists, who believed that the aim of the belief was for monks and nuns to achieve Arahantship, a heightened state of spiritual awareness. On the other side were the Mahasanghikas, (it means 'majority'), who felt that adherents were aiming too low and should be going for full Buddha-hood. And not only that: monks, nuns and lay people should be allowed a shot at it.

So they had a second Buddhist Council to discuss the problem. And it failed miserably. The Mahasanghikas went their own way. But the splitting didn't end there. Even among these two major schools, dozens of sects developed, usually because of some dispute about the practice of Buddhism rather than the theology.

But around 260 BC, Buddhism got its first big break. The biggest political players at the time were the

Mauryans, whose kingdom spread over most of what is modern-day India. After years of conquering and, bloodshed, the then king, Ashoka converted to Buddhism and, to make up for his previous sins, helped the religion to develop.

Ashoka convened the third Buddhist council in 250BC, the aim being to reunite all the various strands and factions and to standardise the Pali Canon. But, surprise surprise, not everyone was thrilled with this: at least two schools of Buddhism, the Sarvastivadin and the Dharmaguptaka, got the hump and walked out.

The Council may not have been a complete success, but other initiatives of Ashoka certainly were: he made it his business to start propagating the faith, and dispatched missionaries to all parts of the known world. It even travelled as far as the then mighty Greek Empire, where there is considerable evidence that they made some progress. Buddhist communities almost certainly existed in Alexandria (now in Egypt, but then part of the Hellenic empire), while contemporary Indian accounts make reference to Buddhist Greek monks and the places they visited. Some speculate that this resulted in some syncretism between Hellenic and Buddhist thought: an intriguing notion, given the central part Greek philosophy would take in the development of Christianity.

There were other contacts with the Greeks via Greek imperial expansion into Bactria: northern Afghanistan. The Greco-Bactrians were there for some centuries and for a while even invaded parts of northern India. One of the Greco-Bactrian kings, Menander, converted to Buddhism, and like Ashoka, became a great patron of the religion. The Greco-Bactrains remained in India right up until the time of Christ, during which it is believed they influenced what eventually became the Mahayana school of Buddhism. We'll come back to this.

And no doubt some influences travelled back to Greece as well: how influential this was will probably never be known. But for a clue, check out the following quotation from the second century Christian scholar Clement of Alexandra. Clement was a dogmatist, meaning that he didn't go in for any of that Gnostic gospel rubbish: you believed what you were told to believe and that was it. Clement wasn't a chap to easily give the heathens their due:

"Thus philosophy, a thing of the highest utility, flourished in antiquity among the barbarians, shedding its light over the nations. And afterwards it came to Greece. First in its ranks were the prophets of the Egyptians; and the Chaldeans among the Assyrians (See **Judaism**); and the Druids among the Gauls; and the *Sramanas* among the Bactrians; and the philosophers of the Celts; and the Magi of the Persians, who foretold the Saviour's birth (See **Zoroastrianism**), and came into the land of Judaea guided by a star. The Indian gymnosophists are also in the number, and the other barbarian philosophers. And of these there are two classes, some of them called Sramanas, and others Brahmins."

Sramanas was another name for wandering monks; the Buddhist version of the naked skinny guys. That even the most dogmatic of early Christians would name-check all these other races demonstrates just how much many of the world's major religions have influenced each other's development.

But back to Buddhism. After Ashoka's death, his kingdom fractured, but a new outfit took over a large lump of eastern India, ruled by Pusyamitra Sunga, a Hindu. We're now in and around 185 BC. Buddhism may have started small, but now it was a threat to the dominant religion. So Sunga got on with a bit of persecuting, destroying Buddhist temples and offering rewards for the heads of Buddhist monks. Disconnected from their bodies, that is.

In northern India, thing were a bit jollier. The Greeks were finally sent home packing and eventually replaced by the Kushan Empire, which, happily, was far better disposed towards Buddhism: so well, in fact, that the Kushan King convened the fourth Buddhist Council. Well, sort of: this, in fact, was the Council to establish the aforementioned Mahayana School of Buddhism; it's often referred to as Mahayana Council. Buddhism in Northern and Southern India had been growing apart for some time: this just made it official. Buddhism as was practised in the south, known as Theravada Buddhism, does not recognise this Council.

Now admittedly, we have been simplifying here: even up to this point Buddhism had dozens of schisms and sects and sub-sects and kissing-and-making-up sessions. But in broad terms, there were now two major schools of Buddhism: *Theravada*, the traditionalists, and *Mahayana*, the new boys. Mahayana had absorbed some influences from the Kushans, and like Mahasanghikas way back at the second Buddhist Council, felt that everyone should aspire to Buddhahood. Probably due to the Greek influence, they had also come to regard Buddha as more of a God-like figure.

So with official support from the state, Mahayana Buddhism began to spread: into South-East Asia, Central Asia, China, Korea, and finally Japan in the fifth century.

This happened under the Kushans and the kings which replaced them, the Guptas, who ruled northern India until the sixth century.

And it was around this time that emerged from eastern Indian the third main school of Buddhism: Vajrayâna, sometimes known as Tantric Buddhism. An offshoot of Mahayana, it didn't develop any major philosophical differences but offered a sort of fast-track to enlightenment by the introduction of new yogic practices, such as visualisation.

Indeed, it could be argued that if it wasn't for this expansion, Buddhism as a religion might have died out altogether. Because of the more unsettled political conditions in the south of India, along with the odd bit of Hindu oppression, Theravada Buddhism hadn't had that much chance to spread much further than Burma and Sri Lanka.

But from the seventh century on, came threats which seriously damaged both schools of Buddhism in India. First there were invasions from the White Huns, a central Asian people about which not that much is known, and then in 1193 came Turkic Muslims. They devastated both schools of Buddhism along the entire length of India. (Not regarding them as People of the Book, the Muslims thought of them as idolaters.) Allied with some Hindu revivals, by the end of the twelfth century, Buddhism was only a minor player in the country in which it was founded.

But as we know, Buddhism had left town and travelled down the Silk Road, settling along the way in central Asia, China, Korea, Japan, Thailand and Vietnam, among others. It was occasionally oppressed in some of these countries, but survived reasonably intact, especially in Japan.

There was something of a fight-back in the eleventh century though with the re-growth of Theravada Buddhism in Burma and the neighbouring countries of Laos, Thailand and Cambodia.

Thanks, mostly to western colonialism, interest in Buddhism in the west has grown significantly. But in India, the numbers remain relatively small.

But if you thought the history of Buddhism was complicated, brace yourself: what they believe ain't too easy to grasp either. And at the risk of sounding like a nag: there are recognised to be three main schools of Buddhism, but this splinters off into dozens of different sub-sects, in various countries around the world who pray in different languages and different styles and have different ideas about what happens when we die. Some think you should help yourself to achieve Nirvana. Others put off their Nirvana to help you and me get it. And while there have been occasions when things have got a little bitchy, (the Mahayana used to call the Theravada the *Hinayana* (Lesser Vehicle), Buddhists have no problem with this. In fact they think it is a good thing.

It's a curious contradiction, but for a religion much concerned with the destruction of the ego, it is quite an egocentric religion in the sense that the individual can choose what is best for them. The collective nature of Buddhism takes place in the next life, not this. If there is a next life. We'll get to that

When Buddha reached enlightenment, he escaped suffering and also realised the nature of reality: which is that most things don't actually exist: everything is in a constant state of change and impermanence – our thoughts, our bodies, our *souls*, the physical world all around us. By realising this, people can divest themselves of craving, which only causes suffering.

This craving goes on for some time though because of reincarnation (known as *samsara*). Reincarnation occurs because of karma: the build-up of good or bad 'credits' due to whatever is done in this life and which carries on to the next.

Now this bears some explanation because, yes, Buddhism doesn't believe there is such a thing as an eternal soul. Think of it this way: your physical body sheds skin all the time, so in an actual, *physical* sense you are a different person now to the one you were born as. This is kind of how Buddhist reincarnation works – you move from life to life, changing all the time, so much so that the terms 'you' or 'I' start to lose meaning. Put another way: it is like a flame being passed from candle to candle.

However, karma also affects this movement by influencing how it will turn out. If you were bad in this life, 'you' won't have such a jolly time in the next. There are six levels you can come back in: as a deva, which is a spiritual being doing very well for itself; an asura, another spiritual being but not so good; a human being; an animal; a hungry ghost; or you can spend some time in Naraka, which is like Hell. And even if you're a deva, you can fall down to Naraka if you're not careful. (This is further divided into 32 meditative planes.)

So: to get rid of the reincarnation and the karma and the horrible earthly life, the first thing you have to accept are the Four Noble Truths. This was the subject of the

Buddha's first-ever sermon and this is what he outlined for them:

1. All worldly is unsatisfactory and contains suffering.

2. Suffering is caused by attachment or desire – which stems from ignorance.

3. There is an end to suffering called Nirvana.

4. The only way to get there is the Noble Eightfold Path.

Now we have met the Eightfold path before, otherwise known as the Middle Way. But we'll have to repeat it. Here comes Buddhist list number two:

1. Right view: realising the Four Noble Truths.

2. Right intention: commitment to spiritual growth (in moderation; it is the Middle Way).

3. Right speech: speaking in a non-hurtful, truthful way.

4. Right action: avoiding actions that hurt others.

5. Right livelihood: not having a job that hurts others.

6. Right effort: making a constant effort to improve.

7. Right mindfulness: the mental ability to see the truth of things.

8. Right concentration: with this, you'll eventually destroy the ego and attain enlightenment.

Other than that there aren't that many 'rules' in Buddhism. They are against abortion because they regard it as killing, but don't have much against artificial contraception. However, do discourage adherents from chasing sensual pleasure as that's all worldly and horrible. So you can use contraceptives. You just can't have sex for fun. Oh.

There isn't much of a marriage rite in Buddhism anyway. It's regarded as a mostly secular affair, though you can receive a blessing from a Buddhist monk. Funerals are a much bigger deal, though again the funeral rites differ from burning the body almost immediately right through to elaborate rituals which can last up to 100 days. If you have the money to pay for it.

Now the aim of doing all this is to achieve Nirvana, just as the Buddha did. It's usually translated as enlightenment, but more accurately means 'awakening' or 'understanding'. Buddhism teaches that when adherents reach Nirvana, they are freed from endless reincarnation.

So, Buddhism says you have to be good, but you're also working towards understanding the nature of truth and everything. That involves study, but also meditation. There are many different techniques, but generally speaking it involves concentrating on an idea or object, until that concentration envelops the mind, the body and everything around the meditator; once that happens they have achieved *jhâna*, a sort of sneak-preview of Nirvana.

Buddhists also go on pilgrimage and pray as in other religions – either in a temple or at home. In Buddhism it is not considered important to worship with others, though whether done alone or collectively, it usually involves sitting cross-legged and facing the Buddha while chanting or reading from religious texts. As for those texts, there is the aforementioned Pali Canon, but that has gone through many revisions and versions, according to the school, subsect and country you practise in. The same applies for a range of additional materials.

But hang on: why would you bother doing all this? To please God? 'Fraid not, because in Buddhism there isn't a God; at least in the old-bloke-with-a-beard-who-made-the-Universe sense. Buddha never claimed to be divine; just a guide for finding Nirvana. Buddhism did inherit some of the Hindu pantheon of gods, but The Buddha explicitly stated that the Hindu creator of the universe, Mahâ-Brahmâ, is not a God but a deva. Indeed, while he was on the earth preaching, the Buddha went to some lengths to rubbish the idea of a creator God, arguing that there couldn't be evil and dissatisfaction in the world if a 'good' God had created it. So rather than 'God', Buddhists have the system of reincarnation and eventual Nirvana: this system has existed forever and will exist forever, so there was no need for a 'God' to create it. Indeed, a creator God would be a direct contradiction to the Buddhist belief as it is based on the idea that nothing can exist outside the 'system'. Thus the Buddhist view of the theistic religions is not that God made people in His own image, but that people created God: a view echoed later on by some European atheistic philosophers.

So are Buddhists atheists? In his book, *Crossing the Threshold of Hope*, Pope John Paul II said exactly that. Buddhists, however, say this is unfair. It is would be more accurate to say they are agnostic: the Buddha himself never answered the question of whether there is a God or not, claiming that it was impossible to answer and therefore a waste of time: and that we should concentrate on attaining Nirvana. Thus Buddhism is highly unusual in relation to most of the other world religions. In answer to some of the Big Questions of Existence, it is prepared to say: we don't know.

Well, is there a heaven then? Er, sorry. Don't know that either. As we've said Buddhism has levels of existence which could be compared to 'heavens' or 'hells'; but these are not final destinations. During his lifetime, the Buddha refused to explain what the final destination is like; or even if there *is* a final destination: all important stuff to know, you would think.

Again, Buddhism teaches that dwelling on such details is pointless and also distracts from the practical business of attaining enlightenment; when you do attain enlightenment, what you will understand cannot be understood with the rational mind: so there's no point in trying to explain it. All the Buddha was prepared to explain is that *something* happens: you go through the endless cycle of rebirth on this earth until you achieve Nirvana. Nirvana is knowledge of God: you are in a state of peace and devoid of all earthly passions and ego. So when you die it is for the last time. And when you die it is *parnirvana*, a full passing away. Now there is some sort of fulfilment here, a sense of everlasting happiness: it's a heavenly state, but it's not as place; more a way of being.

Another way of describing it is this: once the ego, the sense of 'I' has been destroyed, the spirit can finally merge with rest of existence, like a drop into an ocean.

Or put even another way: when you die, that's it. You're extinguished. But because you've reached Nirvana, you don't mind.

At best, it's kinda boring. At worst, it's completely hopeless.

Or is it?

You'll just have to figure that out for yourself.

5

Chinese Traditional Religion

NOW THIS requires some explaining because it might look lazy. But it's not. Really. We haven't just lumped all the Chinese beliefs in together because it's handy: it's because that's what the Chinese do. Or most of them, anyway.

Despite the Chinese government's less than enthusiastic attitude towards religion, beliefs have endured for centuries: the most notable being (for our purposes), Buddhism, that you know about already, Confucianism, Taoism as well as a host of local beliefs and practices.

Obviously, Buddhism is a religion in its own right – and so too is Taoism. (Confucianism is more properly described as a philosophy.) People in most countries would list one of these as their religion – and many people in China do exactly the same. However, the vast majority of religious Chinese make no such distinctions. Rather like the Japanese, the Chinese blend Buddhism, Taoism, Confucianism and local beliefs into a religious culture. It may vary in different areas, but essentially it is the same thing. And there is an awful lot of it. Despite oppression and Cultural Revolutions, it's reckoned that at least 400 million Chinese worship this way. Take that, Commies.

And in fairness, it should be admitted that a lot of Chinese don't even think of it as worshipping. *Culture* is the key word here. Many Chinese, who are, say, Christians, continue with a lot of these practices without seeing any conflict. Many may not have any actual belief in any of the practices but continue with them because, well, that's just what you do in China: and it's been done for centuries, passed down orally and through various rituals, like New Year's celebration and ancestor veneration. Indeed, so engrained is it in the fabric of Chinese life that it doesn't even have a name: it is a spiritual and practical expression of *being* Chinese. 'Chinese Traditional Religion' is just what foreigners call it.

And while we are at it, an interesting aside: CTR is practised by the Han Chinese, which is another way of saying the ethnic Chinese. They constitute 92 per cent of the population of mainland China and are the largest ethnic group in the world. At 1.3 billion, they make up 19 per cent of the population of the world.

There's an awful lot of them, and they've been around a terribly long time. The Han trace their ancestry back to the Huaxia people who lived along the Yellow River around 2,500 BC – though other Neolithic sites have been found in the same region which date back to 5,500 BC.

So because the origins of the Han Chinese stretch back into pre-history, it is impossible to say when their traditional practices began. Taoism and Confucianism, (which we'll get to later), have more of a clearly defined history, but what is sometimes called Chinese Folk Religion appears to have been around as long as the Chinese.

Firstly Chinese Folk Religion doesn't really involve any creed or defined belief system. It is simply made up of practices with assumptions built into them: that being that there is a pantheon of gods, ghosts and ancestral spirits, and it's best to keep all of them sweet. As regards practices, this mainly involves 'sacrifices': of food and objects; even cans of beer.

As you might expect from an ancient religion, mediumship, fortune-telling and astrology are important. There are two sorts of medium: the bog-standard variety who communicates with the dead, (though in China it is through the use of a writing implement), and *jitong* who get up to all sorts of David Blaine-type antics: when communicating with spirits, they walk on hot coals, cut themselves and generally abuse their own bodies.

Straightforward worship involves what is known as *baibai:* bowing towards an altar while holding a stick of incense. This can be done at home or in a Taoist temple overseen by a priest or *Daoshi*; however, only a tiny percentage of people who practise Chinese Traditional Religion go to Taoist temples.

So: the folk religion component of CTR involves the worship of heaven, ancestors and a pantheon of gods and goddesses: some of whom have even crossed over into Chinese Buddhism. The Bodhisattva (an elevated being who helps others achieve Buddha-hood), Kuan Yin, is thought to have evolved out of the traditional Chinese deity, Miao Shan.

Let's start with the worship of heaven; a practice which for centuries was interlinked with the Chinese political system. The heavens above were regarded as God, an omnipotent force but with no physical form. It was referred to as *Shang Di* (Emperor Above). As you might expect, Heaven exhibited its powers through the use of weather and other natural disasters. For centuries, the Chinese believed that their Emperors received the Mandate of Heaven: basically, God would give them the thumbs-up to rule. (Thus many Emperors greatly encouraged belief in this idea.) However, that mandate could be taken away if the Emperor abused his powers. Evil people could be killed by Heaven with lightning, with their crimes inscribed – or burnt – into their spines. Yuk.

So the ancient Chinese sucked up to Heaven a lot, mostly through the building of shrines, the most famous of which is the Altar of Heaven in Beijing – where the Emperor would take part in elaborate rituals dedicated to Heaven: to show the people he still remembered where he got his authority from. One of the most important Heaven-worshipping days of the year was the Winter Solstice, where the Emperor would pray for a good harvest for the coming year.

In normal parlance today, a Chinese person wouldn't say, 'Oh my God', but 'Oh Heaven', and the winter solstice – or *Dong Zhi* – is still celebrated, mostly by family gatherings and the consumption of dumplings, which are believed to keep evil spirits at bay. They are also used as offerings to dead ancestors.

The whole dead relatives thing is a huge deal in Chinese Religion, and is incorrectly termed ancestor worship; more correctly it is ancestor veneration. The simple act of remembering them is important, as it commemorates their deeds while alive. However, there is also a large component of care.

It is the spiritual equivalent of emigrants sending home a few bob to the family. The living Chinese feel it is their duty to 'provide' for their dead relatives and not get anything in return, as they might expect if worshipping a God – though ancestors can provide guidance for the living if they feel so inclined and act as protective 'guardian angels'.

Some literally believe that this helps their ancestors in the next life; others feel that simply the expression of family loyalty is what is important.

But its expression is extremely practical: apart from western-style upkeep of and visits to graves, ancestor veneration also involves giving them what they might need in the great beyond: things like toothbrushes, combs, towels and water are left beside the coffin. But perhaps most importantly, the Chinese give their dead loved ones a few bob. An extremely common form of ancestor veneration is to burn Spirit Notes beside the grave. These are bank-notes made from joss paper, a form of bamboo. They have official-looking seals and tinfoil and come in various forms, one of the most popular being Hell Bank-notes.

They are called *Hell* Bank-notes not because the Chinese reckon their ancestors are being prodded by Lucifer, but because of a misunderstanding with Christian missionaries who told them they would go to Hell if they did not convert – so the Chinese assumed that Hell simply meant the after-life. (However, in Chinese mythology, the belief is that the dead do go to Hell – or *Di Yu* – before being judged.)

The idea is that these notes are intended for the King of Hell – Yama, the Buddhist boss of the Underworld – so as to bribe him into giving the dead a short stay in the fiery pits. It is signed by Yama and usually features picture of the Jade Emperor, who is the King of the gods in the Chinese Folk Religion pantheon. (Told you it is all mixed up together.)

Some of them also feature pictures of various world figures – such as John F. Kennedy and Marilyn Monroe. Some bear the Visa logo, and all come in obscenely high denominations – from $10,000 to $5 million. The assumption seems to be that they accept only US currency in Hell.

It is a bit of fun, but it's also taken extremely seriously. The ritual of burning the money is carried out with great care, with the notes placed respectfully on the fire. (There is another Chinese belief that burning real money brings bad luck.) Keeping Hell Bank-notes around the house is also considered bad, so they are always kept out of sight. It's also a total no-no to give a living person a Hell Bank-note, even as a joke. That is seen to be wishing for their death. This tradition had grown even more elaborate in modern times, with the King of Hell being offered speed boats, servants and laptops made out of joss paper.

As with all ancient religions, the Chinese pantheon runs into hundreds of gods, who are worshipped at different times of the year and for different reasons. Indeed, the Chinese system of gods has a marked similarity to the Christian system of Patron Saints. Here is a selection:

The Jade Emperor. As we've mentioned already, the King or Emperor of the gods.

Tu Di Gong. or god of the earth. There are lots of roadside shrines to this guy, as he is believed to protect localities.

Cai Shen or god of Wealth.

Guan Yu. A real-life military general from the third century. The patron god of policemen, law, and confusingly, criminals, as he is noted for his mercy. He is also the hero of *Romance of the Three Kingdoms,* a novel and 84-part TV series which was a huge hit on Chinese television.

Cheng Huang. This is a class of god rather than a specific one; each city has a Cheng Huang, and usually this is a famous person from the place who was deified after death. The *Cheng Huang Miao* or 'Shrine of the Cheng Huang' was often the focal point of a town in ancient times.

Mazu. The patron goddess of sailors. She is particularly popular in South and South-East China, as well as Taiwan, Hong Kong, and Vietnam.

Baosheng Dadi, or the 'Great Emperor Protecting Life'. He's the doctor of the spirit world, who's so good at his job he can even raise the dead. Again, very popular in Taiwan.

Xi Wangmu , or the 'Queen Mother of the West'. The Jade Emperor's Mammy, she has the power to make others immortal.

The Eight Immortals (*ba xian*). Important literary and artistic figures who were deified after death. However, in Chinese culture, they are sort of like the *X-Men*: each has a special power which can be used for fighting evil. They also have X-Men-type names: Immortal Woman He, Royal Uncle Cao, Iron-crutch Li, Lan Caihe, Lü Dongbin, Philosopher Han Xiang, Elder Zhang Guo and Zhongli Quan.

Zao Shen, or the kitchen god. He is the most important of the Chinese domestic gods. (There are gods for every conceivable part of the home.) His job is to report to Heaven on the behaviour of each Chinese family at Chinese New Year. Families leave out sticky rice for him on New Year's night in order to render his speech incomprehensible.

Wenchangdi, or Emperor Promoting Culture. He's the god of students and gets a lot of attention around exam time.

Zhusheng Niangniang 'Birth-Registry Lady'. Worshipped by people who want children – or who want their child to be a boy.

Yuexia Laoren, Old Man Under the Moon. He's a matchmaker, and prayed to by those seeking a partner.

Heaven is organised pretty much the same way as earth – or more accurately, the way China used to be. The Jade Emperor lives in a palace the way his Chinese counterpart used to, while the other gods are his subjects. All of them have human foibles and failings and, according to one account written in 1122 BC, once had a pitched battle among themselves over who should be the next ruler of China. And like any human society, the various gods can get demotions or promotions.

Much of the worship in Chinese Traditional religion centres around family events, such as funerals and weddings. However, festivals also play a hugely important part. Often they involve lively street parades with fireworks, music and dragon dances. The main ones are:

Chinese New Year: as everything is calculated on a lunar cycle, this takes place on a different date on the western calendar, though it's generally towards the end of January. Lots of ancestor veneration and tricking the kitchen god.

Lantern Festival: takes place in February. Paper lanterns are left everywhere with riddles attached to them, while plentiful amounts of Yuanxiao, a sweet dumpling, are consumed. It marks the end of the New Year celebrations and is also a day for praying to the God of Love.

Qing Ming Festival: takes place in April. It used to be a day when the Chinese ate only cold food, but a few hundred years ago it was transformed into a day for visiting graves and making offerings to dead ancestors.

Dragon Boat Festival: usually takes place in May or June. This day commemorates the second-century BC poet Qu Yaun. One day Qu chucked himself in the Miluo River as a protest against corruption. The people went in dragon boats to save him. They failed, but the festival is there anyway, and consists largely of dragon boat races.

Qi Xi Jie Festival:takes place in July/August and is the Chinese equivalent of St Valentine's Day. It's based on the story of the 7th daughter of the Jade Emperor, who fell in love with an orphaned cowherd. The Emperor didn't approve and so separated them, moving his daughter to the star Vega and the cowherd to the star Altair. They are allowed to meet only once a year on the 7th day of the 7th lunar month.

Ghost Festival: takes place in August/September. During this lunar month, the gates of Hell are opened and ghosts roam the earth. Hell Bank-notes are offered as well as food: this is also known as the hungry ghost festival.

Moon Festival: happens in September/October. A big occasion for family reunions and eating moon cakes: the idea being that people you are distant from are looking at the same moon. There are a number of mythological stories connected to this festival, so it's not known exactly where it originated, though it may have something to do with celebrating the harvest.

Double Nine Festival: usually takes place in October – but on the ninth day of the ninth month in the Chinese lunar calendar, (nine being an auspicious number in Chinese numerology). It is a day for veneration of elders, but also dead relatives.

Winter Solstice Festival. On December 22. Already told you about that.

So they are the broad outlines of what is often called Chinese Folk Religion. But there is often another name given to these practices: sometimes it is called Taoism. Then again, Taoism can mean a philosophical system or a religion whose adherents regard Chinese Folk Religion as little more than debased superstition. The truth is that Taoism is all three.

Not that you'll get adherents of any of the three strands of Taoism to agree on this. 'Tao' means 'Way', and, unsurprisingly, there's a lot of dispute as to when it actually began. One line of argument has it stretching back to the ancient Chinese religion in pre-history and works like the *Dao De Jing* composed in the 4th century BC; others claim it arose as a religion around the time Buddhism arrived from India in the 4th century AD.

However, what is beyond dispute is that Taoism – or early versions of Taoism – played a central role in two thousand years of Chinese political history, with various Emperors deploying Taoist ideas as the source of their authority or even setting up outright theocracies: except the Communists, of course, who suppressed the religion for decades. However, since the early '80s it has gained recognition and many monasteries and temples have been rebuilt – after being destroyed by the Communists in the first place. This, however, is not due to a change of heart, but a rather more cold-hearted recognition of the tourism potential. Although now legal, Taoism is still subject to State control.

The *Dao De Jing was* written by a chap called Laozi, reputed to be the teacher of Confucius, (and some claim, the Buddha), and Laozi was made a divinity himself in the first century. Although Laozi himself didn't invent it, his work did open the way for the introduction of the concept of Yin and Yang: the idea that the universe is balanced between two interdependent forces, the Yin being dark and the Yang bright. Along with this came the concept of the Five Elements, (wood, fire, earth, metal, and water), and how these elements generate or overcome each other. These ideas not only influenced Chinese religion and philosophy, but also medicine and even military strategy. The third big concept is Qi (or Chi: which literally means 'air' or 'breath'). Qi is a kind of life force or spiritual energy that runs through everything which exists and can be marshalled in different ways.

The other major figure in Taoism is Zhang Daoling, who claimed to be getting celestial hotmail from Laozi in the 2nd century AD. The Taoist Zhengyi sect claims continuity with Zhang.

Through the various dynasties, Taoism did come to be seen as a religion in its own right, initially in competition with Confucianism and Buddhism, though later on settling down to a more interactive relationship. (During the Song dynasty, a blend of all three religions known as neo-Confucianism was made the State religion.)

However, the relationship between traditional beliefs and Taoism was particularly interactive: to the point where it was often hard to tell them apart. For instance, it was due to Taoism that the Chinese pantheon of gods was organised into its current 'civil service' structure.

Thus among people who cite Taoism as their religion – as opposed to the vast majority of Chinese – many of the practices are not wildly dissimilar. Ancestor veneration is also important, but the relationship to the Spirit World is somewhat different. While the Folk Chinese religion takes a deferential attitude towards spirits, formal Taoism believes that spirits can be controlled through the use of talismans. Formal Taoism also has more of a stress on health, believing that through various rituals, exercises and substances, adherents can improve their physical well-being and align themselves with cosmic forces. Meditation also plays a part, with use of visualisation, controlled breathing and even 'linking' internal organs to various deities.

Their pantheon is also different: rather than recognising the Jade Emperor as supreme God, formal Taoists worship a trio of gods known as the Three Pure Ones: the Jade Pure, who was there at the formation of the Universe, the Upper Pure, whose job it is to reveal scripture to mankind and the Great Pure, the aforementioned Laozi.

Some texts claim that Laozi decides on which mortals get to be gods.

There is a Taoist canon, divided into three books, the Zhen, the Yuan or the Shen. (The Dao De Jing is an appendix to the Zhen.) But formal Taoists are not too hung up about them; even priests tend to use other texts which have been handed down.

And on top of all this is philosophical Taoism, which concerns itself with studying Taoist texts within the context of modern philosophy. It deals with lots of opaque notions like 'emptiness' and 'the strength of softness' (which sounds like a toilet roll advert). Most Chinese have little to do with it, so we don't have to either.

Now; you may have noticed something missing from Chinese Traditional Religion: any sort of an ethical system. And there isn't one: in all the practices we've described so far, there is no requirement on the Chinese to take part as an investment in getting to heaven or fear of going to hell. Pretty much all of what they do is inspired by a sense of tradition and of duty; *duty* being the key word here. Just as these religious practices are woven into Chinese culture, so too is the moral code. And this comes from Confucianism.

Again, there are disputes: over whether Confucianism actually came from Confucius; over whether it is a religion or a philosophy; whether it is even a philosophy.

Let's explain: Confucius lived between 551 and 479 BC. He was essentially a social philosopher and like many wise men, no one listened to a word he said. He constantly bemoaned the corruption and brutality of the many Chinese kingdoms of the time and for his trouble was ejected from most of them. He also seems to have never taken the time to write anything down, so everything we have of him is second-hand; reported by his disciples. Actually, it's disciples of disciples of disciples, because during the 2nd century BC, the First Emperor of Qin took a notion and burned tonnes of books.

The closest we have to a primary source are the *Analects of Confucius*, which almost certainly was written by a group of people and some time after what the book describes actually happened. It uses a lot of metaphors, so in parts it's pretty vague and open to interpretation: so much that some Chinese dynasties used it to establish autocratic regimes – which run quite counter to what Confucius was actually saying.

As far as we know, that is: it's fair to say that the creation of Confucianism was an ongoing process which lasted two millennia, was added to by philosophers from each generation and sponsored by various Emperors with varying agendas.

However, the gist of what Confucius said remains: and explains on a profound level the psychology of Chinese society.

Confucius believed that people are basically good. Because of this, there are two ways to rule people:

1) Introduce lots of detailed laws, which the people will try not to break to avoid punishments. However, if they do break the law, they will not have a sense of shame.

2) Provide exemplary leadership, and through the

development of various rituals, the people will develop a sense of shame – and therefore not want to break the law.

So in Option (1), the rules are administered by an outside force that will punish after transgressions have taken place. The people will obey, but not necessarily understand why.

In Option (2), because of rituals, patterns of behaviour are absorbed by the people: they don't want to break the law because of shame; because of losing *face*. And in China as well as many eastern societies influenced by Confucius, Face is still extremely important.

Now by 'law', we mean anything from not murdering your neighbour to remembering your mother's birthday: the Confucian idea was to ritualise much of the way society worked so it became a constant reminder of people's duties to each other. From greeting a person to eating to praying to working: everything should have some form of ritual attached to it. And today, in most oriental societies, that is still the case.

The ritualisation also served to remind people what category they and others are in and what is the hierarchical structure. In the ideal society of Confucius, the King, as an example to all, would be at the centre.

Now as we've said, many Emperors put these ideas into practice, so secular ceremonial behaviour got mixed up with religious ceremonial behaviour (taken from Taoism, folk traditions and Buddhism) and all became part of everyday life: it became an intrinsic component of family interaction, with rules about how various members of the family should act towards each other. Indeed, family loyalty became such a strong notion that a criminal would be punished more severely than usual if their crime was committed against a family member.

Loyalty was also highly valued, as was consideration for others: "What you do not want others to do to you, do not do to others," was what Confucius said. We think.

Confucius was also big on the idea of transforming society into a meritocracy: where people got jobs on the basis of merit rather than by being of noble blood. Luckily for him, this was tied into the idea of the Mandate of Heaven: where Heaven gave an Emperor the green light to rule, but only because he really deserved it. Thus Emperors should do the same, and through the centuries increasing numbers of them gave out jobs on the basis of ability.

This resulted in the Imperial Examination System, where anyone who passed an exam could get a job in government, which in turn led to the creation of a civil service: the first in the world.

And it can't be stressed enough how much Confucian ideas have influenced every single Chinese person. For them, many of the laws they live by come from *within* rather than outside: thus their continued observance of a religion which doesn't require them to do anything at all. As such, it is an example of one of the fundamental differences between eastern and western culture.

4

Hinduism

WE'RE INTO the biggies now – and the oldies. Hinduism can boast a whopping 900 million adherents and claim to be the most ancient religion in the world. Chinese Traditional Religion could possibly dispute that, but given that the Chinese don't necessarily regard what they do as 'religion' in the formal sense, they probably wouldn't bother.

The Hindus probably wouldn't be too pushed either, regarding their core beliefs as eternal anyway. But look, this is just how old Hinduism is: the word Hindu derives from the word Sanskrit word *Sindhu* – meaning the Indus River which runs through India and Northern Pakistan. Sanskrit is an Indo-Aryan language; and no, Aryan does not mean blond, blue-eyed Master-Race types, but actually people from this part of the world. Anyway, the Indo-Aryan languages were an offshoot of the Indo-Iranian (or Persian) languages, which in turn came from the Indo-

European languages. (In other words, Sanskrit and Latin probably came from the same linguistic root.) The original Indo-Aryans called their land *Sapta Sindhu*, which corresponds to *Hapta-Hendu* as mentioned in the Zoroastrian scripture, the *Avesta*. Way back then in the dawn of time it simply meant people who lived in India around the Sindhu River. Much later it was borrowed by the Greeks and transformed into *Indos* or *Indikos* – from where we get the term 'Indian'.

It's old, and already we can see that early Hinduism, or Vedic Hinduism, probably had some influence far outside the borders of modern-day India.

So let's go back to way-back-when. When did proto-Hinduism actually start? No one has a clue. It could be 8,000 years ago. It could be later. It would have been great if the ancient civilisation of the Indus Valley had left behind a few temples or even a big book called 'Stuff we did in pre-history', but alas, no. Graveyards have been discovered where people were buried with personal possessions – indicating some belief in an after-life.

A few small religious statues have also been unearthed: of Mother-Goddess-type figures, possibly the ancient precursors to the Hindu *Shakti,* as well as figures of a male figure with a horned head who some believe was called *Pashupat*i – another name in modern Hinduism for the god of destruction, Shiva. And an interesting parallel here: a similar figure appears in ancient European and Celtic religious depictions – possible hinting at a religious continuity that dates from the Stone Age. That's *old.* Similarly, other Indo-Aryan gods have corresponding 'types' in the Indo-European religions. This has generated a (purely speculative) notion that there was originally a proto-Indo-European mythology which would be an ancestor of Hinduism, most European beliefs and Zoroastrianism.

It's also known that the Indus Valley people liked a bit of a swim, as the ruins of a number of public baths have been found. This could be the roots of the Hindu tradition of bathing first thing in the morning and before the evening meal.

Now it's assumed – though not proven as an undisputed fact – that it was these people who gave us the Vedic religion, from which Hinduism grew. There is a theory that there were an even older people here called the Dravidians who were driven south by the Indo-Aryans, and they brought the Vedic traditions with them. Or that the Aryans invaded from central Asia and mingled with a people called the Harappans; or that the Aryans migrated into this area. It is controversial in India as some argue that this is a 'colonial' view of history: that the most ancient Indian religion actually came from elsewhere. But no one knows for absolute sure.

So now that we've given this warning, let's go back to assuming that it was the Indo-Aryans who were behind a collection of works called the Vedas, (which means 'knowledge' in Sanskrit), the oldest being the *Rig Veda*. The Vedas are a collection of songs, spells, prayers and descriptions of various rituals. Hindu belief is that the Vedas were around forever and not composed by anyone – including God. However, those cynical archaeologists reckon they were first written down as early as 1700 BC. Of course, this doesn't entirely dispute the Hindu belief, because the Vedas were almost certainly transmitted orally for some time before that: perhaps for centuries, even

265

millennia. And another intriguing connection with the West: bits of the Vedas show strong similarities with bits of the Zoroastrian Avesta, both in religious concepts and in language.

The early worship probably included some animal sacrifice and fire rituals, though – seeing as no one has found any – the Indo-Aryans didn't build temples or idols. There was a lot of chanting of mantras though: the Vedas are full of them. But the Aryans knew how to have a good time as well: most of the Rig-Veda is concerned with offering Soma – the name of a god – to the gods. Soma was also a drink, possibly made from cannabis or some sort of magic mushroom. (And it's also mentioned in the Avesta.) Party on, dude.

According to the Vedas, the universe came from the *Hiranyagarbha* or Golden Womb. There was also a pantheon of gods, but these were expressions of the varied aspects of the universe. Many of these gods still appear in modern Hinduism, but in much more minor positions. The Vedic religion also seemed to have female priests. Ironically, one of the most significant parts of the Vedas is the Brahmana, which explains the Vedic rituals. It is from here that we get the word Brahmin: a Hindu priest. They're all men.

Brahmana, however, also means 'supreme truth' and it is here that we see some of the fundamentals of Hinduism already being established: the idea that there are supreme and eternal principles which transcend us humans or even our religious ideas. It wasn't a pukey New Age phrase back then, but the idea was that there was such a thing as a cosmic soul: and Hindus constantly strive to get in contact with it.

Now as we'll see later, Hinduism is an extremely diverse religion. There are many, many different varieties: which if anything is a deliberate policy. Again, we see the roots of this idea way back in the Rig Veda: "Truth is One, but sages call it by many names." This in turn has led to a very tolerant attitude within Hinduism to other beliefs. In the main, Hindus do not try to win converts.

Now what we do know for sure is that the practitioners of this Vedic religion were not just a small tribe: they spread their empire across much of northern India and bit of the south too. Militarily, they were obviously a force to be reckoned with, but they also brought with them a complex religious and social structure.

That social structure was known as *Varna*, and in all probability became the Hindu caste system. Again there is some dispute as to exactly how it worked. Some speculate that it was simply two-tier, with nobles on one level and everyone else below. Or that it was organised by the Brahmins, or priests, and consisted of Brahmins at the top, followed by warriors, followed by ordinary people. A third theory has a four-way division, with Brahmins (priests), Kshatriyas, (king-warriors), Vaishyas (merchants, farmers etc) and Harijahns ('untouchables') – those thought to be descended from the Harappans. But again, no one knows exactly what happened: we're still talking 1,000BC here.

Around that time, the second major work of scripture, the *Upanishads*, came into being. Upanishad literally means 'sit down beside': as one would with a guru or teacher. And that's pretty much what it is: a series of conversations between different people in different settings which provide a commentary on the Vedas. (And in some of these, the guru is a woman.) They are generally dated to around 600BC, but some of them could be 300 years older than that. And again there are disputes. By legend, over 200 were composed, but only a percentage of that number exist: they were not catalogued until some 2,000 years later. They are mystical and philosophical and also provide detailed commentaries on *Om*, the most sacred syllable in Hinduism.

Om, pronounced *Aum,* is chanted at the top of most mantras and is believed to be the sound of the cosmic vibration that underpins the universe. Interestingly, modern physics theorises a similar idea: that there is an 'echo' from the Big Bang still in existence.

The other major work which popped up around this time, give or take a few hundred years, is the *Mahabharata,* one of the three Sanskrit epic poems. (The other two are the *Ramayana* and the *Bhagavatam.*) The *Mahabharata* tells the story of the Bharata Dynasty. With over 100,000 verses, it is the third-longest epic poem ever written, the other two being the Tibetan *Epic of King Gesar,* and the *Manas* of the Kyrgyz people. However, what makes it particularly significant is that one of it's chapters is the *Bhagavad Gita,* which summaries the basic tenets of what became Hinduism.

It was a busy period, because it also saw the emergence of Jainism and a bit later, Buddhism. We've already dealt with these two religions, but it's useful to remind ourselves that in part, both came about as a reaction against the early Vedic religion: to the caste system, the Vedas and to animal sacrifice. Both belief systems went on to influence the development of Hinduism to varying degrees. (Buddha is regarded as an Avatar of Vishnu – we'll explain what this means later.) And as we've seen with those two beliefs, Hinduism's fortunes rose and fell according to who was in power.

So let's cheat a bit at this point: the history of Hinduism is so complex, what with various political and religious developments, it's impossible here to go into it in any great detail. Instead, here are some highlights:

*320 BC: the Mauryan Empire, founded by Ashoka, sponsors Buddhism, so the Vedic religion suffers a bit. (Though Ashoka doesn't suppress it.)

*240 AD: the rise of the Gupta Empire. The Guptas are keener on Hinduism so it enjoys a bit of a resurgence, partly due to being State-sponsored but also because it has taken on board some Buddhist and Jainist ideas: such as vegetarianism and non-violence. The Vedic belief has been constantly evolving up to this point and it is from here that we can refer to it as Hinduism. The Gupta Empire was ordered according to Hindu beliefs – which meant a caste system. It was also an architecturally rich period, with many temples being built. The idea of dedicating temples to specific gods was introduced at this time.

600AD: the rise of various devotional movements within Hinduism, known as Bhakti. They were usually devoted to Shiva or Vishnu or Shakti. The Bhakti movement has continued ever since. Today

there are dozens of them. Also around this time –
somewhere between the 6th and 8th centuries, Adi
Shankara was born. Shankara was a great Hindu
thinker and preacher and held many debates with
Buddhists and Jainists. He introduced many new
ideas to the religion and did much to promote its
growth. Hinduism also began to become a presence
overseas, mainly due to trade routes between China
and the Mediterranean – with India being a stop-off
point. As a result, many countries in south-east Asia
embraced Hinduism. This period of expansion has in
turn given birth to various myths about 'lost' Hindu
kingdoms.

700AD. Various esoteric movements based on the
Tantras develop.

850AD. The Chola dynasty arises in southern India
and surrounding islands. It spreads Hindu culture.

1300AD. Islamic invaders spread across India,
damaging Hinduism, Buddhism and Jainism.

1500AD: Europeans arrive, spreading Christianity.
One of the less jolly aspects to this was the Goa
Inquisition. Founded in 1560 by Saint Francis Xavier,
(once he got the Green Light from the Pope), its job
was to convert the heathens – but mostly Hindus –
to Christianity or else, 'or else' consisting of systematic
torture and being burned at the stake. Many Hindu
temples were destroyed and Hindu scriptures burned.

It was finally stopped in the late 1700s – by which time thousands of Hindus had been killed.

1700-1900AD: The Hindu Renaissance. This is in no small part to the rise of the Maratha Empire in the late 1600s. Building from a small base in western India, it took on the might of the Moghul Empire and pushed it back, finally occupying most of India until the early 1800s. The English, of course, did for them, but by then the Empire had spent the best part of two centuries establishing Hinduism as the dominant religion. Between then and the present day, many Hindu reform movements have sprung up, keen to introduce more modern ideas and to move adherents away from the caste system, which continues to dog the image of the religion.

So with the history out of the way, we can concentrate on what Hindus believe. As we've said, beliefs among the 900 million adherents vary: so much so that some still argue that Buddhism and Jainism are not separate beliefs at all, but simply part of the greater Hindu family: the subtext of which is vaguely nationalist. Don't forget how the word Hindu and Indian come from the same root. For many, it is the same thing.

Thus many of the beliefs we will explain here we have come across before. As we've said, a fundamental idea is that certain spiritual principles hold true forever and for everyone. This is often referred to as Eternal *Dharma*: Dharma translating at 'natural law' or 'reality'. Buddhism and Jainism are also Dharmic religions.

Much like their Buddhist cousins, Hindus believe in karma and reincarnation, which can only be escaped through a combination of doing good, belief in God and devotion. Good karma will bring you to a higher plane of existence in the next life until you finally achieve union with the universal spirit: however, different strands of Hinduism disagree on whether this is an impersonal melding rather like that of Buddhism, or a personal relationship. There are Hindu versions of Heaven (*Svarga Loka*) and Hell (*Naraka Loka*), but these are no more than pleasant or unpleasant staging posts on the way to union with the universal spirit. The Hindu pantheon does have some evil spirits, but no equivalent to the devil: evil comes from human ignorance.

However, unlike Buddhism, Hinduism does stick its neck out and say there is a God.

Unlike Buddhists, Hindus do believe in an individual soul which moves through the reincarnation cycle, though various schools dispute what the soul or *atman*, actually is. They also believe that everything living is subject to Dharma and therefore sacred.

The Hindu view of God is well, a little vague and certainly individualistic. It can be known as Brahman: a supreme cosmic spirit that is the source of everything, eternal, genderless, omnipotent, omniscient, and omnipresent. Yet despite this – or because of it – our tiny human brains cannot really describe such a Being. So you can describe God any way you want: you can give him or her any attributes or a variety of names. And seeing than *everything* comes from this spirit, every description of it is equally valid. So God is called Vishnu by some, Shiva by others.

More others consider those names just to be 'aspects' of Brahman.

Thus Hinduism has a pantheon of beings called *Devas*. However, they are not gods: Hinduism is a monotheistic religion. What a Deva actually is, though, varies according to which strand of Hinduism you belong to. And there are lots of them: according to some Hindu traditions, as many as 330 *million* of these spirits. There are three main ideas in Hinduism of what Devas are:

1) They are simply manifestations of the Brahman, the supreme cosmic spirit. Because we can't get our heads around understanding what Brahman is, we worship these Devas because they are easier to understand.

2) They are spiritual beings in their own right, and act as intermediaries between God and the physical world.

3) Some Hindus, (though a minority), don't believe in the one supreme spirit but that Devas are a pantheon of gods which they have to please.

There are also beings called Avatars: physical manifestations of the Devas which come to earth for a specific purpose. Again, depending on which brand of Hinduism you buy, these are angel-like figures come to earth or a visit by the Big Man himself. Depending on which scripture you read, Vishnu, or God, will have either ten or twenty-five avatars: though in both lists we've only got one more to go: the last one was the Buddha (and before that, Krishna) and the one yet to come is Kalki, otherwise known by the cuddly title, 'The Destroyer of Foulness', who will come on a white horse and destroy evil. Good news for us all, except that by most accounts there will be something of a wait: we can expect him in the year 428,899.

A second-level of Avatars are the 'angel' type Devas, some of whom are people we have met already: there's Zoroaster, Mahavira, founder of Jainism, Bahá'u'lláh, founder of the Bah'ai faith, and Jesus. (It is, admittedly, at the fringes of Hindu belief, but some maintain that Jesus had distinct connections with Hinduism and India and may even be buried there. We'll deal with this in **Christianity**.)

The worshipping of these gods takes place in the Hindu temple, called a *Mandir*. All Mandir are built with the principal shrine facing the rising sun and with the entrance facing east: the idea being that it leads from the temporal world and into the spiritual one. Typically, Mandirs are spectacular, colourful places, filled with various icons which represent specific deities – though sometimes the deities are thought to be present within the icon itself. They are also adorned with Hindu symbols such as the Om, representing God in three aspects and the vibration of the universe, and the Swastika, used since the Vedic days, and which stands for purity of soul and the truth: and has nothing to do with Nazism.

(Just to divert from temples for a moment, Hindu symbolism also extends to the bodies of adherents, particularly the *tilaka*, which most familiarly manifests as a red dot worn on the forehead. This symbolises the need for adherents to develop their consciousness to the point of opening up the mystic *Third Eye* with which they can achieve enlightenment. There are other symbols which vary depending on sect.)

Most temples are dedicated to a particular deity, with a few affiliated minor Devas – so many temples receive visitors who are making pilgrimages to that particular Deva. As you might imagine for such an old religion, the rituals are rich and complex, though they are nothing like western-style religious services, involving communal meditation, the singing of devotional songs and the chanting of mantras. Rather like reciting the rosary in Catholicism, mantras involve repeating the same phrases over and over, though in a particular style and tone, and are commonly known as *mantra yoga*. All are recited in Sanskrit – now effectively a dead language.

However, the main form of worship is called *Puja*, and most Hindus perform Puja at least once a day, either at the temple or at home. (Hindus would also have small temples in their home, consisting of a small table and some icons.) It must be undertaken after a ritual wash and before eating and consists of a 27-step programme which is offered to any deity which the adherent feels is a version of the cosmic spirit. It involves 'washing' the deity, offering various foods, lighting candles, prostration, making requests and asking forgiveness for sins. There are specific forms of Puji for various Hindu holy days.

We've only mentioned a few of the Hindu scriptures, but the list is exhaustive, from metaphysical treatises to epic, blood'n'guts poems. Hindus tend to read widely among these, but more for the allegorical nature of these texts rather than to glean specific instruction: just like the other Dharmic religions, Hinduism doesn't have a big list of things you can and cannot do, but it does have the five *Yamas*, or Eternal restraints. They are:

Ahimsa – essentially, this advocates non-violence and respect for all forms of life; a notion which was imported from Buddhism and Jainism. Vegetarianism is not a requirement of Hinduism, though it is recommended. About a third of Hindus don't eat meat, and, of those who do, most abstain from beef. The cow is still a venerated animal in Hinduism.

Satya – truthfulness.

Asteya – the interestingly-phrased 'freedom from stealing'.

Bramacharya – moderation in all things and abstinence.

Aparigraha – freedom from attachment to possessions.

There's also a sort of general (highly idealised) plan as to how the average Hindu's life might go. The first stage is *Brahmacharya* which is spent celibate and in contemplation under the supervision of a guru. *Grihastha* is the marriage/kids/job stage. Stage three is *Vanaprasta,* a gradual detachment from the material world, which involves giving everything away, doing lots of pilgrimages and praying.

Finally there's *Sanyasa*, where one peacefully shuffles off the mortal coil, often in seclusion and after loads more meditation. Well, it's something to aim at.

As we've said repeatedly, Hinduism comes in all shapes and sizes – and with little or no frictions between the various denominations. Indeed, many Hindus don't claim to belong to any particular sect at all. But generally speaking, it breaks down into four strands of belief:

Vaishnavism. The largest of the Hindu sects. Refers to God as Vishnu.

Shaivism. They refer to God as Shiva.

Shaktism. Their God is female and called *Devi.*

Smartism. Believes that all the religions are the same and lead to a pantheistic God.

All of these traditions would share beliefs and rituals but would differ on how to achieve *Moksha* – escape from reincarnation. They would also have slightly different concepts of the nature of God.

Each one of the four would have their own series of sub-sects, while there are also six major schools of Hindu philosophy. Concentrate now:

Nyaya. The major contribution of the Nyaya School of philosophy is in the invention of a system of logic which today the vast majority of Hindu philosophers use. Simply put, it is that knowledge can be gleaned only from perception, inference, comparison and testimony.

Vaisheshika. This school is still recognised, although it eventually merged with Nyaya. Its main contribution was to studies of how the universe is constructed. It said every object in the universe is reducible to a finite number of atoms – but that these atoms are controlled by the Supreme Being.

Samkhya. The oldest of the orthodox Hindu schools, it divides the universe into *Purusha*, consciousness, and *Prakriti*, all physical material. In each person, Purusha is quite separate from Prakriti; just temporarily joined together. Samkhya also believes that the physical universe is in a constant state of change: nothing is ever completely destroyed.

Yoga. Yes, the same as what they teach in the community centre. Well, not quite. In Hinduism, Yoga is a way of reaching spiritual enlightenment. There are four main types, with the stress being on meditation and breathing techniques as a means of understanding the nature of God more fully. What they teach down at the community centre is a more obscure (in Hindu terms) version of Yoga called *Hatha Yoga* which concentrates on the purification of the physical as a way to the purification of the mind. Hatha Yoga is actually derived from Buddhist traditions and the *Tantra*. Tantric practices exist within all the Dharmic religions in India and are touted as a 'fast-track' to enlightenment. However, many Indians regard them as little more than black magic. (And yes, there is such a thing as Tantric sex and it can do what it says on the tin. Except it takes decades of practice, can be quite bad for you and doesn't sound like much fun.)

Purva Mimamsa. This school studied the Vedas from the point of view that they should not be blindly accepted as dogma: and by doing so established the primacy of the Vedas. By developing methods of interpreting the Vedas, it deeply influenced all Hindu ritual, ceremony and religious law.

Vedanta. The principal branch of current Hindu philosophy, it is the main source of interpretation of the Upanishads – which in turn are a commentary on the Vedas. Vedanta was founded by Adi Shankara whom we mentioned earlier.

These six are known as the orthodox schools of philosophy in that they accept the primacy of the Vedas. Despite regarding themselves as separate religions, Buddhism and Jainism are regarded as non-orthodox because the Vedas are not part of their belief system.

Yep, there's an awful lot to it: Hinduism, apart from being a religious belief is also an evolving system of complex philosophical ideas: and in an average lifetime, your average Hindu would only get to explore a small percentage of it.

So it is somewhat ironic that a belief with such depth

and richness is still connected with a social system which runs on myopia and prejudice. Although technically illegal, the caste system is still a force in Indian society. As we've said, the four castes were originally based on job classifications, but later on became based simply on birth – which led to the evolution of several sub-castes, including the *Dalits*: the untouchables, who were beneath the caste system altogether. It is debatable whether Hinduism actually approved of the system: some scriptures barely mention it, while others give detailed descriptions of how it should work. Many Buddhist, Jainist and Hindu theologians have denounced the caste system, yet still it persists. Gradually, it is diminishing, but thousands of years of prejudice are difficult to eradicate.

The position of women within Hindu society isn't great either: in some parts of the country child marriages and the treatment of women as property still goes on. And while this isn't specifically the fault of Hinduism, many local Brahmins do little to discourage it. But on the positive side, there are many reform movements within Hinduism working to bring about change in a massive, ancient country. With so much religious tradition, they can afford to lose a little bit of it.

3

Atheist/Non-religious

YES, YES, yes: obviously, Atheism is not a religion. It is a highly disparate group with varying forms of non-belief, no detailed theology and no rites or practices: and going to a DIY store every Sunday instead of Church is hardly comparing Like with Like.

And what can you say about these people? They don't believe in God and, er, that's about it.

Well, no, actually: as we've said: there may be varying forms of non-belief, but for many of them there are *reasons* why they feel the way they do; which for them are as true as the Truth adhered to by Muslims or Christians. Denial of the existence of God has a long history and has not always been incompatible with religion. Take, for example, just two of the beliefs we have met so far: in some Unitarian churches, belief in God is not a pre-requisite for membership, while Buddhism is *explicitly* agnostic: one of the major religions in the world admits that it doesn't know if there is a God or not.

However, in this chapter we won't be looking at non-theistic religions (if that's not a contradiction), but at people around the world who can be loosely defined as being Secular, Non-religious, Agnostic or Atheistic: a group which totals 1.1 billion, mostly in Europe and the western world and ex-communist countries like Russia. China, which relaxed its suppression of religion only twenty years ago, has the highest numbers of atheists on the planet. (And the figure could be even higher: many strict Muslim countries still maintain that 100 per cent of their citizens believe in Allah. Interestingly, down the road in Israel, 30 per cent of people admit to being Atheists.)

But before we do meet these folks, another reason for including non-believers in a book about religion: by being part of a religion, all adherents are saying, implicitly and explicitly, 'I believe in the existence of a God or gods': an enormously profound statement about the way they view life and the universe. To come to the opposite conclusion, 'I do not believe in the existence of a God or gods' is equally profound and worthy of examination: it is a *religious* point of view.

So let's start with the now-mandatory bit of confusion: non-believers vary in their non-belief and the degree of it. That's not as contradictory as it may first sound. Rafts of sociologists, theologians and various other pointy-headed types have looked at this and come to generally the same conclusions:

Firstly, there are 'hard' non-believers. These are people who have given the matter some thought and come to the definite conclusion that there is no God. This group can range from people who count it as nothing more than a personal opinion to those who contend that belief in God is an actively bad thing because it is untrue; there is also a body of belief – called Ignosticism, which contends that asking questions like 'Does God exist?' is the same as asking 'What colour is Saturday?': essentially meaningless and therefore not worth talking about. As with religious people, this range of belief can come about as a result of personal enquiry or due to societal conditions, such as being born into an atheistic family or society. Because their non-belief is more 'active' we can call these people Atheists, Secularists or Humanists. (There are religious forms of Religious Humanism, but obviously we are not including those.)

The other category is 'soft' non-believers. Typically, they haven't given the matter much or any thought and are 'passive' towards religion. When pushed, they might say they don't know if there is a God or not. Yet the fact that they have not investigated the matter would indicate that they don't care or don't feel it has any relevance to their life. These we can call Non-religious or Agnostic. According to pretty much all the surveys carried out around the globe, this is the larger category of the two.

Why this is, is, of course, the source of endless speculation by academics: it could be a result of the western-style consumer society, where the acquisition of goods and services has replaced religious belief; it could be a failure of the Churches to make themselves more 'relevant'. Or perhaps it was always this way: it's only been since the 18th century in Europe that people could freely express their non-belief without fear of being beheaded or burnt at the stake; even today, words like 'Atheist' and 'Godless' have pejorative connotations. And in some countries it's still downright dangerous to express atheistic ideas.

So perhaps the truth is more mundane: there's always been a proportion of humanity who simply don't believe or simply couldn't be bothered.

But before we simply chalk non-belief down to laziness, let's examine some of the reasons why Atheists don't buy it.

Religious people can't prove it. Based simply on the evidence of our senses, some Atheists contend that it is up to believers to prove a God exists – and they can't.

Scriptures are unreliable. As we've seen, the various scriptures are hardly paragons of historical accuracy. They contradict each other and often contradict themselves: many of them were written hundreds of years after the 'events' they describe. They also contain profound theological discrepancies: Christian believe Jesus is the son of the God, but Jews and Muslims do not – despite the fact that they all worship the same God. Hindus believe in a God while Buddhists are agnostic: despite the fact their picture of how the universe is structured is largely the same.

And given that there are so many conflicting 'versions' of God, potential adherents could choose the 'wrong' one. (The other side to this argument is that it is safer to choose belief in a God – given that the alternative might be eternal damnation.)

*Science can disprove scriptural accounts. For instance: the formation of the world did not take place as described in *Genesis* or many other scriptural accounts. There wasn't a worldwide flood either. Science has also demonstrated that many gods in ancient society were actually based on natural phenomena that hadn't been explained yet: like thunder. For religions which have a more vague impersonal God, the scientific rebuttal comes from branches of Scientific Logic; specifically, two ideas, *Hume's dictum* and *Occam's razor*, which essentially argue that the existence of God is, at best, unprovable and theistic accounts of the creation of the universe make everything far more complicated than they have to be.

*The Problem of Evil. In most religions, God is omnipotent and omni-benevolent. Yet evil exists in the world. If God created the world, then he must have created the evil. But if God created evil, he can't be omni-benevolent. If the evil exists separate from God, then God is not omnipotent; and if God is not omnipotent, he or she is not God. Similarly, why would God allow people to kill each other in God's name? No one has ever totted up a figure, but definitely millions and possibly billions have died as a result of religion.

*Poor Design. If God created the universe, then why did he make such a sloppy job of it? To get to where we are now, in evolutionary terms, has involved the destruction of millions of species and untold misery for so many others. And why have dead planets and empty space and stars that blow up? It's all terribly wasteful – and not very kind. Many religions claim humans were created in God's image, yet we share 98% of our genetic code with chimps, 90% with mice and 21% with roundworms. Similarly, if humans are so special, how come we have only existed for 0.0015% of the age of the Universe?

*The problem of belief. If God wants us to believe in him, why does he make it so difficult to do so by not providing any evidence?

*The Free Will problem. According to religion, we have been given free will to make the right or wrong choices; so it's up to us if we go to Heaven or Hell. God, however, is omniscient, meaning he knows everything – including every choice you are going to make. Therefore God already knows what the outcome is going to be. Which means it's not really Free Will at all. This is a profound contradiction.

*Why Create the Universe? Why did God bother making the universe? As a perfect being, everything would have been perfect with God beforehand. So why do it?

Whew. There are many, many more arguments against the existence of God but they tend to fairly heavy-duty philosophical notions, so we don't need to explore them here. Instead let's look at the history of all this Godlessness.

No doubt in Stone Age societies all over the world there were people exclaiming how they didn't believe a word of this. However, the first recorded instances of Atheism (apart from Buddhism in India) come from Ancient Greece. (The word Atheist originally derives from the Greek *atheos,* meaning 'without God'.)

First up is the Greek philosopher Epicurus, who actually invented the problem with God and evil that we mentioned earlier. It's known as the *Epicurean paradox* and it goes like this:

"God either wants to eliminate bad things and cannot, or can but does not want to, or neither wishes to nor can, or both wants to and can. If he wants to and cannot, he is weak — and this does not apply to God. If he can but does not want to, then he is spiteful — which is equally foreign to God's nature. If he neither wants to nor can, he is both weak and spiteful and so not a God. If he wants to and can, which is the only thing fitting for a God, where then do bad things come from? Or why does he not eliminate them?"

Read it a few times; you'll get the gist of it.

This was a brave thing to say, because less than two hundred years before, the Granddaddy of Greek Philosophy, Socrates, was executed on suspicion that he had dissed some of the gods. (Which he denied.) To even imply that they might not exist at all ran the same risks. Another notable figure from this period was another philosopher Lucretius, who, although he believed in God, posited the idea that God isn't interested in us and there isn't an after-life.

And after that, well: nothing, for several centuries in Europe. Christianity arrived and as we've seen, you could be burned alive for questioning the finer points of theology, don't mind debunking the whole thing. So if there were any doubters, they kept quiet. The word 'Epicurean' became an insult.

During the Middle Ages, about the only sniff of Atheism came, ironically, from a Pope. Pope Boniface VIII was in charge from 1294 to 1303, and the main thrust of his papacy seems to have been temporal rather than spiritual: in a papal bull he claimed that it was 'necessary for salvation that every living creature be under submission to the Roman pontiff'.

He wasn't a popular man and did some pretty dodgy things when he was in charge: to such an extent that after his death an investigation was held and the title of Pope was retrospectively taken off him; making him an 'anti-pope'. The authenticity of these quotes cannot be verified, (Boniface had a lot of enemies keen to make stuff up about him), but here are some of things he was alleged by the Vatican investigation to have said:

> "The Christian religion is a human invention like the faith of the Jews and the Arab."

> "The dead will rise just as little as my horse which died yesterday."

"Mary, when she bore Christ, was just as little a virgin as my own mother when she gave birth to me."

"Paradise and hell exist only on earth. The healthy, rich and happy people live in the earthly paradise, the poor and the sick are in the earthly hell."

"The world will exist forever, only we do not."

"Any religion and especially Christianity does not contain only some truth, but also many errors. The long list of Christian untruth includes the Trinity, the virgin birth, the godly nature of Jesus, the Eucharistic transformation of bread and wine into the body of Christ and the resurrection of the dead."

Whoops. Whether Boniface said all or any of things can never be known for sure; but it does prove that such ideas were floating around at the time. However, an outfit called the Brethren of the Free Spirit in Germany did come close to Atheism in the 14th century, in a Buddhist sort of way. Rejecting much of Christian theology, the Brethren taught that everything is God: similar to the impersonal spirit of Buddhism. And if everything is God, they figured, then there really is no such thing as sin: so we can do whatever we want. They used to celebrate Mass naked. Until the Church burned the lot of them.

Things got a little more liberal during the Renaissance. There weren't any naked Masses, but at least some criticism of the Church was allowed – which in turn led to the

Reformation, during which there was quite a lot of criticism of the Church. And curiously, it's because of this that the term Atheist came into common use. As we've said, the word was around in ancient Greece, but in the intervening period there had been no need for it, given that everyone except for Pope Boniface believed in God. It came into use in France in the 16th century, where it was aimed at anyone with 'irregular' views – and could result in being burned at the stake. It was also a simple term of abuse, hurled at people who were viewed to have committed bad acts. In this context, it really meant 'God-hater' rather than non-believer: the assumption of the time being that a person actually coming – by means of reason – to the conclusion that God didn't exist was an impossibility.

It wasn't until the late 1700s that anyone could deny the existence of God without losing their own existence. The first recorded incidence of it was a pamphlet published by the German philosopher Paul Baron d'Holbach called the *System of Nature*, in which he described the Universe as being strictly a material place, with no soul, after-life or God. It also included the particularly inflammatory phrase "All children are born Atheists; they have no idea of God".

Just to be safe, he did publish it under a pseudonym. It was promptly banned and the pamphlet was burned. Better than the alternative, though.

There were a few other lone voices here and there, but the big breakthrough in Godlessness came after the French revolution of 1789. This paved the way for movements such as Rationalism and Liberalism, and one of its early pioneers was the German philosopher Ludwig Feuerbach. With his book *The Essence of Christianity*, he proposed the idea that God is in fact an amalgam of human traits: in short, that we created God to reflect ourselves rather than the other way around. Feuerbach's ideas were hugely influential among other thinkers, particularly other Germans like Arthur Schopenhauer, Friedrich Nietzsche – who declared that God was dead – and Karl Marx, who suggested religion was just another method of social control.

Various scriptures, but particularly the Bible started coming in for criticism for their inconsistencies, while even people like the writer George Eliot opined that there was something wrong with the idea of a God who behaved like a 'revengeful tyrant'. Comparative religion studies which sprouted up in the late Victorian era began to suggest that basically all religions contained the same ideas. In 1880 Charles Bradlaugh was the first openly atheistic person to be elected to the British House of Commons – though he didn't take his seat for five years because he refused to swear a religious oath.

In the twentieth century, these ideas were deployed in the running of the Chinese and Soviet communist systems. Religion was tolerated, but not exactly encouraged. However in Albania between 1967 and 1990, all religion was banned outright.

Today, Atheism is more respectable, though still distrusted in many parts of the world where anti-blasphemy laws remain on the books, if rarely used. During the presidential primaries in the 1988 US election, the then candidate George Bush (dad of George W) said: "I don't know that atheists should be regarded as citizens, nor should they be regarded as patriotic. This is one nation under God." And old George knew his constituency: a 2006 poll conducted in the US found Atheists to be the *most* distrusted minority: more so than Muslims.

Partly because of that residue of suspicion which still sticks to Atheism, it has morphed into various other guises in the modern age and developed belief systems.

One is *Antitheism* or militant Atheism: a philosophical school of thought which argues that religion is actually harmful. Another is Naturalism. It contends that everything is natural. It does not necessarily deny phenomena that are usually described as 'supernatural' – just that, if they do exist, there is a natural explanation for them.

But, probably the best known form of Atheistic belief is Humanism. Sometimes it can be called Secular Humanism, though the two terms appear to be slightly different; Humanists can sometimes embrace quasi-religious rites such as marriages or births, while Secular Humanists would reject such things. Some have argued that Humanism is in fact a religion; just without the God bit. Secular Humanists particularly would be horrified by this suggestion, though there are Humanist Organisations all over the globe and an International Humanist and Ethical Union which has been in existence since 1952.

However, all Humanists are keen on stressing that Humanism is about what they believe *in* rather than what they do not. These are the basic tenets:

Test all beliefs – nothing should be accepted on faith, but should be tested using logic and science. And similar rigour should be applied to all human questions.

Fulfilment – Humanists should concentrate on finding fulfilment and encouraging creativity for both the individual and humankind. This also applies to striving for a better understanding of Humanity, through History and Art, and of opposing points of view.

Truth – Humanists should always search for objective truth.

Ethics – Humanists should search for Ethical Systems to improve the lot of humanity.

Building a better world – Humanists believe that by doing all the above in an open-hearted manner, they can help build a better world.

Over time, Atheism has done much to shake off the image of being a synonym for 'evil': atheists have feelings too, and are just as concerned as anyone with ethics, the structure of society and the good of humanity. The only difference is their insistence that God doesn't exist. And despite the many arguments in favour of this position, it suffers from one basic flaw: it can't be proven.

But that's not the same as saying God *does* exist.

It all boils down to this: you can't prove a negative.

Let's pretend we're not talking about God at all, but Leprechauns. There is no evidence that Leprechauns exist – but that doesn't mean that Leprechauns *definitely* don't exist.

But because there is no evidence that Leprechauns don't exist is no reason for believing that they *do*.

In short, both the pro- and anti- God points of view are ultimately unprovable.

There is lots of circumstantial evidence to consider, some impressive theories, but it seems to come down to making an educated guess; what some religious people call Faith. As they say in the church of *Big Brother*: you decide.

2

Islam

HERE ARE two quotations for you:

> "*I came not to bring peace, but a sword. For I am come to set a man at variance against his father, and the daughter-in-law against her mother-in-law . . .*"

> "*. . . became consumed into ashes. Indeed, for their destruction, Canra produced a fierce iron thunderbolt that looked like a gigantic messenger of death . . .*"

Yep, it's violent, grizzly stuff. Except that neither quotation has anything to do with Islam: the first is from the Bible and the second is from the Hindu epic, the *Mahabharata*.

We're making a Big Point here: Islamic history and scripture might not be too full of holding hands and cuddling, but then neither are most of the other religions we have met so far: especially in the case of the Abrahamic religions, violence has played a large part in their being spread around the world. Similarly, all religious scripture has parts that contain, let us say, intemperate language, or stuff that simply isn't relevant any more. Or stuff that's just plain daft. Islam is no different

Obviously, this point needs to be made in the light of world events today: of violence from fundamentalists and the conflicting images of Islam as a religion of peace or one that has sneaking regard for nutcases who blow up schoolchildren. So what is Islam? Even on a religious level, is it a threat to the western world? There are, after all, 1.2 billion of them

The truth, as it annoyingly tends to be, is complicated: Islam – in the hands of various political powers – has been grindingly oppressive and blissfully open-minded. But it's a long story; so relax.

First the roots of the word Islam: it comes from the Arabic, obviously, and literally means 'submission to Allah'. However, a number of other words stem from the same linguistic root. They are:

Salaam: 'peace'; a common salutation.

Assalamu alaikum: 'peace be upon you'.

Muslim: 'one who submits to God'.

Salamah: 'safety', commonly used in the phrase *ma' as-salamah* 'go with safety'.

Now Muhammad is the founder of Islam, but before we get to him, let's spin back in time to a few other big names you may be familiar with.

Adam: you know, the very first bloke ever. Islam regards him as a prophet, and a big one at that: in some Islamic accounts he was thirty metres tall. There are various accounts of where he went after the Fall, but one is that he went to Sri Lanka: a mountain there named Adam's Peak is said to contain his giant footprint.

Noah: known as Nuh in the Qur'an, where his story is pretty similar to that in the Bible.

Abraham: Ibrahim to Muslims, but the same guy. The Biblical and Qur'an accounts differ on some points. In Judaism and Christianity, Ibrahim's father sold idols; in Islam this was his Uncle. In the Qur'an though, Ibrahim isn't a Muslim or a Jew but a Hanif: it means 'follower of the right path' and is the Muslim term for pre-Muhammad monotheists.

Now: this is where it gets contentious because the Old Testament and the Qur'an have different versions of the same story. Where they agree is that Ibrahim had two sons, Isaac and Ishmael.

Here's the Old Testament version, or the relevant bits for our purposes: from the start, there is a bit of needle between the two boys – possibly because while Ishmael is the eldest, Isaac is 'legitimate'. So when God tests Abraham by asking him to kill his only son, he means Isaac. Ishmael is sent off to the desert with his mother by Isaac's mother, Sarah, and the two of them nearly die, but are rescued by God. When Abraham dies, he leaves everything to Isaac.

Poor Ishmael gets zip. The sons of Isaac become the twelve tribes of Israel.

Here's the Qur'anic version. Ishmael was the eldest son and was legitimate. On instruction from God, Hagar and Ishmael take off for the Arabian Desert, eventually settling in Mecca. In them days though, Mecca was just, well, a large bit of sand and the two of them nearly died of thirst. Hagar ran around like a mad thing looking for water until the *Zamzam Well* miraculously appeared, saving them both. Later on, Ibrahim came to visit and together with Ishmael they built the Ka'aba, the holiest site in Mecca. Ishmael remained in Mecca and Muhammad was one of his many descendants. And it was Ishmael that God asked Ibrahim to kill, not Isaac.

Moses: or Musa in the Qur'an. In fact the Qur'an has more references to Musa than any other prophet: which is odd, as you'd expect the whole focus of the story of Islam to now switch to what was happening in Mecca. But no: here we learn all about the burning bush and the Ten Commandments and leading the Israelites out of Egypt.

Jesus: like all the above, Jesus was a prophet – not the Son of God – who came to guide the children of Israel. As in the Bible, there was a virgin birth, strict non-violence and preaching. However, Muslims believe what is known as the New Testament is actually a distortion of a scripture given to Jesus by God. (They believe the same thing happened to the Hebrew Bible.) Nor do they believe he was crucified. There are various variations of the story, but in the main they believe that God made it appear Jesus was crucified and then lifted him up to heaven, Muslims believe Jesus lives in heaven and will return to battle the Anti-Christ.

As we know already, given the shared history of Jews and Arabs, it's not at all surprising that characters who populate the story of the Bible also appear in the Qur'an. (The Arabic name for God, Allah, shares the same Aramaic (the language spoken at the time of Jesus) root with one of the Hebrew names for God, Elohim.) But where things really start to diverge is in the 6th century, when the last in this line of prophets is born: Muhammad.

It's reckoned he was born around the year 570 in Mecca, though, as always, not everyone agrees with this. Accounts of his life are sketchy as a lot of it came through the *hadith*: oral accounts which were not written down for several hundred years after Muhammad's death. Thus academics squabble over the details and allege that some of the accounts may have been 'adjusted' over the years to suit political conditions at the time. Similarly, Sunni and Shi'a accounts also differ.

Nonetheless, the picture we get of Muhammad is as a *human being*, not a flawless super-holy man. At the time Arabia was a scantily populated place, with various Bedouin nomadic tribes and farmers. The religions among these Arabs were mixed: some were Christians or Nestorians, (a Christian sect which believed Christ was actually two people), some were Jews or Zoroastrians. There was also an Arabic polytheistic religion which worshipped three goddesses, Allat, Uzza and Manat.

Muhammad was born into the well-off Banu Hashim clan of the Quraish tribe. In those days, different clans had different areas of expertise, and the Banu Hashim were in charge of the Ka'aba shrine that we've mentioned already, and which, by Muslim accounts, was built by Ibrahim: except that by then it wasn't dedicated to the Hebrew God but to all of them. It was full of idols: the three goddesses were represented along with a host of other deities and religious figures, including Jesus. So when, later on, Muhammad started giving out about idol worship, he was taking on his own family.

Muhammad's father died six months before he was born, while his mother died when he was but six years of age. He was cared for by his paternal grandfather and later on his uncle, Abu Talib, the leader of the Hashim clan. By all accounts he was a dreamy, serious boy but with a reputation for honesty. He received no formal education, and may well have been illiterate.

While still in his teens, Muhammad embarked on various trade missions with his uncle. Because the Ka'aba shrine was a place of pilgrimage, Mecca had also developed as a trading post. He regularly travelled to Syria and it's believed this contributed to his education: he almost certainly would have come into contact with a range of religious beliefs, which in turn may well have shaped his attitudes towards the religious practices of the time.

Eventually, Muhammad went into the trading business for himself, and not only made a living from it but also got a wife: one of his employers was Khadijah, a forty-year old widow who became so impressed with the 25-year old Muhammad that she asked him to marry her. Muhammad accepted, and together they had five children together. (Though the number of kids is disputed.)

The marriage was by all accounts a happy one: so much so that Muhammad took no other wives until after Khadijah's death. He made up for it then, but we'll get to that.

He had been a reflective boy and this continued into manhood: troubled by the slew of religious belief he saw around him, it was his habit to meditate in a cave on which was the right path to take. Then in 610, while meditating in a cave in Hira, just outside Mecca, he was visited by the Angel Gabriel. It was here that Gabriel relayed to Muhammad the first few lines of the Qur'an. The gist of it was that idol worship was wrong and that there is only one God – the God of the Jews and Christians – but that they had debased this belief.

Understandably, Muhammad was a bit freaked out about this, so he went home and told the wife. She then relayed this story to her Nestorian Christian cousin, a monk called Waraqah ibn Nawfal. He recognised that Muhammad had been chosen as a prophet and identified his visitor as being Gabriel. Waraqah encouraged Muhammad to begin preaching this message but also predicted that Muhammad would be driven out of Mecca for it. Waraqah died a few days after this.

It was some time before Muhammad received another visit from Gabriel – and three years before he began preaching in public, though in the meantime a few friends and family members did pledge their allegiance.

And you can guess the reaction when he did go public: the economy of Mecca depended in no small part on pilgrimages coming into the Ka'aba – so to suggest that all the icons be taken out of the Temple, was to many at the time clearly bonkers: especially coming from a member of the clan who looked after it. Some listened, and many more laughed at him. But no action was taken: the fact that Muhammad was a member of a powerful clan did afford him a measure of protection. For a while.

But as his support grew, the patience of the authorities began to shrink. Some Muslims were forced out – one group fleeing to Ethiopia where a Christian king offered his protection.

Then in 619 came the Year of Sorrows: his wife, Khadijah and his uncle, Abu Talib, both died – and with his powerful uncle out of the way, the Quraysh tribe withdrew their protection of Muhammad. Muslims were suddenly subject to social and economic exclusion, beatings and death threats. They were on their own.

But the following year Muhammad had an experience which has ramifications to this day. Muhammad told his followers that he had experienced two miraculous journeys, the Isra and the Miraj, both in the company of the Angel Gabriel. In the first, he travelled to the 'furthest mosque' – which most Muslims take to be Jerusalem. From there he embarked on the second journey, where he ascended into heaven and met various prophets, including Jesus and eventually, God.

By 622, things hadn't got any better, including several attempts to assassinate Muhammad – who decided enough was enough. He instructed his followers to pack their bags and move with him to Medina. For the time, this was considered an almost unthinkable notion: tribal and family loyalties were considered the most important, even more so than religion. By rejecting his clan, Muhammad was making the point that God was paramount.

The flight to Medina is known as *Hijira* and marks the beginning of the Islamic year. (As well as having different year-numbers, the Islamic calendar is calculated by their own version of the lunar cycle.)

Now at the time, Medina was hardly an estate agent's dream: it was an oasis with a few farmers. But it did have a small Muslim community and a problem which Muhammad fancied he could solve: a feud between two local tribes. Muhammad converted them all to Islam and forbade bloodshed among Muslims. Problem solved. There was also a number of Jews in Medina, (whether ethnic Jews or Judaic Arabs isn't known for sure), at least one of whom converted to Islam. Muhammad hoped the rest would follow, but he was disappointed.

Now interestingly, it was about this time that Muslims changed the direction of their prayer or *qibla*: before this they had prayed facing Jerusalem, the site of the original Hebrew temple. Now Muhammad instructed them to face Mecca. Historians speculate that this may have been due to Muhammad's failure to win the support of the Jews. Islam teaches that it was a simple instruction from Allah.

However, Muhammad did negotiate the Constitution of Medina, which laid out how Jews and other groups could exist within the State. This agreement became the template for future Muslim States down to the present day.

And yes: within a short time, Medina *had* become the world's first Muslim State, with Muhammad as its ruler. Within an equally short time, relations with Mecca got seriously bad. The Meccans confiscated all property left behind by the Muslims. In retaliation, Muhammad began raiding caravans bound for Mecca – a process which culminated in the battle of Badr, where the Medinans triumphed, despite being outnumbered three to one. The victory gave credence to the notion that God was on the side of Muhammad and his new State.

The Meccans launched two more attacks against Medina, both of which failed, but which did result in accusations that a local Jewish tribe the Banu Qurayza, had provided help to the Meccans. Muhammad's forces attacked the Jews and executed hundreds of them. Understandably, this is a controversial bit of Muslim history.

All the while, Medina's sphere of influence and power was growing, so by 628, Muhammad was ready to march on Mecca. Now at first it wasn't an invasion; it was a 'pilgrimage' in the company of 1,600 heavily armed men. A peace agreement was even signed. But before entering Mecca there were more battles with Jewish tribes – during which most of the Jewish men were killed and the Jewish women 'divided up' among the Muslims. Muhammad himself claimed Safiyya bint Huyayy, the daughter of the chieftain of one of the tribes.

As we've said, Muhammad had only one wife up until the death of Khadijah. But after her, he collected a few more. Safiyya was his ninth, and there were two more after that. Some of the unions were for political purposes – to strengthen ties among his growing empire, but most of the women he seems to have had genuine affection for. By marrying women from various tribes, Muhammad did manage finally to unite the Arabs – who previously had spent most of their time fighting with each other. He also broke another taboo by mostly marrying widows: widows were previously regarded as 'used goods' in Arabic society. And it was also a way of taking care of the wives of dead comrades.

So it's a good time now to pause our story and examine Muslim attitudes towards polygamy. One criticism of Muhammad is that during the second, polygamous phase of his married life, he broke the rule, as issued through him from Allah, that men are allowed no more than four wives. The Muslim response is that the rule didn't apply to him: he was Muhammad after all. And his marriage choices set examples for Islamic society: he married a woman far older than himself; he married a Jew; he married a Christian. (Though both converted.) In all the stories concerning Muhammad's wives, he demonstrates great kindness and gives each of them the free choice to marry him or not. He was *kind* to women; that's the point.

Thus the Muslim regulations state that a man is permitted no more than four wives, but that each of these wives must come with their own property and assets. Usually the wives have no contact with each other and lead separate lives.

In the modern world, the logic is that polygamy reduces instances of adultery and divorce, and therefore the number of children in 'broken homes' or born 'out of wedlock'. It also gives more women the chance to be married, which is a good thing as there are more women than men. Apparently.

In reality, however, it is far more influenced by

economic and cultural factors. It is most widely practised in west Africa, where many non-Muslims do it as well, and a few of the more conservative Arab states such as Saudi Arabia. It is also a practise limited to the rich: four wives ain't cheap. But in many parts of the Muslim world, it's not done at all: in effect, only a minority of Muslim men take more than one wife; and there is a growing mood in some Muslim societies that it is a 'backward' practice.

But back to the 7th century: followed by scraps with some Meccan allies, Muhammad finally marched on Mecca with a force of 10,000 behind him. They walked into the city and encountered virtually no resistance.

Muhammad proclaimed a general amnesty and the vast majority of Meccans wisely converted to Islam. The idols were quickly cleared out of the Ka'aba temple, and Mecca became the capital of the Muslim world.

After that, Islam was an unstoppable force in the Arabian Peninsula. The remaining Arab tribes converted and were ruled by Muhammad through a series of tribal treaties.

And so it remained until June 8, 632. After a visit to a cemetery, Muhammad grew ill and died. He is buried in the Mosque of the Prophet in Medina. He was 63 years of age.

But the march of Empire didn't stop with Muhammad's death: Islam went on to conquer Iran, Iraq, Egypt, Palestine, Syria, Armenia and a big chunk of Northern Africa. In subsequent centuries it spread to the Iberian Peninsula and much of Asia.

We are, however, getting ahead of ourselves here, because the death of Muhammad left the Arabs something of a problem: who would succeed him and how that person would rule. All power, spiritual, political and legal, had rested with Muhammad – but this was possible because he was the Prophet of God. No one else could make such a claim.

So instantly, we are into controversy – and from this point on, it depends on whose version of history you believe, the Sunni or Shi'a. However, what is generally agreed is that the followers of Muhammad were a confederation of various tribes – who unified behind their loyalty to Muhammad and Islam. When he died, reasons for that unity were far less compelling. As a result, each subsequent Caliph had to fight military battles to establish his authority.

After the death of Muhammad, a series of four men were Caliphs – or leaders of the Islamic state. Sunnis refer to them as Rashidun, or 'rightly-guided Caliphs'. Shi'as don't. The first three were Abu Bakr, Umar and Uthman. The Sunni view is that these three men were the rightful rulers. The Shi'a, however, believe that Muhammad wanted his cousin, Alî ibn Abî Tòâlib, to take over the job. Therefore, the first three men are usurpers. Shi'a is actually a shortened form of the historic phrase *Shi`at `Ali*: followers of Ali.

What is certain is that the appointment of the first three Caliphs generated some controversy. All three had to deal with rebellious tribes and unhappiness with their leadership; Umar was assassinated, while Uthman had to fight a full-scale civil war – or *Fitna* – and was assassinated as well. Tough job. However, all three managed to extend the borders of the Muslim empire.

Finally, the man whom the Shi'a regard as the rightful

successor to Muhammad, Alî ibn Abî Tòâlib, got the job. But he didn't have much better luck: he also had to fight internal battles and was eventually slain by an assassin.

So again, the question was: who would succeed Alî? The Shi'a belief was that only someone who was a blood relative of Mohammad could be a proper interpreter of the Sunnah, or 'way' of Islam. So they plumped for Alî's son, Hasan ibn Ali. Hasan did briefly claim the Caliphate, but almost instantly was challenged by Muawiyah I, the ambitious Governor of Syria who had previously tried to get the job after Uthman was killed. They fought a few skirmishes, but it seems that Hasan's heart wasn't in it: eventually, some of his own soldiers rebelled against him and Muawiyah I seized power.

And this is the root of the Sunni-Shi'a split. Since that time the Shi'a acknowledge a completely different set of people as the spiritual head of their religion, all of whom, they believe, are descendants of the Prophet, (though they've had internal splits on this subject since then). Today, the Shi'a make up about ten per cent of the worldwide Muslim population. We'll return to them.

So back to the Caliphate. Muawiyah I seized power and he, and his descendants, ruled for the next hundred years. From now on, the Caliphate would be ruled by a series of Dynasties.

Now you'd think that all this internal bickering would have weakened the Empire, but not a bit of it; even when civil wars were raging, (there was a second Fitna in 680), the Caliphate steadily grew. By the 8th century it stretched from North Africa to Pakistan – nearly one-quarter of the planet.

However, this doesn't mean that all the people in these territories were forced or even volunteered to become Muslims; actually, quite the opposite. The vast majority of subjects in the Caliphate were non-Muslims, and, based on the Constitution of Medina, were allowed to live as *Dhimmis* and practise their own beliefs. This was originally applied only to Jews and Christians as 'People of the Book', but later on was extended to Zoroastrians, Mandeans (an Iraqi sect based on John the Baptist), and even Hindus.

Dhimmis were required to pay *jizya,* a tax to the state, and in return they would receive a measure of protection. However, the non-Muslims were required to wear distinctive clothing (usually a badge; blue for Christians, yellow for Jews), were forbidden to carry arms and were not allowed to testify in Sharia, or Islamic courts.

Again, the whole area is one of massive dispute, but it is fair to say that, on the face of it, this wasn't such a great deal for non-Muslims. But let's be clear here: payment of the Jizya is mentioned in the Qur'an, but there were political and economic aims as well.

The political reason was, simply, to show the subject people who was boss. However, in practice, the perception of the Dhimmi system was quite different: in many territories it was hardly enforced at all, while in others it worked more as a system of self-government; the various religions were allowed to develop their own economies and legal systems in parallel with the Muslim power, and as long as they didn't get in each other's way, everyone was happy. Indeed, the Muslim rule of Spain from the 7th to the 11th century is referred to by Jewish scholars as a 'Golden Age' and a period of great cultural development.

That's not to say that it was all fun and sunshine for non-Muslims. Today the Dhimmi laws are still applied in some strict Muslim states and can be rightly interpreted as oppressive. In the Caliphate, however, the idea was to keep them in their place – but not too much.

And one of the reasons for this was money. Muslims were required to give money to the state for charitable purposes, known as Zakkah, but as this was, in practice, a voluntary contribution, it didn't supply the Caliphate with a steady revenue stream. The *jizya* tax, however, supplied regular cash: so it wasn't in the interests of the State to have everyone convert to Islam. Indeed, under the first dynasty, the Ummayad, it seems to have been made deliberately difficult. This is not to say that mass, enforced conversions didn't happen – they did – but it was in a minority of cases.

Nonetheless, over a period of centuries the majority of subjects did convert to Islam. Whether this was because they felt they would enjoy more rights as Muslims, or because they simply felt Islam was a better religion, remains a subject of furious debate.

Back the story again. As we've said, the Ummayad dynasty, with its capital in Damascus, lasted around a century. After the death of Muawiyah I, he was succeeded by his son Abd al-Malik ibn Marwan. By all accounts an educated and capable man, and his rule was relatively peaceful. However, he did make one controversial decision: he built the Dome on the Rock.

The Dome is a shrine (not a mosque), at the spot where Muhammad embarked on his tour of heaven. However, the Dome is built on the site of the Temple Mount: the last Jewish temple and as such one of the holiest sites in Judaism.

That Abd might have built the Dome as a deliberate snub to Judaism is, again, the subject of debate. Jews believe that the Dome will be destroyed and the Temple re-built when the Messiah comes; Christians believe this will happen at the time of Armageddon. All very jolly.

Anyway, the Ummayad dynasty was overthrown in 758 by the Abbasids who set up their capital in Baghdad. During the rule of the Abbasids, Baghdad became arguably the greatest cultural centre in the world. The arts and sciences flourished, Sharia, Islamic law, was codified and the various Hadith (oral accounts) were collated. This era also saw the arrival of Sufi Islam, a more mystical form of Islam.

But, as is always the way of such things, the political empire founded by Muhammad (according to Sunnis anyway) was beginning to crumble. It had grown too large and unwieldy and difficult to run. Some territories claimed independence, while crusades from the west further weakened the empire. Finally, the Mongols invaded Baghdad in the thirteenth century. The Muslim Caliphate disintegrated.

But let's not forget that the Caliphate was a *political* entity: Islam the religion had spread around the world; so it wasn't long before new Islamic empires (or empires where Islam happened to the religion) emerged: the Ottoman Empire in the Middle East, the Safavid Empire in Iran; the Moghuls of India. But they too eventually crumbled. In the modern age, many 'Muslim' countries have been founded: some with a separation of Church and State, such as Turkey, and some outright theocracies, such as Iran.

So let's get down to it: what do Muslims believe? Again, it varies between sects and the many sub-sects; especially in terms of how 'strict' a religion it should be.

But there are some basic tenets: there is one God, Allah, who spoke through Muhammad. Muhammad is the final prophet before the day of resurrection. Allah narrated the Qur'an to Muhammad and it is flawless. The Qur'an had to be revealed by God to correct the 'distortions' of the Hebrew Bible and the Old Testament.

As we've also said, the two main sects in Islam are Sunni and Shi'a, with Sunni being the vast majority. (Though both Iran and Iraq have a Shi'a majority.) However, many Muslims refuse to be identified with either group, as the Qur'an specifically bans sects within Islam.

A fundamental of the religion is what Sunnis call the Five Pillars of Islam and Shi'as call The Roots of Religion, but they are basically the same thing. They are:

*Shahadah. Profession of faith in Allah and Muhammad, his messenger.

*Salat. Performing the five daily prayers while facing Mecca. (21°25'24N, 39°49'24E, if you want to know.)

*Sawm. Fasting from dawn to dusk in the month of Ramadan.

*Zakat. Giving of alms.

*Hajj. Pilgrimage to Mecca during the month of Dhu al-Hijjah. If possible, this must be undertaken at least once in the lifetime of each Muslim.

Other central tenets of belief are listed in the Muslim creed:

I testify that there is no god but God Almighty, Who is One (and only One) and there is no associate with Him; and I testify that Muhammad (peace and blessings of God be upon him) is His Messenger.
I believe in God; and in His Angels; and in His Scriptures; and in His Messengers; and in The Final Day; and in Fate, that all things are from God, and Resurrection after death be Truth.

Now the God referred to here is the Abrahamic God, though in the Qur'an God shows no gender. Or plural either: Muslims regard the Christian doctrine of the Trinity to be polytheism. As with Muhammad, Islam makes no visual representations of God – because it's impossible to do and also because such depictions might lead to idolatry.

Obviously, central to all this belief is the Qur'an, which Muslims believe was gradually revealed to Muhammad by the Angel Gabriel over a period of 23 years, and which goes some way to explaining apparent inconsistencies in the text. The argument goes that by revealing the Qur'an gradually, Gabriel and Muhammad were gently leading Muslims to full realisation of the Muslim way of life: which is why a ban on drunkenness early in the Qur'an is replaced later on by a ban on alcohol outright.

The transmission of the text was carried out orally, as it is believed Muhammad couldn't read or write. He would recite what Gabriel told him and others would write it down. Some time after his death these various writings were collated. And this can't be stressed enough: in Islam, the Qur'an is a perfect book: there are no versions or omissions; this is literally the word of God, so even printed versions of the book are treated with great reverence. Muslims undergo a ritual washing even before touching it. And damaging a copy is considered deeply offensive.

The 'true' Qur'an is also the one in the original language: classical Arabic. Translations are considered guides but not the Qur'an itself. But given its poetic style, the Qur'an is a book which was intended to be spoken aloud – and Muslims are required to recite passages from the book every day. Most have learned large sections of it, while it's not uncommon for adherents to have memorised the entire book. Such a person is known as a *hafiz*.

The Qur'an is divided into 114 *Surah*, chapters, and 6,236 *ayat,* or verses, and involves many versions of stories also in the Bible: those of Adam, Noah, Abraham, Moses, Jesus and others. Some of the details are different – and obviously Jesus is depicted as a prophet rather than the Son of God, but the gist of them is largely the same. A line of twenty-five prophets is mentioned, starting from Adam. (However, a hadith claims there were 124,000 prophets in the course of history.) The Surah are not arranged in temporal order – the order it is believed they were revealed to Muhammad – but in accordance with various hadith believed to have also come from the prophet. As well as the stories of various figures from Muslim history, the Qur'an contains exhortations to worship God and rules for living the Islamic life.

But although the Qur'an is regarded as the pure word of God, that doesn't mean that it is always easy to understand: in fact Muslims regard its often opaque style as evidence of its divine source. The version of Arabic it was composed in is quite different to the one used today, while many of the allusions and allegories included in the text may make sense only to people living in 7th century Arabia. Because of that, huge squads of Muslim academics have produced mountains of interpretative material explaining the history of the time and in what sequence the Surah were revealed: which in many cases has meant that some sections of the Qur'an can have more than one meaning.

Which is where Islam, and most other religions, can run into trouble. As we've already said, the Qur'an, like most holy books, has its share of what seems to be intemperate and warlike language: but in the modern age, is this meant to be interpreted literally? Take this quotation:

> "*Fight those who believe not in Allah nor the Last Day, nor hold that forbidden which hath been forbidden by Allah and His Messenger, nor acknowledge the religion of Truth, (even if they are of the People of the Book), until they pay the Jizya with willing submission, and feel themselves subdued.*" (*Qur'an 9:29*)

Leaving aside the problems of translating from an ancient language, does this mean 'fight' in the literal sense? Are Muslims being told to 'subdue' the rest of us?

Depends on who you listen to. Some in the Islamic world do take this literally; and some, as we know, have done something about it. But a closer examination of the various militant Islamic groups which have emerged in this and the last century usually reveal a parallel political agenda: one is used to justify the other.

Other Muslim scholars place such quotations in the context of the time, when warlike metaphors were commonly used. They were, after all, warlike times.

Thankfully, the vast majority of Muslims don't take such quotations literally: if they did, our world would be engulfed by a conflict far greater than the so-called 'War on Terror'. The Qur'an, while instructing Muslims to establish their own states, also clearly says that these states should not attack others, even if they are non-Muslim; instead Muslims should issue a *Dawah*, or invitation to others to worship Allah. "Invite to the way of your Lord with wisdom and beautiful preaching and argue with them in ways that are best."

However, while the Qur'an is full of instructions for determining the *Sunnah*, or Islamic way of life, as well as Islamic law, it is not a *complete* set of instructions. To fill in the rest, Muslim scholars turn to the Hadith: a set of descriptions of what Muhammad said, what he did and what he approved of. There are also Hadith of some of his contemporaries.

They fall into three main categories: stories about Muhammad, commentary on the Qur'an and juristic reasoning.

And there are problems here too: there are tens of thousands of these, all of which were passed down orally and can be sourced back to various contemporaries of the prophet. Scholars have literally spent centuries studying these hadith and trying to establish their reliability, mainly by tracing back the people through whom the hadith were transmitted. Many of them tell the same stories, with inconsistencies; many flatly contradict each other. Many were rejected on the basis that the people transmitting the stories were clearly biased. As a result, few hadith scholars are ready to stick their necks out and claim that all the hadith are completely reliable. After throwing out the stuff that was completely bogus, they came up with three 'grades' of hadith: *sahih,* 'genuine'; *hasa,* 'fair' and *da'if* 'weak'. As you might expect, not everyone agrees on which hadith falls into which category – and the Sunni and Shi'a have a completely different set of hadith.

So: there are six Sunni hadith, originally collated by six different men. They tend to be referred to by the man who put it together rather than the name of the book. They are:

1. Sahih Bukhari, collected by al-Bukhari

2. Sahih Muslim, collected by Muslim

3. Sunan Abi Da'ud, collected by Abu Da'ud

4. Sunan al-Tirmidhi, collected by al-Tirmidhi

5. Sunan al-Sughra, collected by al-Nasa'i

6. Sunan Ibn Maja, collected by Ibn Maja

In terms of reliability, they go from 1 to 6: al-Bukhari being the most reliable. In practice, most Muslims tend to stick with the first two, al-Bukhari and Muslim. (His full name was Abul Husayn Muslim ibn al-Hajjaj Qushayri al-Nisaburi. Phew.)

Thus for Muslims on an individual level, much of what they believe is a matter of choice, personal study and interpretation. On a practical level, of course, most don't have the time to engage in such intensive study – so they rely on their Imam to do it for them.

An Imam is not a priest. (And it is usually a man: female Imams can lead female congregations, though there is a controversy over whether females Imams should be allowed to lead mixed congregations.) Islam does not have a formal clergy at all. Imams are scholars who lead prayers and interpret the sacred text. There isn't any formal process to become an Imam: you simply have to put in the hours.

Similarly, Islam has no hierarchy: there is no Muslim 'Pope' or College of Cardinals. (There are national and international federations of Muslims, but these have little power.) The 'version' of Islam adherents receive depends on what mosque they attend and what Imam they listen to.

Thus it is a considerable achievement that a belief system which allows such autonomy among its mosques has also managed to maintain such a strong sense of identity: despite coming from all parts of the world, Muslims routinely refer to themselves as a 'nation' or *Ummah*. (Though this is not to be taken literally – or as code for a secret plan to re-establish the Caliphate.) This is probably due in no small part to Sharia – Islamic law.

Again, Sharia has its basis in the Qur'an and the hadith, and again, it can vary in practice, yet Sharia provides an incredibly detailed set of prescriptions for all aspects of life: from the governance of the State down to various crimes, diet, marriage, inheritance, fasting, prayer, banking and even how they speak: Muslims routinely refer to each other as 'sister' and 'brother', while all references to Muhammad must come with the phrase 'Peace Be Upon Him'. Thus Muslims all over the world, despite ethnic differences, can lead very similar lives. And even in the law, there is choice. Sunni Islam recognises four different legal traditions, Maliki, Shafi'i, Hanafi, and Hanbali, which differ mostly in how much reliance they place on various texts. Adherents are free to choose the one that suits them best.

However, probably the most controversial aspect of Sharia, at least from a western perspective, is the treatment of women. Again, it varies depending on the cultural conditions of each country. Yet it is fair to say that, in general, Muslim women have fewer civil rights than men.

As we've said, Muslim men can have up to four wives. However, Muslim law gives women the right to demand a marriage contract. In this she can stipulate how many other, if any, wives the man can have and whether she has to give her permission. The contract can also give the woman the right to divorce and specify what the terms of that divorce will be. In practice, most Muslim women do not do this, though there is a growing movement in many Muslim countries to inform women of these rights.

Even if there is no marriage contract, a woman can divorce her husband – theoretically. In practice it only happens if she can convince a *Qadi*, or Sharia judge, that her problem is serious. Men, however, can divorce their wives with relative ease.

You may well have noticed that the list of well-known muslim female politicians is not a long one – though there are exceptions in non-theocratic Muslim societies. There is a (disputed) hadith in al-Bukhari, (the most reliable), that a country with a female leader will never be successful. However, women are allowed to be elected to the Iranian parliament, the Mejlis.

However, the right to vote is increasing for women, just as the level of democracy is increasing in Muslim countries: there is a growing view that democracy is related to the Islamic concept of *Shura* – or consultation – a system used by many of the Arab tribes to arrive at major decisions.

Clothing is another contentious issue. Yet another quotation from the Qur'an:

> *And tell the believing women to lower their gaze and guard their private parts and not to display their adornment except that which ordinarily appears thereof and to draw their headcovers over their chests and not to display their adornment except to their husbands, their fathers, their husbands' fathers, their sons.*

In other words, dress modestly: which in most Muslim societies means covering the head and the avoidance of belly-tops and hot pants. However, in the more theocratic societies, women are forced in *chadors*: a huge black robe with only the face exposed, (popular in Iran) or the even more extreme *burqas* which hide all but the eyes. There is by no means agreement in the Islamic world on these practices: some argue that to cover up more than is required by the Qur'an is in fact un-Islamic. (There are also dress codes for men, though they are less strict.)

The logic behind the dress code is that it protects the woman by not revealing any details of her body and therefore not stirring the passions of any passing men. Thus it protects her from rape and enables her to go about her business without sexual distractions. The concept of men simply controlling themselves doesn't seem to be considered.

It might be something of a simplification, but the Muslim logic towards many issues relating to women – polygamy and the dress code – seems simply to be that 'Boys will be boys' and there's nothing that can be done about it: because men are not monogamous 'by nature', they should have more than one wife; because men cannot help but regard women as only sexual beings, the women must dress in large black bags.

In some Muslim countries, women are required to walk behind men. But this practice is cultural, not Islamic.

But this *is* Islamic: the Qur'an allows men to beat their wives.

There are strict conditions laid out: if the husband has a problem with his wife, first he must admonish her. If it continues, he seriously adds to her punishment by refusing to have sex with her. And if that cruel and unusual treatment doesn't work, he can hit her.

No doubt you'll be relieved to know that there are strict rules on how severely a man can beat his wife. He's not allowed to leave bruises. Sweet.

Curiously, there are several hadith which condemn domestic violence. But they are not considered that reliable.

Women inherit less than men, they are generally discouraged from giving evidence in Sharia courts, and in the *diyah* system, where those convicted of crimes pay compensation to their victims, women are literally worth less. In the more hard-line Islamic states, women are not allowed to vote, drive, work, travel without written permission or even be seen in public without a male relative.

But it's not all grim: there are many women's movements within the Muslim world: and they are vocal. Recently in Iran, (where 60 per cent of university students are female), women staged a protest against a programme on Iranian television which promoted polygamy.

So now let's have a quick look at the varieties of Islam on offer. As we know, the vast majority are Sunni, and a lot of the history and practices related so far stem from that tradition. Here are some others:

Shi'a. As we know, they originated from a row over who should succeed Muhammad. They contend that Muhammad's daughter Fatima and twelve other descendants of the Prophet were the rightful rulers of the religion, and that they were infallible. However, this subdivides into three schools called 'twelvers', 'seveners' and 'fivers' who disagree over how many infallible leaders there were. (The twelvers are the largest.) As a result, Shi'a Islam has separate hadith and legal systems. Imams are much more powerful in Shi'a than their Sunni counterparts – being regarded not just as teachers but sacred people appointed by Allah. Shi'as live mostly around the Middle East, though another sub-sect, the Shi'a Ismaili, which further divides into two other sects (or sub-sub-sects), live mainly in Pakistan and India. One of the sub-sub-sects, the Nizari Ismaili, is led by the Aga Khan.

As the recent history of Iraq demonstrates, relations between Sunni and Shi'a are not exactly convivial; in the case of Iraq this is exacerbated by a Sunni minority ruling the Shi'a majority for decades. However, on the religious level alone there is a mutual grudge which dates back to the death of Muhammad and who should have taken over. There are elements in both sects which regard the others are heretics – or not Muslims at all. (Which means for some – once they've interpreted the Qur'an in a way that suits them – killing the 'non-Muslims' is permitted.) If you think there's some bad feeling between Islam and Judaism, try sticking some Sunnis and Shi'as in the same room and see what happens.

Sufism. Not a sect, but a practice engaged in by both Shi'a and Sunni. The idea is that following Islamic law is all fine and well, but that's only the first step; the adherent needs then to start working on his or her own spiritual development. Yes, it is all very mystical and some maintain that it has been influenced by pre-Islamic Iranian beliefs and perhaps some eastern religions. The basic idea is that everything is a reflection of God and therefore the aim of the Sufi is to find beauty in everything – even the ugly. Sufis have a pantheon of 'saints' whom their revere – leading some other Muslims to suspect them of pantheism. There's lot of meditation and coming to an awareness of God, singing, dancing and chanting. (Which some Muslims also find suspect.) Some schools of Sufi are more traditionally Islamic, but others, (especially in India), pay barely any attention to the Qur'an at all.

Wahhabism. Again, not a sect but a movement within Islam. They don't like to be called Wahhabis either – that's what we call them in the west. However, there was a time when they didn't mind the term, especially after the movement's foundation by Muhammad ibn Abd al Wahhab in what is now Saudi Arabia. The idea was that they would practise a 'pure' form of Islam in line with the teachings of the first three Caliphs: their contention being that the religion had been debased since then by 'innovations'. Wahhabism, as it was called then, was made the State version of Islam when Saudi Arabia was founded. Wahhabism in turn influenced the formation of an outfit called The Muslim Brotherhood in Egypt, in 1928. Equally conservative, its religious-political aim was the establishment of Muslim government in Egypt and the re-establishment of the Caliphate, which, as it did before, would stretch a quarter ways around the world. They were banned and kicked out of most middle-eastern countries, but did find a home in Saudi Arabia where they mingled with Wahhabis to form a movement called Salifism: just as religiously conservative, but now with a bit of a political edge. (The Muslim Brotherhood, which still survives elsewhere as a political force, has gone through many mutations but now is mainly political, pro-democracy and peaceful.) Salifism, however, contains many members who – such as Osama Bin Laden – support violent *Jihad*; even against Muslim countries which they regard as having strayed. They are extremely scary.

(And while we are here, a word on two words: *Jihad* and *Fatwa*. Jihad means, more or less 'struggle', but in the broadest possible sense: you can, for instance, have a Jihad of the Heart, which would be an inner struggle against evil. A Fatwa is a legal pronouncement: and in the vast, vast majority of cases these pronouncements are on utterly mundane subjects. Unfortunately, the word came into parlance in the west when Iran issued a Fatwa for the execution of the writer Salman Rushdie.)

Ibadi. Now: remember Alî ibn Abî Tòâlib? He was the fourth Caliph; the guy who the Shi'a believe should have got the job in the first place. Just prior to assuming the position, he had a spat with one of the tribes supporting him, the Kharijites. The Kharijites withdrew their support for Alî , but didn't give it to anyone else, deciding to keep themselves to themselves. The only remaining descendants of the Kharijites are the Ibadi. Oman is the sole country in the world to practise Ibadi Islam. One of the main differences is that they accept the legitimacy of some of the Caliphs, but not all of them. (Especially Alî ibn Abî Tòâlib; who they think was good at the start, but then made a complete mess of it.) Their interpretation of Islam is quite strict, and (again), they feel they are the only ones practising 'pure' Islam. Many of them regard other Muslims as *Kafir*, a term meaning 'unbeliever' or 'one who covers the truth'. In the Islamic world it is a racist insult with the same force as 'nigger'.

Ijtihadists. A liberal movement within Islam with a

big stress on personal interpretation of the Qur'an and hadith. They too feel they have gone back to the core values of the religion by stressing greater pluralism. They favour equality for women and the separation of Church and State. They seek reform, not schism and are a small, but growing movement.

Druze. Based mainly in the Middle East, especially Lebanon, the Druze aren't regarded as real Muslims by the rest of Islam because, yes, you guessed it, they don't practise a pure form of the religion. Which in fairness, they don't. It evolved in the tenth century with a mixture of Islam and Greek philosophy (they regard Plato as a prophet), and is a belief which is mostly kept secret by its adherents: in fact, even most of the adherents don't know what the secrets are.

Alawites. Like the Shi'a, the Alawites were big fans of the fourth Caliph, Alî ibn Abî Tâlib: but just a bit too much. At the time, some of them claimed he was God incarnate and for that, Alî banished them. Again, they are a secretive lot about their beliefs so it's not known if they still regard Alî as a God or another prophet like Muhammad or a kind of saint. Whatever the truth, it's just not a pure form of Islam. They live mostly in Syria.

Now we have mentioned intemperate language, but one of the most controversial of allegations is that in Islam, suicide bombers believe that by becoming 'Martyrs' they will go to straight to heaven and receive 72 virgins. Certainly,

Islamic teaching is that martyrs do go straight to the highest level of heaven (there are seven of them).

First check out this Hadith:

Abu Hurairah (May Allah be pleased with him) reported: The Messenger of Allah (PBUH) said, "Whom do you reckon to be a martyr amongst you?" The Companions replied: "The one who is killed in Allah's way." He said, "In that case, the martyrs among my people would be few." The Companions asked: "O Messenger of Allah! Then who are the martyrs?" He replied, "He who is killed in the way of Allah is a martyr; he who dies naturally in the Cause of Allah is a martyr; he who dies of plague is a martyr; and he who dies of a belly disease is a martyr; and he who is drowned is a martyr." (This is from Al-Bukhari and Muslim, who compiled the two most reliable hadith.)

In other words, *anyone* who lives a righteous life and dies is a Martyr. You don't need to strap yourself with plastic explosives to get it: the 'promise' of paradise for suicide bombers is more probably used by militant groups to distract from the repeated instructions in the Qur'an not to harm innocent people.

So what's the deal with the virgins? The word for them in the Qur'an is *Houri*, which more correctly translates a 'pure being' – though it is made clear that these beings have not been touched by any man. The Qur'an says they are there, and that the devout will get to marry them.

However, there is no mention of numbers. Some of the

hadith claim that devout men will get 72 wives and eighty thousand servants – others do not mention it at all. Others say it is just two. The hadith compiled by al-Bukhari – considered the most reliable – does not mention a number at all.

In 2000, a German academic published a book (under the pseudonym Christoph Luxenberg), which claimed that, due to mistakes in translation, what the Qur'an actually promises are white raisins. You can imagine the reception he got. And why he published the book under a pseudonym.

Increasingly, many Muslim women are questioning this promise: on the basis that the raw deal Muslim women get in this life seems to be continued into the next. Muslim scholars counter this by claiming that in Paradise, women will also get whatever they want – even if this is apparently contradictory to the desires of their husbands.

It's also fair to go back to the point made earlier: the Qur'an was revealed to a desert people at a time when polygamy was the norm and the acquisition of wives was a status symbol. Elsewhere in the Qur'an, the description of Paradise is an idealised version of life in the desert: with sand, camps and bazaars; not the kind of heaven which might necessarily appeal to westerners or Orientals or Africans. And some Muslim scholars do make the point that this may be taken more as an allegorical description, given the historical background.

Nonetheless, many Muslim men do believe in the 72 virgins promise. Well, they would, wouldn't they? The point is that they don't have to: it's not a fundamental article of faith, but it is used as a propaganda tool by people both within Islam and outside.

Islam has much in common with other religions: like many of them, it believes that it is the one true religion with a message for all humanity: but in Islam that belief is so fervent that the notion of secular life, in some versions of the religion at least, is almost extinguished.

It's also a religion with great internal tensions: most Muslims don't approve of suicide bombing or hijacking planes, yet feel that much of western society regards Islam as threatening and perhaps even uncivilised. Mainstream Islam is caught between what for them are two unattractive options. Yet secular western society has to find a way to communicate with Islam, before the mutual suspicion turns into something far more ugly.

But take heart: history shows us that sooner or later, all the great political/religious conflicts have played themselves out. (To be replaced by other ones.) In the Muslim version of the final judgement, all people will be resurrected and brought to earth for one day – a day which will last 50,000 years – to be judged. Good Muslims will go straight to heaven, of course, but so too will the virtuous People of the Book, Jews and Christians. And then Allah will dispatch angels to Hell to search for people with even one atom's measure of goodness in their hearts. And they too will be saved.

There's hope for us all yet.

1

Christianity

SAY WHAT you like about Christianity, but one fact is undeniable: it's fierce popular. The largest belief system on the planet with 2.1 billion adherents, it's even well in with the other religions: out of the twenty in this book, eight of them consider Jesus to be some form of prophet, saint or holy man – and that's excluding Christianity.

It's also handy because – for our purposes – there are many things about Jesus that we don't need to tell you, because you know them already. In **Judaism** we covered some of the history up to the point of his birth, so let's start from there. And almost immediately, we're into controversy.

First, the name: Jesus was an Aramaic name, that being the language spoken at the time he was born. In a rough English translation it would be pronounced as *Yeshua* or *Yehoshua,* which among Jews in first-century Jerusalem would have meant, appropriately enough, 'Yahweh Saves'.

It was also a very common name. The first century

Jewish historian Josephus, (no relation to Jesus' stepfather), names at least twenty other blokes called Jesus.

Which is where the controversy starts. But first let's tell you about Josephus himself. Before getting in the history game, Josephus was a Hebrew priest and then a military leader in the Jewish revolt against the Romans which started in 67AD. However, in 68AD, so the story goes, Josephus and forty of his men were trapped in a cave by the Romans. Rather than surrender, the men all decided to kill themselves. Yet curiously, Josephus survived. It's not certain what happened, but the suspicion is that Josephus simply gave up. Some time later he moved to Rome and became a Roman citizen, and then spent the rest of his life writing books which extolled the virtues of the Jewish people.

So: as you can imagine, many regard Josephus as a sneak and a traitor and that his historical accounts should be dismissed.

In the light of this, here's the controversial bit: Josephus claimed Jesus had a brother. The claim is made in his work *Antiquities of the Jews*, in which he makes reference to 'the brother of Jesus who was called Christ, whose name was James'.

As you might expect – and we'll explain why in a moment – such a claim has been fiercely contested. But what makes it a wee bit more difficult to dismiss is that the New Testament *also* make reference to James as the brother of Jesus.

The James we are talking about is called James the Just. He was the first Bishop of Jerusalem, he wrote parts of the New Testament, and was a hugely important figure in the early Christian church. He was stoned to death by the Roman authorities in 62AD.

Actually, it gets more complicated: while Saint Paul makes a reference to 'James, the Lord's brother', Matthew refers to *four* brothers: James, Jude (possibly the apostle Jude), Simon and Joseph. Mark refers to brothers *and* sisters. Now theologically, this is a no-no because Mary, Jesus' mother, was a virgin when she gave birth – therefore it would have been impossible to give birth to any siblings: at least before Jesus. The Roman Catholic and Eastern Orthodox churches (as well as Islam) maintain it couldn't have happened afterwards either, as Mary stayed a virgin for the rest of her life. (Though this is not mentioned in any scriptures.) But the Roman Catholic and Eastern Orthodox churches differ in their explanations of the 'brother' reference in the New Testament. The Eastern Orthodox Church believes that Joseph had children from a previous wife (though there are no Biblical references to this either). Catholicism maintains that the problem is one of translation: James was not a brother of Jesus, but a cousin from Joseph's side of the family. (And given that Joseph was only Jesus' stepfather, not even a blood-relation.)

However, many of the Protestant churches take the Biblical references at face value. They believe that Joseph and Mary had a normal married life after Jesus: and that Mary did indeed give birth to siblings. Thus if you believe in this version of the story, you can also assume that there are still people on the earth biologically related to the Son of God. Cool.

But once again, we're ahead of ourselves. Let's go back to the parents and start with the one you don't hear that much about: Joseph.

The gospel accounts don't tell us much about him. We know that he was a carpenter, and that he was betrothed to Mary when she conceived Jesus – which means, by the custom of the time, that they were legally married but not yet allowed to live together. Around this time Joseph was informed in a dream by an angel of Mary's conception and accepted this. We know that he lived in Nazareth with Jesus and Mary and that he probably died before Jesus' ministry started: the last mention of Joseph is when Jesus is twelve and travels to Jerusalem. However, he wasn't at the wedding feast of Cana (when Jesus did his water into wine trick), nor was he present at the crucifixion.

In the two centuries after the death of Jesus, there was an avalanche of apocryphal 'testaments' which add to the story of the time. One called *The History of Joseph the Carpenter* claims that Joseph had indeed been married before, and had four sons and two daughters, Assia and Lydia. It claims that Joseph was betrothed to Mary when he was ninety and she was twelve and that he died at the age of 111. (Which might explain Mary's continuing virginity.) However, none of the mainstream churches accept that this has any validity.

The New Testament accounts, though, do leave us with a slight puzzle: both Mathew and Luke go to some pains to establish that Jesus is literally the 'King of the Jews' by being a descendant of the House of David. Both of them present (differing) lines of genealogy – but both portray Jesus as a descendant on his *father's* side. Which, of course, is impossible because Joseph wasn't Jesus' 'real' father. Back then, some tried to get around this problem by suggesting that Joseph was in fact Jesus' biological father and that the spirit of God didn't enter Jesus until he was baptised by John the Baptist. But this was rejected by the First Council of Nicaea. We'll get to that later.

Some have theorised that perhaps Jesus was related to David through Mary, though there is virtually no evidence of this either. Some non-scriptural accounts, which are quite widely accepted, state that Mary was the daughter of Saint Joachim and Saint Anne, who were well-off and also lived in Nazareth. (The only relation mentioned in the New Testament is Elizabeth, mother of John the Baptist.) It is believed that Joachim and Anne were quite old when Mary arrived – by which time it had been assumed that Anne was barren: in those days interpreted as a sign of divine displeasure. The good news was delivered to them by an angel. (Angels seemed to do a lot of this at the time.)

As to Mary's age when she conceived Jesus, there is no concrete evidence, though most academics agree that she was young: almost certainly in her teens. As we've already said, she was present at the Wedding Feast at Cana and the Crucifixion, and after that she was present when Matthias was appointed as a replacement to Judas in the Twelve Apostles. But virtually nothing is known about her death: it could have occurred anywhere between three and fifteen years after the crucifixion. However, it is stated in the New Testament that after her death, her tomb was found to be empty; the assumption being that she ascended into heaven. A tomb in the Kidron Valley, close to Jerusalem, is believed by many to be where this happened.

So let's move on to the one son everyone agrees Joseph and Mary did have. As is well known, it will never be known for certain if Jesus was born on December 25, or that the western calendar is correct in its calculation of how many years ago this happened. Many Christian churches celebrate Christmas on January 6th, while the actual year could be out by as much as four years either way. The calculation we currently go by was done by Dionysius Exiguus, a Romanian monk who made it, (the calculation), in the year 532. Or that's what he reckoned. However, most Christian churches don't get too hung up about the dates.

As we've mentioned, the language Jesus spoke was Aramaic. However, the balance of opinion is that Jesus received some education (there are instances in the Bible when he reads) and probably had a smattering of Hebrew and Greek as well; which he was probably lucky to get: a carpenter was not a posh job in those days. And education was anything but universal.

Let's get on with it: Mary is pregnant. Because of a census at the time, Joseph and Mary are forced to travel to Joseph's ancestral home – Bethlehem, where King David was born – and where the birth of Jesus also takes place. It must have been the busy time of year though because the hotels were all full: so Jesus is born in a stable, and Mary is forced to use a manger as a crib. Word of the birth is spread in the area by an angel to local shepherds and some of them come to see the child. Jesus was also visited by the Magi, or three wise men. As we've seen (see **Zoroastrianism**), these men were probably Zoroastrians: specifically, the priestly caste of a Zoroastrian offshoot known as Zurvanism. Central to their practices was the study of the stars and astrology – hence the account that these men followed a star to get there.

On the way, according to the Biblical accounts, they

also bumped into the wildly paranoid King Herod, (Herod killed several of his own sons, viewing them as a threat), who attempted, but failed, to trick them into revealing the baby's whereabouts.

(Interesting aside: the traditional birthplace of Jesus is Bethlehem – which means 'House of Meat' in Hebrew – located in Judah, the heart of ancient Judaism. However, there is another Bethlehem in Galilee, about ten miles from Nazareth, and some have proposed that Jesus was born there. At the time though, Galilee was regarded by Jews as, well, a bit of a dump, and its residents as ill-educated muck-savages who could barely speak properly: to have 'sold' Jesus to the Jews as a man of royal lineage would have been far more difficult, so the theory goes, had Jesus been a Galilean. However, this theory falls down somewhat because Jesus is routinely referred to in the Gospels and elsewhere as 'Jesus of Nazareth' – which is in Galilee anyway. Nonetheless, it does seem as if Jesus' Galilean background did count against him in his dealings with the Hebrew clergy: their attitude being that a prophet – don't mind the Son of God – could never come from such a backwater.)

Anyway, once Jesus is born, Mary and Joseph decide to make themselves scarce for a while: in another fit of neurosis, Herod has ordered all male babies in the area to be killed. They flee to Egypt and return when the danger passes and settle down to normal life in Nazareth.

Again, we don't know much about it, at least from the Biblical accounts: there is an almost twelve-year gap from the time of the flight to Egypt up until Jesus' first visit to the Temple. However some of the apocryphal gospels fill in the gaps: the *Infancy Gospel of Saint Thomas* claims

Jesus performed many miracles as a boy, some of a mischievous and gruesome nature: he struck adults blind, turned other kids into pigs, and as a result, wasn't invited for many sleep-overs. Other stories present the young Jesus more as he was as an adult: healing the sick, bringing the dead back to life and even improving the weather. Babies, according to these accounts, never cried in his presence.

But in the official Bible accounts, of course, none of these things happened. We learn that at the age of twelve he went on a pilgrimage to Jerusalem with Joseph and Mary – and once there Jesus disappeared for three days, leaving his parents to frantically search. Eventually they found him in the Temple debating with religious teachers. When Mary, as any good mother would, asked him what he thought he was playing at (or words to that effect), Jesus replied "Why did you seek Me? Did you not know that I must be about My Father's business?" So even the Son of God gave his mother lip occasionally.

And then we have yet *another* gap: this time up until Jesus gets baptised and starts his ministry; when he was believed to be thirty years of age. Now the New Testament isn't trying to suppress any interesting information here: obviously, the whole *point* of Jesus was what he did between the ages of 30 and 33; the only clue we have of what he might have been getting up to in the intervening period is just one quote in Mark. "Is this fellow not the carpenter?" So perhaps Jesus trained in the family business and spent his time putting up shelves and saying, "That'll cost you, Bud."

There is, however, a different theory which doesn't

come from Christianity but from Hinduism – which also reveres Jesus. Views among Hindus of Jesus vary as to his status, (whether he was simply a holy man or a manifestation of God), but some believe that he spent his 'lost' years in India.

In Jerusalem of the time, there was a Judaic cult known as the Essenes. According to the Hindu view, the Essenes had been deeply influenced by Hinduism and shared many of its beliefs, such as non-violence and vegetarianism. (It's believed John the Baptist was Essenian.) And when Mary finally found Jesus in the Temple, it was a group of Essenes he was talking to – and he was asking them to be sent to India. About a year later, the Essenes arranged for Jesus to travel to Kashmir, where he spent his time learning from both Hindus and Buddhists and while there received the name *Isha* – which is what Hindus still call him. Later on he taught in the area and spent a lot of time meditating in the Himalayas. Champions of this idea claim they know the specific caves he visited and also maintain that some Buddhist monasteries have records of his visits – as does the Vatican. But these are buried in its vaults.

There are also two 'relics' of Jesus still in Kashmir. One is His staff – which originally belonged to Moses and which now is kept in a monastery called Aish-Muqan.

The other is the Stone of Moses, which belonged to Moses and which Jesus brought with him. It is located at a temple called Bijbehara. It is one hundred and eight pounds in weight, and the tradition is that if eleven people put one finger on the stone and recite 'Ka' for long enough, it will levitate.

Much of what Jesus taught, they say, was the message

of eastern religions but was misinterpreted. And they reckon he didn't die on the cross either. Or ascend into heaven. Instead, they believe he went back to India. And Mary went with him. Near a mountain called Pindi Point in the Kashmir there is old tomb called *Mai Mari da Asthan* or 'The final resting place of Mary'. Locals believe this is the mother of Jesus. Nearby, Jesus is 'buried' in a town called Srinagar. The tomb has footprints carved into it, believed to be those of the Son of God. The feet have scars from the crucifixion. Some Buddhists, Hindus and even Muslims in Kashmir believe that this is the final resting place of Jesus, and that he died anywhere between the ages of 50 and 80.

As you might expect, Christian historians have roundly rubbished this theory, disputing the existence of much of this evidence and the people who produced it, some of whom have been decidedly dodgy. Nonetheless, this belief does persist among Hindus in Kashmir; and many western conspiracy theorists are keen on it as well. However, critics of this theory have been unable to explain how this belief – which is at least 1,000 years old – came into existence.

Whatever, the truth, what is agreed upon is that Jesus began his ministry by turning up to John the Baptist and asking to be baptised. Despite some early reluctance – John felt that Jesus should baptise him – John did what he was asked. As soon as this happened, the skies opened up and a voice from heaven announced that Jesus was the Son of God. Following this, Jesus took off to the desert for forty days of fasting, during which time Satan attempted three times to tempt Jesus, but failed miserably on each occasion.

When his sojourn in the desert was over, it was time to begin his ministry in earnest. First on the agenda was to get some help, so Jesus recruited the twelve apostles, some of whom, but not all, were fishermen. Contrary to the popular image, the twelve didn't follow Jesus around the Middle East like a bunch of ancient Yes Men, agreeing with everything he said. In fact, Jesus dispatched them in pairs to different towns around Galilee to preach. The gospels largely agree on who the apostles were, though there are some slight discrepancies on names. They were:

Simon, given the name Peter by Jesus

Andrew brother of Peter

James, otherwise known as James the Great. *Not* the aforementioned James the Just

John

Philip

Bartholomew

Thomas

James, otherwise known as James the Lesser

Matthew, a former tax collector, and therefore a controversial choice

Simon the Canaanite

Judas Iscariot

Thaddeus/Judas, son of James

However, the Gospel of Luke doesn't mention *twelve*

disciples going to do this work – but *seventy*. (Or in some versions of the New Testament, seventy-two.) This larger group includes the twelve apostles and many other well-known figures of the time, including Jesus' 'brother', James the Just. The eastern Orthodox churches accept that this group existed; the Roman Catholic and Protestant churches do not.

This part of the story is so well known we don't need to dwell on it here for too long. Jesus spent three years preaching and performing miracles, most of the time within what is modern-day Israel, though he is believed to have made two trips into Lebanon. He hung out with people regarded by society then as outcasts and debated with the various Judaic sects, the main two being the Sadducees and the Pharisees. Some speculate that Jesus was a Pharisee, others than he was an Essene, though the latter are not even mentioned in the Bible.

What's agreed is that Jesus built up a large following – and something of a stink for the authorities, both of which culminated in his triumphal arrival into Jerusalem on Palm Sunday. Large crowds greeted Jesus, who went on to overturn the money-lenders' tables in the Temple. Some time later, in the Garden of Gethsemane, he was arrested by Roman soldiers – having been first identified by Judas.

Jesus was arrested on the say of the *Sanhedrin*, a council of Jewish clergy and elders. Their problem with Jesus was not just blasphemy, but also politics: by claiming to be the Son of God, he was directly challenging their position as leaders of the Hebrew Church. However, the Sanhedrin didn't have the authority to have Jesus crucified, so they kicked it upstairs to the Governor of Judaea, Pontius Pilate.

341

In the Israel of the time, there were already movements which proposed the violent overthrow of Roman rule. And although Jesus never suggested such a thing, his claim to be King of the Jews might imply that he wanted to replace Roman rule with a re-established House of David.

Pilate wasn't entirely convinced by this argument, but after consulting that wise and august body, the screaming mob outside his palace, he condemned Jesus to death. According to all the accounts, Jesus died in the early afternoon, after which there was a darkening of the sky and an earthquake.

We all know what happened next: Jesus was placed in the tomb and three days later came back to life. According to the Acts of the Apostles he spent the next forty days appearing to various people: to all the apostles, of course, but also to travellers and some crowds. He also appeared to Saul on the road to Damascus, (though this could have happened a year or two later). Saul became St. Paul, one of the most influential figures in the early Church.

However, before returning to heaven, Jesus specifically instructed the now eleven apostles to go forth and spread the word: which is why Christianity, unlike many other religions, believes in proselytising non-believers: Jesus' instruction to the apostles is today regarded as an instruction to all Christians.

The apostles carried out their orders. The generally accepted account is that they remained in Palestine for about twelve years, but then scattered to various parts of the Roman Empire. However, reports of where they went and how they died are extremely sketchy, and often seem to 'mix-up' the various apostles with each other. This version is just one of the many available:

Peter, regarded by Catholics as the first Pope, ended up as Bishop of Rome, where he was crucified – according to some accounts, upside down.

Andrew preached in Asia Minor and was also crucified. According to some accounts, fragments of his body were later brought to Scotland, of which he is patron saint.

James the Great is thought to have preached in Spain, though it's not known exactly where he died.

John also went to Asia Minor.

Philip preached in Greece, Syria, and Turkey.

Bartholomew went to India and later, Armenia.

Thomas went to Egypt and also India.

James the Lesser also went to Egypt and was martyred.

Matthew, went to either Iran or Ethiopia, according to differing accounts.

Simon the Canaanite. Some traditions have it that he preached in Armenia and Persia.

343

Thaddaeus/Jude also went to Armenia.

Matthias. Replacement for Judas who killed himself after betraying Jesus. May have preached in Ethiopia, or died in Jerusalem.

However, according to one reference in the New Testament, this group consisted of 120 others who did similar work; there is also a reference to 3,000 people converting when Jesus entered Jerusalem prior to his crucifixion. Thus the early Christian church already had something of a foundation.

It's thought that all these people were Jews, and it wasn't until Peter converted a Roman centurion that it became accepted that Gentiles (non-Jews) could also become Christians. However, this in turn generated a further controversy: should Gentile Christians follow the traditions of Judaism – should they be circumcised? It is believed that many of the major players in the Bible – St. Paul, Peter and James the Just, met in Jerusalem around the year 50 for the Council of Jerusalem to discuss this very matter. It was agreed that Gentiles didn't have to be circumcised. (However, Christian churches in Ethiopia and Egypt still require circumcision.)

This was a significant moment in the gradual split between Christianity and Judaism: to many at the time, the followers of Christ were no more than a Judaic sect.

During the next two centuries, despite persecution, Christianity grew around the Mediterranean, though it did have competition: a huge variety of other beliefs also emerged; some of which had differing views of Jesus, some of which included Jesus in a pantheon of gods – not to mention religions which had no connection with Jesus at all.

Similarly, there were also a number of gospels and pseudo-gospels in circulation which we've already mentioned: and arguments over what were genuine or not have raged since then. The New Testament as it now exists – consisting of the gospels of Matthew, Mark, Luke and John, Acts, which details some of what the apostles got up to after Jesus, the epistles of Paul and others along with the prophecies of Revelations – was not agreed for the first three centuries of the early church. It is believed that St Athanasius, Bishop of Alexandria, put it together in this form in 367 AD, though even then not everyone bought it. It did, however, gain wider acceptance after the Third Council of Carthage gave it the thumbs-up in 397. Contrary to some popular beliefs, the current New Testament was not decided on by the Council of Trent of 1546 – after which lots of other versions of the Bible were 'suppressed'. The process was far more gradual, and Trent for the most part simply rubber-stamped what had been agreed already.

Of course, this doesn't stop many from speculating as to whether what today we call the New Testament is, as Christians believe, the word of God or a heavily abridged version. Almost certainly, it was transmitted orally for some years after the death of Jesus and may have many more authors than in the official account. And some other completely legitimate accounts of the life of Christ may have been omitted. Speculation and research about this is a huge industry: and different sects of Christianity today have differing versions of the same book.

But back to the fourth century: in 313 the Roman Empire officially declared itself neutral in relation to religion. This not only legalised Christianity, but also de-established Mithraism, a belief system which borrowed from Zoroastrianism and some Persian beliefs.

This was good news for Christianity, which was further helped by the interest taken in it by the then Roman Emperor, Constantine I. Although officially a follower of Mithraism, he had taken an interest in an internal Christian debate over the doctrine of the Trinity: whether Jesus was God, and had therefore existed forever, or whether he came into existence only when he was born. (See **Unitarianism**). So to resolve this question, he organised the Council of Nicaea in 325.

The Council – basically the first-ever meeting of Christian bishops from around the world – voted in favour of the Trinity, while also establishing the dates of Easter and Christmas. (It also voted down that Joseph was the biological father of Jesus theory we mentioned earlier.) It established the Nicene Creed – the prayer which eventually became the Credo and the declaration of what Christians believe in.

With the added bonus of what was seen as the official approval of the State, (there are stories that Constantine made a death-bed conversion to Christianity), Christianity spread rapidly through the empire, with Rome as its capital.

This made the Bishop of Rome an extremely powerful figure – but not the Pope. That concept, as we understand it today, did not come about for another 500 years or so. The Council of Chalcedon in 451, however, did declare that the bishopric of Rome 'speaks with the voice of Peter', which may well have been one of the first factors in the Great Schism which occurred 500 years later.

And let's spin forward to that now – what happened in the intervening period was more of the same: the steady spread of Christianity, both through preaching and the point of a sword; there were regular Councils to debate Christian dogma, with the aim of regularising belief. However, these often caused as many problems as they solved.

In the first 1,000 years of Christianity, certain bishops had a special position, they being the Bishop of Rome, the Bishop of Alexandria, the Bishop of Antioch and later, the Bishops of Constantinople and Jerusalem, Among them, the Bishops of Rome and Constantinople were senior, the former because it was the seat of Saint Peter, and the latter because it was capital of the Roman Empire.

However, after the death of Theodosius the Great in 395, the Roman Empire was split into eastern and western halves: with Greek being spoken in one and Latin in the other. This added to a cultural drift between the two parts of the Church, which was added to when the western empire essentially disintegrated, thanks to invasions from the Barbarian hordes. The rise of Islam also saw a weakening of the Bishoprics of Antioch, Jerusalem, and Alexandria: slowly it turned into Rome versus Constantinople, with both jockeying for position and trying to establish their seniority over the other. There were also disputes over elements of the Nicene Creed, territorial spats over who had jurisdiction in the Balkans and disagreements over rites and practices, such as the use of unleavened bread for communion in the Western Church.

But as we've said, this was a gradual process: ostensibly, the row which led to the schism was over the use of unleavened bread, which caused the Eastern Church to excommunicate some western envoys. Most historians date the Great Schism to this event, which took place in 1054. However, it didn't technically take place until the Ottoman Turks invaded Constantinople in 1453, and under pressure from their new Muslim rulers, the Eastern Church repudiated any link with Rome. Many attempts at reconciliation have taken place, but none with any success.

Technically, each Church regards the other as practising a debased form of Christianity: though this is not a phrase which would be spoken out loud any more. In 2005, Patriarch Bartholomew I of the Eastern Church attended the funeral of Pope John II, the first time an Eastern Patriarch has turned up in Rome for such a funeral in many centuries. So relations are a bit friendlier nowadays.

But back to the past. Despite the 1054 row, the Church was still committed to spreading the word – and between the 11th and 13th centuries the Church opted to do this with physical force. The Crusades were for the most part intended to capture Jerusalem back from Muslims who had occupied it since the 7th century. However, prior to this most Christians weren't too pushed about Jerusalem: they could still make pilgrimages to the Holy Land without any interference from the Muslim authorities. But when a local Muslim leader in Jerusalem destroyed the Church of the Holy Sepulchre, this fostered a perception in the west of barbarous and cruel Muslims – as did threats to the

Byzantine Empire (and Eastern Church) from Muslim forces.

So the concept of the just 'Holy War' emerged within the Western Church, and over two centuries nine different crusades were launched, from different countries and involving various orders of soldiers – such as the Knights Templar as made famous by the DaVinci Code. The crusades were popular not just out of religious fervour in Europe but also because, relatively speaking, it was a politically stable time and there were not that many wars to fight at home. Also in those days, the nation-state in Europe was not such a strong concept: the Church was the pre-eminent political power.

However, it could be argued that the Crusades were a complete failure: the aim was always to re-capture Jerusalem and Christianise the Middle East. That didn't happen.

The idea of fighting for Christianity overseas had a logical extension: that the Church should also do it at home. So while Our Boys were killing the dreaded Muslim, they were also doing it all around Europe in the form of the Inquisitions. Another group made famous by Dan Brown, the Cathars in southern France, were the initial cause. A heretical sect whose beliefs may have been influenced by old Gnostic ideas, the Church at first tried to convert them back to regular Christianity, but when that didn't work, the Vatican rustled up an army and had them all killed.

As we've seen elsewhere in this book, (see **Unitarianism**), this began centuries of religious-inspired butchery in Europe, where the burning of heretics was all the rage and those accused of heresy were considered guilty before being proven otherwise.

But even by those standards, the Spanish Inquisition was spectacularly brutal. Of course, there was also a political subtext: with Spain now taken back from Muslim control, there was increasing paranoia among the Spanish royal family that the country was still under Muslim and Jewish influences – Spanish Jews now having been in the country for well over 1,000 years. In 1478, this process received the official *imprimatur* of the Vatican, giving rise to thousands of show trials, torturing and *auto-da-fé*: the burning of heretics. These practices were continued in some Spanish colonies such as Mexico and Peru. Not too long after, the Portuguese established their own inquisition which carried out similar atrocities in India. (See **Hinduism**.)

Afterwards, somewhat shocked by this brutality, the Vatican established a permanent congregation of cardinals with the job of defending the integrity of the faith. The Congregation of the Holy Office kept a tight control of any local inquisitions, and while the violence was more restrained, the Holy Office didn't always get it right: in 1616 it decreed that Galileo's idea of the earth moving around the sun was 'foolish and absurd.' The Congregation of the Holy Office is now known as the Congregation for the Doctrine of the Faith, and they haven't set fire to anyone for ages.

Unfortunately for people in many other parts of the world, the rise of the Inquisitions also roughly coincided with the birth of European Colonialism – which meant that Christianity also travelled overseas: with the tacit approval of the Pope that heathens could be 'persuaded' into conversion.

But despite all the heathen-incineration, it still wasn't a happy time for the Roman Catholic Church: during the

1300s, the papacy had moved to Avignon in France, then back to Rome. But when the next Pope, the Italian Urban VI, turned out to be clearly bonkers, the Cardinals took off to the Italian town of Fondi and elected yet another Pope, Clement VII, who established a rival papacy back at Avignon. There then followed decades of farce where competing popes vied for the support of various European nations, which was eventually brought to an end in 1418.

This, plus the arrogance of the Church, plus widespread corruption, plus the birth of nationalism brought many in Europe to feel that the Roman Church had become way too big for its britches – and more importantly, had strayed theologically. Some, such as Wyclif in England argued for a more Bible-centred faith, unmediated by the Catholic Church: which meant a Bible published in local languages, not Latin.

The Reformation eventually erupted over a row about the sale of indulgences, or Get-Out-of-Hell-Free cards, which were being flogged at the time to finance the renovation of Saint Peter's basilica in Rome. (Indulgences had been sold by the Church for centuries: thus the richer you were, the more sin you could be absolved from.) Objecting to this, an Augustinian monk and Professor at the University of Wittenberg named Martin Luther wrote 95 theses – or objections to the idea of selling indulgences at all – and, so the tradition goes, nailed them to the door of the local church. This happened in 1517.

Thanks to the printing press and a lot of people who wanted reform in the Church anyway, this quickly turned into a movement. In Switzerland, a parallel group led by Huldrych Zwingli had also been launched and was going even further, actually establishing branches of a Reform Church.

Luther, meanwhile was tried for heresy in the tastily-named Diet of Worms. (A Diet is a general assembly; Worms is a place in Germany.) Luther stood his ground, arguing for extensive reform within the Catholic Church. Unsurprisingly, he was excommunicated and his books banned. He was branded an outlaw and the Church decreed that anyone could kill him without legal consequence: a sort of Roman Catholic *fatwa*. Luther, wisely, went into hiding and began work on a German translation of the Bible. But the severity of the punishment only prompted more support for him within Germany. The law banning his books was never enforced. Luther eventually came out of hiding and continued to call for reform until his death in 1546. (from natural causes.)

However, this might have been a small-scale revolt were it not for the writings of John Calvin; he was only eight when Luther stuck his theses to the door. Although born and educated in France, it is in Switzerland where he made the greatest impression, publishing his *Institutes of the Christian Religion*, a seminal Protestant critique of the Bible. Together with William Farel, the founder of the Reformed Church in Switzerland, Calvin introduced a theology and a church structure that has influenced pretty much all of the Protestant churches.

As a pastor of the new church, he also made the very deliberate point of getting married – one in the eye for the Roman Church's celibacy rules.

(The idea that clergy should be unmarried goes back as far as the Council of Elvira in 295AD – the argument of the time being mainly theological and based upon the

352

teachings of Saint Paul (not a big fan of marriage), and the example of Jesus. However, that doesn't mean anyone paid great attention to this. Priests and even bishops getting married was commonplace right up until the first Lateran Council of 1123 which expressly forbade marriage for clergy – and nullified any previous marriages clergy had entered into.)

In 1539, England under Henry VIII separated from Rome, (though for a quite different set of reasons, and at first the English were not particularly keen Protestants), but it was another body blow to the authority of Roman Catholicism: now gaining support among various princes, the ideas of Luther and Calvin spread across northern Europe. Local editions of Bibles were published, (the most notable being the King James Version in the UK), and the establishment of various Protestant denominations: Anabaptist, Lutheran, Calvinist and Zwinglian.

Because of the fiercely independent nature of the Protestant movement, there was no attempt to bring them all together in any sort of Catholic-style hierarchy: the whole idea was that religion be local, with the individual dealing on a personal level with God through the Bible.

There were, however, five *Solas* (Latin for Slogans), which characterised Protestant belief:

*Christ is the only mediator between humans
and God – not the Pope or anyone else.

*Scripture should not be mediated by anyone else.

*Faith alone wins justification before God. However . . .

*Grace alone earns salvation. No one deserves to
be saved. But God gives it anyway.

*God alone deserve glory – not the Pope or any
bishops.

Of course none of this took place easily or peacefully.
As was the fashion at the time, the rise of Protestantism
sparked violence all across Europe, but especially in
Germany. Protestant and Catholics happily burned each
other, eventually prompting the Thirty Years War which
involved many countries in Europe and had reverberations
for centuries afterwards.

The Roman Church also responded with the Council of
Trent in 1545, which re-affirmed basic Catholic beliefs and
standardised the Tridentine Mass across the entire Church.
It also launched many new religious orders in an attempt
to 're-brand' Catholicism as a belief of piety and honesty.

But it didn't do much good. Protestantism continued to
spread and develop across Europe and into the New
World, producing even more variations. The development
of rationalist and more scientific ways of looking at the
world during the Age of Reason also caused the Catholic
Church to find itself reacting to the changes taking place
in society rather than prompting them. In 1757, the Roman
Church eventually allowed the translation of the Bible into
local languages.

In 1870, the First Vatican Council issued the dogma of
Papal Infallibility: an idea which had been doing the
rounds since the early days of the Church. However, it
doesn't mean that the Pope is perfect, but that in a very

specific set of circumstances, the Pope can issue statements on matters of belief, that are free from error.

In 1929, the Vatican became an independent state, protecting it during World War II. (The Vatican State also remains one of the few countries in Europe which is still ruled by an elected monarch with absolute control – the Pope.) The Second Vatican Council in 1962-65 was seen as a liberalising move, as it allowed Mass in native languages and gave a greater stress to Ecumenism.

In April 2005, German-born Cardinal Joseph Ratzinger was elected as Pope Benedict XVI. Although viewed as a doctrinal conservative on matters such as contraception and gay relationships, he has commissioned an internal study into the possibility of married couples who have sexually transmitted diseases to be allowed to use condoms. For liberals within the Roman Catholic Church, this would be viewed as a massive step forward.

Christianity is the biggest belief system on the planet, but it is as much characterised by its variety as its size. Indeed, in researching this book, it proved impossible to find any source which provided a definitive list of all the various Christian denominations: mainly because new ones pop up so regularly, it's impossible to keep track. So here's a non-definitive list. But it's still pretty long. You don't really have to read the next few pages if you don't want to; just flick through them and you'll get the point. Normal service is resumed on page 384.

Catholic Churches. After the great schism of 1054, a number of Catholic Churches maintained their link to the

Vatican. And while, legally, the Vatican regards them as no different to the rest of the Catholic Church, they do have their own rites and are, in practice, ever so slightly different. They are:

Albanian Catholic Church

Armenian Catholic Church	Maronite Catholic Church
Belarusian Catholic Church	Melkite Catholic Church
Bulgarian Catholic Church	Romanian Catholic Church
Byzantine Catholic Church	Russian Catholic Church
Chaldean Catholic Church	Ruthenian Catholic Church
Coptic Catholic Church	Serbian Catholic Church
Ethiopian Catholic Church	Slovak Catholic Church
Georgian Catholic Church	Syrian Catholic Church
Greek Catholic Church	Syro-Malabar Catholic Church
Hungarian Catholic Church	Syro-Malankara Catholic Church
Italo-Albanian Catholic Church	Ukrainian Greek Catholic Church

---

Catholic churches which are similar to Roman Catholic but which do not accept the primacy of the Pope. (A lot of these are American and relatively recent)

American Catholic Church in the United States	Catholic Apostolic National Church of Brazil
Ancient Apostolic Communion	Catholic Apostolic Church
The Arian Holy Catholic and Apostolic Church	Catholic Apostolic Church in North America

Celtic Catholic Church

Charismatic Episcopal Church

Chinese Patriotic Catholic
Association

Free Catholic Church

Liberal Catholic Church

Mariavite Church

Old Catholic Church

Palmarian Catholic Church

Philippine Independent
Church

Polish National Catholic
Church

Sedevacantism

Society of Saint Pius X

True Catholic Church

Eastern Orthodox

Orthodox Church of
Constantinople: the
Ecumenical Patriarchate

Orthodox Church of Mount
Sinai

Orthodox Church of Finland

Orthodox Church of Estonia

Orthodox Church of
Alexandria

Antiochian Orthodox Church

Antiochian Orthodox
Christian Archdiocese of
North America

Western Rite Vicariate of the
North American Archdiocese

Orthodox Church of Jerusalem

Russian Orthodox Church

Chinese Orthodox Church

Japanese Orthodox Church

Ukrainian Orthodox Church

Metropolia of Western Europe

Georgian Orthodox and
Apostolic Church

Serbian Orthodox Church

Orthodox Ohrid Archbishopric

Romanian Orthodox Church

Bulgarian Orthodox Church

Cypriot Orthodox Church

Church of Greece

Polish Orthodox Church

Albanian Orthodox Church

Czech and Slovak Orthodox Church

Orthodox Church in America

Orthodox Syrian Church in India

Greek Old Calendarists

Belorussian Orthodox Church

Macedonian Orthodox Church

Russian Old Believers

Russian Orthodox Church outside Russia

Ukrainian Autocephalous Orthodox Church

Ukrainian Orthodox Church – Kiev Patriarchy

Western-Rite Orthodox Churches

Orthodox-Catholic Church of America

Western Orthodox Church in America

Oriental Orthodox Communion

Armenian Apostolic Church

Coptic Orthodox Church

Eritrean Orthodox Church

Ethiopian Orthodox Church

Indian Orthodox Church ('Malankara Syrian')

Syrian Orthodox Church ('Jacobite Syrian')

Nestorian

Holy Apostolic Catholic Assyrian Church of the East

Chaldean Syrian Church of the East

Protestantism:

Anglican Communion

Anglican Church in Aotearoa, New Zealand and Polynesia

Anglican Church of Australia

Anglican Church of Canada

Anglican Church of Kenya

Anglican Church of Korea

Anglican Church of Papua New Guinea

Church in Wales

Church of England

Church of Ireland

Church of Nigeria

Church of Uganda

Church of the Province of Burundi

Church of the Province of Central Africa

Church of the Province of Melanesia

Church of the Province of Myanmar

Church of the Province of Rwanda

Church of the Province of South East Asia

Church of the Province of Southern Africa

Church of the Province of Tanzania

Church of the Province of the Indian Ocean

Church of the Province of the West Indies

Church of the Province of West Africa

Episcopal Church in Jerusalem and the Middle East

Episcopal Church in the United States of America

Episcopal Church of Cuba

Episcopal Church of the Sudan

Hong Kong Sheng Kung Hui

Iglesia Anglicana de la Region Central America

Iglesia Anglicana de México

Iglesia Anglicana del Cono Sud de las Americas

Igreja Episcopal Anglicana do Brasil

Kerala Christian Assembly

Lusitanian Church of Portugal

Nippon Sei Ko Kai

Philippine Episcopal Church

Scottish Episcopal Church

Spanish Reformed Episcopal Church

Independent Anglican Churches

African Orthodox Church

African Anglican Orthodox Church Worldwide

American Anglican Church

Anglican Catholic Church

Anglican Church in America

Anglican Church International Communion

Anglican Mission in America

Anglican Orthodox Church

Anglican Province of America

Anglican Province of Christ the King

Christian Episcopal Church

Church of England in South Africa

Communion of Evangelical Episcopal Churches

Episcopal Missionary Church

Free Church of England

Free Protestant Episcopal Church

Reformed Episcopal Church

Southern Episcopal Church

United Episcopal Church

Lutheranism

American Association of Lutheran Churches (AALC)

Apostolic Lutheran Church of America

Association of Free Lutheran Congregations

Church of the Lutheran Brethren of America

Church of the Lutheran Confession

Concordia Lutheran Conference

Confessional Evangelical Lutheran Conference

All Saints Lutheran Church of Nigeria

Bulgarian Lutheran Church

Christ the King Lutheran

Confessional Evangelical Lutheran Church

Evangelical Lutheran Church

Confessional Lutheran Church

Czech Evangelical Lutheran Church

Evangelical Lutheran Free Church (Germany)

Evangelical Lutheran Synod (Peru)

Evangelical Lutheran Synod – United States

The Lutheran Church of Cameroon

Lutheran Church of Central Africa Malawi Conference

Lutheran Church of Central Africa Zambia Conference

Lutheran Confessional Church (Sweden and Norway)

Lutheran Evangelical Christian Church (Japan)

Ukrainian Lutheran Church

Wisconsin Evangelical Lutheran Synod

Evangelical Catholic Church

China Evangelical Lutheran Church

Christian Evangelical Lutheran Church of Bolivia

Evangelical Lutheran Church – Synod of France and Belgium

Evangelical Lutheran Church
of Argentina

Evangelical Lutheran Church
of Brazil

Evangelical Lutheran Church
of England

Evangelical Lutheran Church
of Ghana

Evangelical Lutheran Church
of Haiti

Evangelical Lutheran Church
of Ingria in Russia

Evangelical Lutheran Church
of Paraguay

Evangelical Lutheran Church
of the Republic of Chile

Evangelical Lutheran Free
Church of Denmark

Free Evangelical Lutheran
Synod in South Africa

Gutnius Lutheran Church

Independent Evangelical-
Lutheran Church

India Evangelical Lutheran
Church

Japan Lutheran Church

Lanka Lutheran Church

Lutheran Church –
Canada

Lutheran Church –
Hong Kong Synod

Lutheran Church –
Missouri Synod

Lutheran Church in Korea

Lutheran Church in
Southern Africa

Lutheran Church in the
Philippines

Lutheran Church
of Australia

Lutheran Church
of Guatemala

Lutheran Church
of Nigeria

Lutheran Church in
Singapore and Malaysia

Lutheran Church of
Venezuela

Lutheran Synod of Mexico

Laestadian Lutheran Church

Lutheran Congregations in
Mission for Christ – USA

Latvian Evangelical Lutheran
Church in America

Lutheran Church of
New Zealand

Lutheran Ministerium and
Synod – USA

Lutheran World Federation

Bolivian Evangelical Lutheran
Church

Christian Lutheran Church
of Honduras

Church of Denmark
(Evangelical Lutheran
Church in Denmark)

Church of Iceland
(Evangelical Lutheran Church
of Iceland)

Church of Norway
(Evangelical Lutheran Church
of Norway)

Church of Sweden

Estonian Evangelical
Lutheran Church

Evangelical Church of the
Augsburg Confession in
Slovakia

Evangelical Church of the
Lutheran Confession in Brazil

Evangelical Lutheran Free
Church of Norway
(Associate member)

Evangelical Lutheran Church
in America

Evangelical Lutheran Church
in Canada

Evangelical Lutheran Church
in Chile

Evangelical Lutheran Church
in Guyana

Evangelical Lutheran Church
of Papua New Guinea

Evangelical Lutheran Church
in Russia and Other States

Evangelical Lutheran Church
in Southern Africa

Evangelical Lutheran Church
in Surinam

Evangelical Lutheran Church
in Venezuela

Evangelical Lutheran Church
of Colombia

Evangelical Lutheran Church
of Finland

Evangelical Lutheran Church
of France

Evangelical Lutheran Church
of Hong Kong

Evangelical Lutheran Church
of Latvia

Evangelical Lutheran Church in Tanzania

India Evangelical Lutheran Church

Japan Evangelical Lutheran Church

Lutheran Church in Chile

Lutheran Church in Great Britain

Lutheran Church of Australia

Lutheran Costarican Church

Mexican Lutheran Church

Nicaraguan Lutheran Church of Faith and Hope

Salvadoran Lutheran Synod

United Evangelical Lutheran Church (Argentina)

Presbyterianism

Associate Reformed Presbyterian Church

Bible Presbyterian Church

Church of Scotland

Confederation of Reformed Evangelical Churches

Cumberland Presbyterian Church

Evangelical Presbyterian Church

Evangelical Presbyterian Church in England and Wales

Evangelical Presbyterian Church of Australia

First Presbyterian Church of Buffalo, New York

Free Church of Scotland

Free Church of Scotland Continuing

Free Presbyterian Church of Scotland

Free Presbyterian Church of Ulster

Korean Presbyterian Church in America

Orthodox Presbyterian Church

Presbyterian Church in America

Presbyterian Church of
Aotearoa New Zealand

Presbyterian Church of
Australia

Presbyterian Church in Canada

Presbyterian Church of Eastern
Australia

Presbyterian Church of India

Presbyterian Church in Ireland

Presbyterian Church of Korea

Presbyterian Church in the
Republic of Korea

Presbyterian Church in Taiwan

Presbyterian Church of Wales

Presbyterian Church USA

Presbyterian Reformed Church

Presbyterian Reformed
Church (Australia)

Reformed Presbyterian
Church of Australia

Reformed Presbyterian
Church – Covenanted

Reformed Presbyterian
Church of Ireland

Reformed Presbyterian
Church of North America

Reformed Presbytery in
North America

United Free Church of
Scotland

Uniting Presbyterian Church
in Southern Africa

Westminster Presbyterian
Church

Reformed / Congregationalist Churches

Congregational Federation of
Australia

Dutch Reformed Church

Evangelical Reformed Baptist
Churches in Italy

Evangelical Reformed Church
of Singapore

Evangelical Reformed Church
in Republic of Poland

Federation of Swiss Protestant
Churches

Federation of Reformed Churches

Fellowship of Congregational
Churches (Australia)

Free Reformed Churches of North America

Heritage Reformed Congregations

Hungarian Reformed Church in America

Orthodox Christian Reformed Church

Protestant Reformed Churches in America

Reformed Christian Church in Croatia

Reformed Church in America

Reformed Church in Bavaria and Northwestern Germany

Reformed Church in Hungary

Reformed Church in the United States

Reformed Church of Alsace and Lorraine

Reformed Church of Japan

Remonstrant Brotherhood

United Church of Christ

United Reformed Church

United Reformed Churches in North America

Anabaptists

Beachy Amish

Nebraska Amish

Old Order Amish

Swartzendruber Amish

Bruderhof Communities

Alliance of Mennonite Evangelical Congregations

Anabaptist Association of Australia and New Zealand

Brethren in Christ

Chortitzer Mennonite Conference

Church of God in Christ, Mennonite

Conservative Mennonite Conference

Evangelical Mennonite Church

Evangelical Mennonite Conference

Evangelical Mennonite Mission Conference

Fellowship of Evangelical Bible Churches

Canadian Conference of Mennonite Brethren Churches

Japan Mennonite Brethren Conference

US Conference of Mennonite Brethren Churches

Mennonite Church Canada

Mennonite Church in the Netherlands

Mennonite Church USA

Old Order Mennonites

Swiss Mennonite Conference

Pietists and Holiness Churches

Apostolic Christian Church

Bible Fellowship Church

Christian & Missionary Alliance

Christians Missionary Church

Church of Christ (Holiness) U.S.A.

Church of God (Anderson)

Church of God (Guthrie, Oklahoma)

Church of God (Holiness)

Churches of God General Conference (Winebrenner)

Church of the Nazarene

Evangelical Covenant Church

Missionary Church

United Christian Church

Methodists

African Methodist –
Southern Africa

African Methodist Church –
Zimbabwe

African Methodist Episcopal
Church

African Methodist Episcopal
Zion Church

Bible Methodist Church

British Methodist Episcopal
Church

Central Congo United
Methodist Church

Chinese Methodist Church

Chinese Methodist Church –
Australia

Christian Methodist Episcopal
Church – Dallas, TX

Congregational Methodist
Church

Church of Christ – Hong Kong
& People's Republic of China

Church of North India

Church of Pakistan

Church of South India

Church of the Nazarene –
Kansas City, MO

Evangelical Church

Evangelical Church of the
Dominican Republic

Evangelical Church of
Uruguay

Evangelical Methodist Church

Evangelical Methodist Church
of Argentina

Evangelical Methodist Church
of Bolivia

Evangelical Methodist Church
of Costa Rica

Evangelical Methodist Church
of Panama

Evangelical Methodist Church
of Philippines

Evangelical Methodist Church
of Portugal

Evangelical Methodist
Community – Paraguay

The Evangelical Church –
Spain

Evangelical United Church –
Ecuador

Finnish United Methodist Church – Finland

The Free Methodist Church – North America

Free Wesleyan Church – Tonga

Fellowship of Independent Methodist Churches

Fundamental Methodist Conference, Inc.

Independent Methodist Church

Korean Methodist Church

Methodist Church – Hong Kong

Methodist Church in Ireland

Methodist Church in Singapore

Methodist Church of Bangladesh

Methodist Church of Brazil

Methodist Church of the Caribbean and Americas

Methodist Church of Chile

Methodist Church of Colombia

Methodist Church of Cuba

Methodist Church of Fiji and Rotuma

Methodist Church of Ghana

Methodist Church of Great Britain

Methodist Church of Hong Kong & People's Republic of China

Methodist Church of India

Methodist Church of Indonesia

Methodist Church of Italy

Methodist Church of Kenya

Methodist Church of Korea

Methodist Church of Malaysia

Methodist Church of Mexico Iglesia Metodista de México, Sitio Oficial

Methodist Church of (Lower) Myanmar

Methodist Church of
(Upper) Myanmar

Methodist Church of
New Zealand

Methodist Church of
Nigeria

Methodist Church of
Peru

Methodist Church of
Puerto Rico

Methodist Church of
Republic of China

Methodist Church of
Samoa

Methodist Church of
Sierra Leone

Methodist Church of
Southern Africa

Methodist Church of
Sri Lanka

Methodist Church of
Togo

Methodist Church of
Zimbabwe

North Katanga United
Methodist Church – Kitwe
Zambia

Primitive Methodist Church

Protestant Methodist Church –
Benin

Protestant Methodist Church –
Côte d'Ivoire

Salvation Army

South Congo United
Methodist Church

Swedish United Methodist
Church – Finland

United Church – Zambia

The United Church of
Canada

United Church of Christ of
Philippines

United Methodist Church

United Methodist Church of
Albania

United Methodist Church of
Algeria/Tunisia

United Methodist Church of
Austria –

United Methodist Church of
Bosnia and Herzegovina

United Methodist Church of
Bulgaria

United Methodist Church of
Czech Republic

United Methodist Church of
Denmark

United Methodist Church of
East Angola

United Methodist Church of
Estonia

United Methodist Church of
France

United Methodist Church of
Germany

United Methodist Church of
Hungary

United Methodist Church of
Croatia

The United Methodist Church
of Latvia

United Methodist Church of
Liberia

United Methodist Church of
Lithuania

United Methodist Church of
Macedonia

United Methodist Church of
Mozambique

United Methodist Church of
Nigeria

United Methodist Church of
Norway

The United Methodist Church
of Russia

United Methodist Church of
Serbia and Montenegro

Methodist Church of
Sierra Leone

United Methodist Church of
Slovak Republic

United Methodist Church of
Sweden

United Methodist Church of
Switzerland

United Methodist Church of
West Angola

United Methodist Church of
Zimbabwe

United Protestant Church –
Belgium

Uniting Church of Australia

The Wesleyan Church –
Indianapolis IN

Wesleyan Reform Union

West Africa African Methodist
– Philadelphia PA

West African Methodist
Church – Sierra Leone

Baptists

American Baptist Association

American Baptist Churches USA

Association of Baptist Churches in Ireland

Association of Grace Baptist Churches

Association of Reformed Baptist Churches of America

Association of Regular Baptist Churches

Baptist Bible Fellowship International

Baptist Conference of the Philippines

Baptist Convention of Ontario and Quebec

Baptist Convention of Western Cuba

Baptist General Conference (formally Swedish Baptist General Conference)

Baptist General Conference of Canada

Baptist General Convention of Texas

Baptist Missionary Association of America

Baptist Union of Australia

Baptist Union of Great Britain

Baptist Union of New Zealand

Baptist Union of Scotland

Baptist Union of Western Canada

Baptist World Alliance

Bible Baptist

Canadian Baptist Ministries

Canadian Convention of Southern Baptists

Central Baptist Association

Central Canada Baptist Conference

Christian Unity Baptist Association

Coloured Primitive Baptists

Conservative Baptist Association

Conservative Baptist
Association of America

Conservative Baptists

Continental Baptist Churches

Convención Nacional
Bautista de Mexico

Convention of Atlantic Baptist
Churches

Cooperative Baptist Fellowship

European Baptist Convention

European Baptist Federation

Evangelical Baptist Mission of
South Haiti

Evangelical Free Baptist Church

Fellowship of Evangelical
Baptist Churches in Canada

Free Will Baptist Church

Fundamental Baptist Fellowship
of America

General Association of Baptists

General Association of General
Baptists

General Association of Regular
Baptist Churches

General Conference of the
Evangelical Baptist Church, Inc.

General Six-Principle
Baptists

Ghana Baptist Convention

Global Independent Baptist
Fellowship

Grace Baptist Assembly

Independent Baptist Church
of America

Independent Baptist
Fellowship International

Independent Baptist
Fellowship of North America

Interstate & Foreign
Landmark Missionary Baptist
Association

Landmark Baptist Church

Liberty Baptist Fellowship

Myanmar Baptist Convention

National Baptist Convention
of America, Inc.

National Baptist Convention,
USA, Inc.

National Baptist Evangelical
Life and Soul Saving Assembly
of the U.S.A.

National Missionary Baptist
Convention of America

National Primitive Baptist Convention of the U.S.A.

New England Evangelical Baptist Fellowship

New Testament Association of Independent Baptist Churches

Nigerian Baptist Convention

North American Baptist Conference

Norwegian Baptist Union

Old Baptist Union

Old Regular Baptists

Old Time Missionary Baptists

Primitive Baptists

Progressive Baptists

Progressive National Baptist Convention

Reformed Baptists

Regular Baptist Churches, General Association of Regular Baptists

Separate Baptists

Separate Baptists in Christ

Seventh Day Baptists

Sierra Leone Baptist Convention

Southeast Conservative Baptists

Southern Baptist Convention

Southern Baptists of Texas

Sovereign Grace Baptists

Strict Baptists

Two-Seed-in-the-Spirit Predestinarian Baptists

Union D'Églises Baptistes Francaises Au Canada

United American Free Will Baptist Church

United American Free Will Baptist Conference

United Baptist Convention of the Atlantic Provinces

United Baptists

United Free Will Baptist

Unregistered Baptist Fellowship

World Baptist Alliance

World Baptist Fellowship

Brethren Denominations

Church of the United Brethren in Christ

Plymouth Brethren

Open Brethren

Exclusive Brethren

Indian Brethren

Kerala Brethren

River Brethren

Brethren in Christ Church

Old Order River Brethren

United Zion Church

Schwarzenau Brethren

Church of the Brethren

Conservative Grace Brethren Churches, International

Dunkard Brethren

Ephrata Cloister

Fellowship of Grace Brethren Churches

Old German Baptist Brethren

Old Order German Baptist Brethren

The Brethren Church (Ashland Brethren)

Social Brethren

Apostolic Churches

Catholic Apostolic Church

Restored Apostolic Mission Church

New Apostolic Church

United Apostolic Church

Pentecostalism

Abundant Life Worship
Centres

Apostolic Assemblies of
Christ

Apostolic Church of
Pentecost of Canada

Apostolic Faith Church

Assemblies of God

Assembly of Pentecostal
Churches of Jesus Christ

Bible-Pattern Church
Fellowship

Calvary Holiness Association

Charismatic Episcopal Church

Christian City Churches

Christ Gospel Churches
International

Christian Church of
North America

Christian Congregation of
Brazil

Christian Outreach Centre

Christian Revival Crusade

Church of God (Charleston,
Tennessee)

Church of God
(Chattanooga)

Church of God
(Cleveland)

Church of God
(Huntsville, Alabama)

Church of God
(Jerusalem Acres)

Church of God for All Nations

Church of God by Faith

Church of God, House
of Prayer

Church of God in Christ

Church of God Mountain
Assembly

Church of God of Prophecy

Church of God with Signs
Following

Church of God of the Union
Assembly

Church of the Little Children
of Jesus Christ

Congregational Holiness
Church

CRC Churches International

Destiny Church

Elim Fellowship

Elim Pentecostal Church

Fire Baptized Holiness Church of God of the Americas

God is Love Pentecostal Church

Holiness Baptist Association

House of Prayer Christian Church

Independent Assemblies of God, International

International Church of the Foursquare Gospel

International Pentecostal Church of Christ

International Pentecostal Holiness Church

Ministers Fellowship International

New Life Churches

New Testament Christian Churches of America, Inc

Open Bible Standard Churches

Pentecostal Mission

Pentecostal Assemblies of Canada

Pentecostal Assemblies of Newfoundland

Pentecostal Church of God

Pentecostal Free Will Baptist Church

Pentecostal/Charismatic Churches of North America

Pentecostal Churches of the Apostolic Faith

Pentecostal World Conference

Redeemed Christian Church of God

The Church of God (Jerusalem Acres)

The Church of God for All Nations

The Fellowship (FGFCMI)

United Gospel Tabernacles

United Holy Church of America

United Pentecostal Churches of Christ

Zimbabwe Assemblies of God Africa

Oneness Pentecostalism

Apostolic Assembly of the Faith in Christ Jesus

Apostolic Brethren

Apostolic Church of the Faith in Jesus Christ

Assemblies of the Lord Jesus Christ

Bible Way Church of Our Lord Jesus Christ

Church of Jesus Christ of Prophecy

Church of Our Lord Jesus Christ of the Apostolic Faith

House of Prayer Christian Church

International Church of Jesus Christ

Pentecostal Assemblies of the World

Potter's House Christian Fellowship

United Pentecostal Church International

Charismatics

Charismatic Episcopal Church

Full Gospel

New Frontiers

Sovereign Grace Ministries

Vineyard Movement

Neo-Charismatic Churches

Believers' Churches in India

Bible Christian Mission

Church Assembly Hall

Filadelfia Fellowship

Montagnard Evangelical Church

New Birth Movement

New Life Fellowship

New Life Outreach

Rajasthan Bible Institute

Reaching Indians Ministries

True Jesus Church

United and Uniting Churches

China Christian Council

Church of Bangladesh

Church of Pakistan

Church of North India

Church of South India

Evangelical Church in Germany

International Council of Community Churches

Protestant Church in the Netherlands from 1 May 2004

Syrian Marthoma Church in India

United Church of Canada

United Church of Christ

United Church in Jamaica and the Cayman Islands

United Church in Papua New Guinea and the Solomon Islands

Uniting Church in Australia

Other Protestant Denominations

Greater Grace World Outreach

Calvary Chapel

Church of Christ, Instrumental

Christian City Church

City Harvest Church

Eternal Grace

Evangelical Covenant Church of America

Evangelical Free Church of America

Fellowship of Fundamental Bible Churches

Grace Movement Churches

Great Commission Association

Hope Church Singapore

Indian Shakers

The Jesus Movement

The Family International

Metropolitan Community Churches

New Frontiers

Schwenkfelder Church

Christian Conventions

Society of Friends (Quakers)

Evangelical Friends
International

Friends General Conference

Friends United Meeting

Shakers

Messianic Judaism

Chosen People Ministries

Jews for Jesus

Messianic Bureau International

The Messianic Jewish Alliance
of America

Union of Messianic Jewish
Congregations

Messianic Believers in Yeshua

Restorationism

Disciples of Christ

Christian Church

Churches of Christ

Churches of Christ
(non-institutional)

Churches of Christ in
Australia

International Churches of
Christ (Boston Movement)

Southcottites

Christian Israelite Church

Israelite House of David

Israelite House of David as
Reorganised by Mary Purnell

Yahweh's New Covenant
Assembly

Church of the East and
Abroad

Sabbath-Keeping Churches, Adventist

Branch Davidians

Branch Seventh Day Adventists

Creation Seventh Day
Adventist Church

Davidian Seventh-Day
Adventist Association

General Association of
Davidian Seventh-Day
Adventists

International Missionary
Society of the Seventh-Day
Adventist Church Reform
Movement

People's Christian Church

Promise Adventist Church
(Brazilian Pentecostal
Adventists)

Seventh-day Adventist Church

Seventh Day Adventist Reform
Movement

Sabbath Rest Advent Church

Sabbath-Keeping Churches, Non-Adventist

Assembly of God in Christ
Jesus

Associated Churches, Inc.

Associates for Scriptural
Knowledge

Biblical Church of God

Body of Christ Church of God

Church of God (Anadarko)

Church of God (Jesus Christ
the Head)

Church of God (O'Brien)

Church of God (Philadelphia
Era)

Church of God (Sabbatarian)

Church of God (Seventh Day,
Salem, West Virginia)

Church of God Evangelical
Association

Church of God's Truth

Church of the Great God

381

Congregation of God, Seventh Day

Congregation of God

Congregation of Yah

Foundation of Life Fellowship

General Conference of the Church of God Seventh-Day)

General Council of the Churches of God

Global Church of God

Harmony of Life Fellowship

International Church of God (ICG)

Philadelphia Church of God

Restoration Church of God

Seventh-Day Church of God

The Eternal Church of God

The Pure Truth

Triumph Prophetic Ministries (Church of God)

Twentieth Century Church of God (Pennsylvania)

Twentieth Century Church of God

United Biblical Church of God

United Church of God

United Seventh-Day Brethren

Universal Church of God

World Insight International

Worldwide Church of God

Sunday Adventists

Advent Christian Church

Church of God General Conference (Abrahamic Faith)

Church of the Blessed Hope

Primitive Advent Christian Church

Sacred Name Groups

Assemblies of Yah

Assemblies of Yahvah

Assembly of Yahweh (Easton Rapids, MI)

Assemblies of Yahweh (Bethel, PA)

Assemblies of the Called Out Ones of Yah

Bible Study Association

Church of God (Jerusalem)

House of Yahweh (Abilene, Texas)

House of Yahweh (Odessa, Texas)

Missionary Dispensary Bible Research New Life Fellowship

Scripture Research Association Workers Together with Elohim

Yahweh's Assembly of Messiah

Other Adventists

Christian Nations – Eagle Warriors

Church of God (Reinersten)

Kingdom of God on Earth Within Man

Remnant Church

Restored Israel of Yahweh

Shiloh True Light Church of Christ

Star of Truth Foundation

True Church

Church of God world mission society

Mormonism

Church of Jesus Christ of Latter-day Saints (Mormons)

Community of Christ

Fundamentalist Church of Jesus Christ of Latter-day Saints

And there's bound to be a few missed out there. Of all the world religions, Christianity has had to grapple the most with the new challenges of secularisation and a strict separation of Church and State. In many western European States especially, the Christian churches are struggling to appear relevant.

Christianity prospered due to the Roman Empire, European Imperialism and a strong ethic within the religion itself to proselytise. However, that strength could also be viewed as a weakness: Christianity has mutated into so many different forms that many of its sects and sub-sects have virtually nothing in common with each other. Some have a social or political agenda, but again there seems to be no agreement as to what party Jesus might vote for if he was on earth today: it ranges from the left-wing vision of Liberation Theology to the right-wing views of some strains of American evangelism.

Yet you would be hard-pressed to find any member of the groups listed above willing to admit that they are doing anything but practising a 'purer' form of Christianity than the others.

As with all the other subdivisions of all the other religions, there appears to be an ongoing process of change; a search to discover exactly what it is that God wants us to do. And perhaps one day, we might find out.

STARK RAVING RULERS

SEAN MONCRIEFF

Stark Raving Rulers: Twenty Minor Despots of the Twenty-First Century is a series of profiles of world leaders who still rule their countries through anti-democratic means.

In many forgotten or ignored parts of the world, there are still men who have inherited entire countries from their families, or blatantly rig elections to stay in power. Like latter-day Roman Emperors, they rule according to their whim.

* *Uzbekistan, where political opponents are boiled to death*
* *Cameroon, where the President intervenes in the national football team*

* *Belarus, where rather than divorce his wife, the President had her*

* *North Korea, where Kim Il-Sung is still President – despite the fact that he's been dead for ten years*
* *Mauritania, where slavery is still widely practised*
* *Turkmenistan, where the president renamed Tuesday after his mother*

All of them are fascinating characters. While they all share a ruthlessness, their personalities differ wildly: from the coldly messianic to the downright bizarre.

Based on a series of reports originally broadcast on The Marian Finucane Show, *Stark Raving Rulers* is sometimes hilarious, sometimes horrific. It reminds us that most of our planet's citizens don't get to choose who governs them: often with the tacit cooperation of the Western World.

ISBN 1-84223-210-X

Typically, items such as an engine crankshaft, connecting rod, camshaft, piston pin, rocker arm, gears, bolts, etc. are inspected by this method.

The inspection process consists of magnetizing the part and then applying small magnetic particles to the surface to be inspected. If a crack, lap, seam, inclusion, porosity or other such defect is present in the part, the magnetic field is distorted about the defect and the magnetic particles, usually in a solution liquid, form a pattern the approximate shape of the discontinuity.

This method of test will locate defects on or below the surface of the test item. The test part can be magnetized by passing an electric current directly through the part (circular magnetization) or by passing the part through a solenoid magnetizing coil (longitudinal magnetization). The two magnetization techniques provide magnetic flux paths which are located at 90 degrees to each other. A defect which is "in line" with the longitudinal magnetic field could escape detection because its axis is the same as the magnetizing field. However, this same defect will be readily detected when exposed to circular magnetization. Conversely, a defect lying in the axis of circular magnetization is readily detected when exposed to a longitudinal magnetization field.

Magnaglow inspection is similar to the magnaflux procedure with the exception that a flourescent particle solution is used and the inspection is made under black light. Efficiency of inspection by this method is increased due to the neon-like glow of defects and small flaw indications are more readily visible.

Following magnaflux or magnaglow inspection, the permanent magnetism is removed by a demagnetizing process. This is necessary to minimize extraneous magnetic fields and their potential effects on the aircraft compass system.

Inspection by a dye-penetrant is a non-destructive test of non-porous, non-magnetic material such as aluminum, magnesium, brass, copper, cast-iron and stainless steel. This form of inspection will detect surface defects. Porosity, heat-treat cracks, seams and defects caused by fatigue are revealed. In use, a test item (after cleaning) is coated with the dye-penetrant material. After development, surface defects will appear as bright red indications for the case of a visible penetrant-type developer. Flourescent type inspection will show defects as a brilliant yellow-green color and sound areas as deep blue-violet. The location and shape of surface defects is provided by this method. Of course, the knowledge of a surface defect will give rise to inspection by other means in the event a deep or subsurface flaw is suspected.

X-rays, because of their unique ability to penetrate both plastic, ferrous and non-ferrous materials, represent still another non-destructive means of inspection. Examination of an X-ray photograph must be accomplished by a trained interpreter to judge the structural integrity of the part under test.

Visual inspection is of course the most common and oldest means of non-destructive testing. Defects which would normally escape the naked eye can be detected by telescopes, microscopes and magnifying glasses. During overhaul, all critical part dimensions are measured by micrometer, dial indicators and various gauge measurement devices.

Parts Refurbishment

There are several parts of an aircraft engine which can be returned to service by refinishing critical surfaces—grinding valves, valve seats, etc. An item of special interest is the cylinder. Because cylinders can cost from $225.00 to $500.00 each (exchange), the method of refurbishing is an important consideration in an overhaul cost. Restoring cylinder walls to original dimensions by chrome plating is becoming an increasingly popular method of cylinder refurbishment. The following technical information supplied by Chrome Plate of San Antonio, Texas, 78286, describes the principle features of the technique.

"The properties of electrolytically deposited chromium are ideally suited for air cooled cylinders. The material is harder than steel. It can occupy space and restore a worn cylinder bore to any desired size. Chromium is machineable, chromium can be plated upon chromium, and chromium will not rust! The surface finish of chromium (porosity), can be controlled to provide an oil wetable

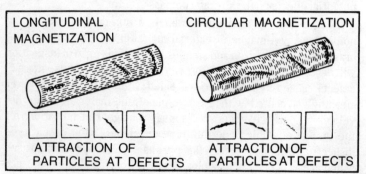

Fig. 7-1. Magnaflux detection of defects (courtesy of FAA).

surface (micro-grooved) that will distribute the necessary amount of lubrication for pistons and sealing rings operating in a combustion environment.

"The conventional process of grinding an aircraft cylinder oversize means that the diameter of the cylinder bore has been increased by a specific amount. FAA Regulations govern the amount of oversize to which a cylinder may be ground. To establish the maximum legal oversize for any given cylinder, the cylinder must withstand certain tests regarding barrel strength. These tests are established by the manufacturer and approved by the FAA. To maintain proper strength, cylinders used on opposed aircraft engines are usually not ground more than 20 thousandths of an inch oversize.

"Cylinders can be ground oversize to remove score marks, usually caused by broken piston rings, or to remove rust or rust pits. One of the most common reasons for grinding a cylinder oversize is an attempt to compensate for uneven wear. After a cylinder has been ground oversize, an oversize piston and rings must be used to maintain the proper compression seal in the cylinder. Before grinding a cylinder oversize and using it, there are several negative factors to be considered. First, oversize pistons and rings will be slightly heavier than standard parts. Second, oversize parts are more expensive than standard parts. Third, a

Fig. 7-2. Newest in the Continental family of opposed engines, the Tiara 6-285-B is rated at 285hp and weighs only 406 pounds. The Tiara is geared at a 2:1 reduction ratio and features a unique vibratory torque control unit to eliminate the need for crankshaft counterweights. Initial use of the engine is in the Piper Brave (courtesy of Teledyne Continental Motors).

cylinder barrel that has been ground oversize and then worn to its maximum wear limit is of no further use and must be replaced.

"There is a better alternative to running an engine with oversize cylinders. A cylinder can be ground just enough to remove the rust, rust pits or score marks, and to reshape the bore to the proper contour. Then the cylinder bore can be restored to new dimensions by chrome plating. A very important function is to return a used cylinder bore surface to its original new dimensions and this includes the all important contour (choke). The function of a dimensionally correct choke is to provide the sealing rings with a straight barrel at operating temperature. The constriction or choke is toward the head and this is simply because the head of a cylinder operates at a much hotter temperature than the flange end. Cylinder choke is the cold barrel contour required to maintain a straight cylinder barrel at normal operating cylinder temperature."

As chrome cylinders can be fitted to an engine already installed in an aircraft, engine checkout and break-in might have to be accomplished without a test cell. Chrome Plate Inc., recommends the following procedure for an in-flight engine break-in.

Use non-detergent mineral oil of correct viscosity. See the engine manufacturer's overhaul manual or service bulletins. After break-in is accomplished and oil consumption is satisfactory, AD oil may be used as recommended by engine manufacturer. This is normally done between 25 and 50 hours.

Prelubricate engine. Remove lower spark plug from each cylinder and crank engine until normal idle oil pressure is shown.

Cold weather starts will require preheated lubricating oil.

Limit initial run to 3 or 4 minutes. Do not exceed 1200 RPM.

Allow engine to cool to approximately 120F and repeat short runs of 3 minutes each. Do this as many times as necessary to correct discrepancies. Do not exceed 1600 RPM.

After all discrepancies are corrected, a very brief power run, 15 or 20 seconds, will determine if the engine is ready for in-flight break-in.

Under no circumstances attempt to clear a fouled spark plug by a power run during this critical period. Stop engine and change fouled spark plug.

In hot weather, select the coolest time of day for in-flight break-in.

Keep aircraft weight to minimum.

Do not cycle propeller on ground.